Please Don't Cry

MARIA HERKAL

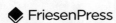 FriesenPress

Suite 300 - 990 Fort St
Victoria, BC, V8V 3K2
Canada

www.friesenpress.com

Copyright © 2017 by Maria Herkal
First Edition — 2017

Some names and places have been changed to protect the identities of individuals involved.

All rights reserved.

No part of this publication may be reproduced in any form, or by any means, electronic or mechanical, including photocopying, recording, or any information browsing, storage, or retrieval system, without permission in writing from FriesenPress.

ISBN
978-1-5255-1267-4 (Hardcover)
978-1-5255-1268-1 (Paperback)
978-1-5255-1269-8 (eBook)

1. FAMILY & RELATIONSHIPS, ABUSE, CHILD ABUSE

Distributed to the trade by The Ingram Book Company

CHAPTER I

Ramona in the Orphan Village 1947-1960

Clara:
Dozing off, or daydreaming sometimes comes along with a big confusion. You hear things that you don't want to hear, and then your daydream becomes confused with reality. And that's exactly what happened to me.

I was heading back to my girls. Well, they weren't exactly my girls. You see I worked in an orphan village so that's why I call them that. But the truth is they were nobody's girls. They were the one left on streets and they eventually ended up in the orphan village, or God knows where.

After World War II, Eastern Europe was badly damaged and much of it had been destroyed. Orphan children were everywhere, and in my town of Kosin in Yugoslavia, there was a big property that had been donated as an orphanage by the wealthy Tekish family. The site was very well organized, and the government paid for each child that lived there. It was set up for girls up to eighteen years of age.

At the time I was dozing off though, I was on the train headed back to Kosin and I heard a little boy asking his mother, "Where are we going?"

There was no answer, so I went back to my daydream.

Then again, I heard the boy's voice. "Mommy, are we going home? I am hungry and tired."

In an angry voice, the mother said, "I will see if I can find you some food. I'll be right back. Meanwhile, just sit there, and wait."

Somehow, that didn't sound right to me. I turned around to see the boy, thinking I could give the kid some food I hadn't eaten. I wondered if he'd like a chicken sandwich. That's when I I saw the mother was holding another child, all wrapped up. I though it must be a newborn since I hadn't heard any crying or noise.

I didn't like the way she was talking to her little boy; it sounded like trouble. I thought if I could speak to them, I might offer some help; the mother looked so lost and scared. She was carrying her baby and walking towards to the end of the train, leaving the boy sitting in his place with tears in his eyes.

It made me sad and I wondered where she was going. Something was not right... so I followed.

When I got closer to her, she was standing at the open door, with the baby in her arms. Suddenly I was sure she was planning to jump or to throw the baby out. As fast I could, I grabbed her and yelled, "What in the world are you trying to do? Are you mad?"

She just looked at me—sad and scared. I manage to grab her and pull her over to the center aisle.

"Please let me go," she said. "I don't want her, she is nothing but trouble for me. I can't go home with her. I don't want her."

I just stood there, not believing the words she was saying. For a moment I went speechless, and then I realized that I would have to do something very fast.

The train was slowing, and the next stop was mine, but I knew that I'd have to find out more about her before my stop. If not, she would more than likely try again. Then I remembered she had left a little boy back at the other end. I turned to check if he was still there, and what I saw made me sadder. The look on his face was very strange. I wondered if he was healthy, but as long he was still sitting there I could return to the young woman.

"Look, let us go back to your seat," I said, "and we can talk about your situation. I'd like to help if you'll let me. Throwing the baby out like that or jumping is not a good solution. You have a little boy over there. On the other hand, is that boy yours?"

With a sad voice, she finally spoke. "Yes, he's my son. His name is Sasha. He is a great boy, and he only will listen to me."

"Is he scared of you?"

She looked startled. "No. Why would you ask me that?"

I'd asked because we had been on this train for three days, and he was hungry and tired, all because of her.

She pointed at the baby with tears in her eyes, and I saw that deep inside her, she really didn't love her child.

"Let us start again," I said. "What is your name?"

In a small voice, she said, "My name is Elsa."

"Okay Elsa, my name is Clara Slavich; I am a teacher, and we have about seventeen girls that we look after. I work in the Orphan Village for girls in the next town of Kosin. I'd like to help you. I have some food and water I can give to Sasha and you. So, let us go back to your seat and see if Sasha is all right. Now tell me what is wrong with the baby, and why don't you want her? Also, if you did throw her off the train or if you jumped, what do you think would happen to Sasha? What would happen to both of you if you just threw your baby out? Could you just walk away and forget what you have done? On the other hand, do you think you could have lived in peace the rest of your life? I don't believe so; I don't think you have thought about that at all."

I waited for a response, but there was none. I tried again: "Can you tell me why you don't want to keep your baby? What is so horrible about her that you were willing to kill her?"

Her eyes shifted down to the floor. "I was not going to kill her. I was getting some fresh air. Please leave me alone."

"Then why were you standing right at the edge of this fast-running train? Were you interested in a field? And why did you open the door so wide? Please, Elsa, tell me the truth. You know I am willing to help you, but if you don't say anything, I can't assist. Like I said before, I will help you, but we have to talk first. I'm willing to listen to you and right now we don't have much time. The train is going to stop any minute, so please let us start again. I beg you to trust me. I'd like to help you, Elsa."

There were tears in my eyes. I knew that there was very little I could do if Elsa wouldn't talk.

Then in a tiny voice, she said, "Please, can you take her? I cannot keep her—she is trouble for me."

"Why, Elsa? Why can't you keep the baby? Do you mean the baby is a girl? What is her name?"

"You are asking too many questions, and you are confusing me. She, she's not wanted by me, or our relatives, or cousins, or anybody in the village. In my village, you don't bring a baby into this world unless you are married. Moreover, I was not married to her father, I didn't even know him that well. I saw him sometimes with my husband and that is all. So now do you see my problem? The problem is her."

"I don't see a problem. You don't throw babies off the train just because people in your village or your relatives don't like her or want her. That is a just poor excuse—stupid and morose. I want the truth—all the facts. You are the mother so let's start again, and one more time before this train stops. Let's start with where your husband is. And are you running away from someone or are you afraid of someone? What happened to the father of this baby? And are Sasha and the baby from the same father? Please tell me."

She took a deep breath. "Miss Slavich, this is hard for me to explain, but I will try. It is not easy to remember and live through those horrible moments again. I would like to forget them all, and to be honest I will try as much as I can. My husband died in a horrifying accident on our farm, and I was left alone with my son. Lots of people were trying to help and one of them was Nenad, the chief of police.

"Well, you see, Nenad was an important man in our village. He was the only one in charge of all the villages around there, so he took advantage of that and did whatever he liked. He had known my late husband a long time ago, and they were always fighting; the truth is they hated each other, I'm not sure why.

"When my husband died two years ago, Chief Nenad was always kind to me, and he always asked about Sasha. First, I thought that was nice and that maybe he cared for us, but that was completely not so. He started to come over just to say hello or to take Sasha out to the village. I often wondered what his wife thought of him always talking to me and looking out for me. You see Miss Clara, they didn't have any children; I thought maybe he felt sorry for Sasha not having a father, so I ignored all the signs.

"One day everything changed. Nenad came into my house when Sasha was out playing with some other kids. I saw a strange look in Nenad's eyes, and I got scared. My first instinct was to run, but I had my child outside. Where would I run? So, I just stood there. Nenad grabbed me and started kissing me and touching me all over. I begged him to stop, saying that it wasn't right. But he wouldn't. He took me to my bedroom, ripped off all my clothes, and forced himself on me; he raped me twice that time. I was crying, begging him to stop, but he was mumbling about how I was his from the beginning—that my husband had taken me away from him. I had not a clue what he was talking about. Then he got up, and in an angry voice he told me if I told anybody about this, he would take Sasha. I was so scared, hurt, and shaking, I just yelled at him to get out. Sasha heard me screaming, and then he came running in. 'Mommy, mommy what is wrong?' Seeing Sasha, Nenad took off.

"I stood there like a zombie asking myself what had just happened. Sasha was crying, and I cried with him. Finally, for my child's sake, I told him, 'Mommy, fell and got hurt. Not to worry, everything is going to be okay. Nevertheless, deep inside of me I knew that from then on, my life would never be the same.

"From that day and almost every day, he bullied me, called me names, and many times made fun of me in stores or at the market. My nightmare continued every day. He would come and just pretend to ask about Sasha, with a warning look. I knew what he wanted, and then one day I realized that I was pregnant with his child. I didn't know what to do! The nightmare continued, and he was always there. He was usually drunk and had eyes like a devil. I was so scared of him, but I knew I had to tell him, thinking maybe if he knew, things would be better.

It took all the courage I had, but I told him that I was pregnant. He was very upset and angry, and then he hit me so hard and ran out.

"I sat in my kitchen wondering if I should tell anybody, but my answer was who could I tell? His brother was the mayor of our village. We didn't have lawyers in town, and I was alone. I knew that no one would believe my story, so I kept it all to myself.

"After that, I didn't see him often. Days went by, and months, and I was getting big, and everybody noticed. There were rumours about who the father was. Nenad came quite often to warn me to keep my mouth shut, or he would make sure they took Sasha from me. I told him not to do that—that I would keep quiet, but I knew I had to get out of there as soon as the baby was born.

"There were a couple of people that I'd told about the chief and his abuse, but I had no help from anyone. So when she was born I waited for a couple of months to make sure I had enough money, and then I took a train to nowhere. I called it nowhere because I was not certain where I was going."

I couldn't be sure if she was finished with her story or not, so I said, "Elsa that is not a reason you should have to drop your child anywhere. There is a lot of help if you ask the right people."

Her face grew darker. "I didn't have any people where I came from, and you are making me confused. I wish you would go away and mind your business. I am not asking you for any help. Please go away."

I put my hand on her arm. "Perhaps if you listened to me, you would see that all I am trying to do is help you. The train will be coming to a full stop soon, so please tell me more about you and your children. What happened when the chief found out you had a baby?"

"When the baby was born, I told him that was a girl. At first I thought he was happy, and then out of the blue, he hit me so hard and told me that I'd better keep my mouth shut and not tell anybody that the baby was his. He did say that he would help me time to time, but I knew I had to get out of my village, because he would always be there...

"My friend Branko and my best friend, Sofia, from across the street pretended that nothing was going on, but they all knew that Chief Nenad had been abusing me for a long time. I decided to sell my house and move on. Two months passed and then some people were very interested in buying my place, so I decided to sell everything. However, what happened in the meantime was very strange. I happened to go into town, and I noticed everybody was at the police station. Wondering what was going on, I asked a woman who was walking by. She said that Chief Nenad and his wife had been in a car accident and that they both had died.

"I stood there wondering whether I should laugh or cry from happiness. The first thing that came to my mind was that I was free; no more abuse. I could go on with my life."

The story didn't make sense to me. "So then, why didn't you stay in your village, since he was not around anymore? Is there anything wrong with the baby that you are hiding her?"

"Miss Clara, you are asking too many questions. Nothing is wrong with her; I don't want her because she will always remind me of him, and I cannot take that anymore. Since you asked me for my entire story, then why don't you keep her?"

"Elsa, I would love to keep a baby, but you don't just give children away like that. We have to talk about that first. Right now, the train is at a full stop, and this is my town. Are you getting off, or what are your plans?"

"I am getting off as well, and I will find a room for us for now. Don't worry about us."

We both got off, and before I knew what was going on, Elsa threw the baby into my arms and said, "She is yours. I don't want her, and I will never take care of her."

I fumbled with the baby for a second, trying not to drop her, and while my eyes were down, Elsa just disappeared.

Turning around I saw her running toward the other side of the station. The next thing I knew she was on the train again, but going back. I had no time to do anything. I was in shock. There were a couple of police officers nearby, and I was going to call to them for help. But I knew that in those days police and many other people didn't care about single mothers—they were on their own. Almost immediately, the train started to go at full speed, and Elsa was gone; where I don't know. She'd left me her baby without any information, and I couldn't believe that a mother could be as cold as that. I managed to take down the train's number so I could research it the next day, but that was all I was able to do at that moment. When I checked the baby to see if she was all right, I noticed a piece of paper attached to her blanket. Right away, I grabbed it, hoping that there would be information about her, but my hope disappeared in a second.

The paper said that the baby's name was Ramona, that she'd been born on October 9, 1948...and that was all. I was in shock, now understanding that Elsa had planned all this just to get rid of the baby no matter what it took. I still couldn't believe that a mother could do that to her child. It was so sad.

There was only one thing to do, and that was all. Ramona was going home with me.

CHAPTER 2

"My dear Ramona," I whispered as I fit my key into the front door of the Orphan Village. "This is going to be difficult from now on. It will be like a bumpy road, especially when it comes to Mr. Tekish, but those are my worries, not yours for now. I am giving you my promise, Ramona. I will look after you no matter what happens."

The door creaked open, and I stopped for a moment, hoping it wouldn't wake everyone up. There was no noise from anywhere. "Let's go in. Please don't cry Ramona. It's very late and we don't want to wake up everybody. Soon I will find some milk for you; just hold on one more minute." I tiptoed down the hall. "So here we are, this is my place. Welcome to your new home Ramona, and from now on, I will look after you. Let's go to the kitchen and get you some milk."

There was the sound of footsteps coming from the kitchen. "Uh oh, somebody heard us. I hope it's Krina. She's an excellent worker and my best friend. Krina hates Mr. Tekish, but she loves kids, She'll help us. I know it."

Sure enough, it was Krina coming through the kitchen door. "Clara, what is that crying noise? Sounds like a baby." She stared at the bundle in my arms. "I know we don't have babies. Or do we? Apparently, we do now."

I patted my friend on the arm. "Please, Krina don't panic. Let me just warm up some milk, and I will explain everything."

Krina looked anxious. "Yes, okay. I'll warm up some milk for you, Clara, but how are you planning to give her the milk? Would you like me to put it in a glass? She is a baby; two or three months. We don't have baby bottles or anything else that babies need. What were you thinking?"

"Krina, please find something; I know you can do that. Tomorrow I will go to town, and I will get everything she needs. Just for tonight, though, please do this for me."

"Okay Clara. Give me a minute, and I will bring you a cup of tea—you look like a zombie. Just hold the baby, and I'll be right back."

"Thank you, Krina."

I don't remember going to my room or feeding Ramona. I must have been so tired that I passed out. When I opened my eyes, Krina was standing there with her hands crossed, looking at me.

"It's about time you woke up."

"Oh Krina, I'm sorry. How long was I asleep?"

"Well, not for long and don't worry about that, but let me hear the whole story. How did you end up bringing a baby to the orphan village when you know we don't take infants? And especially when you know we have a monster in charge? It won't be long before that monster finds out, so let me hear the story."

"Krina, does Mr. Tekish know about Ramona?"

'No, I don't think so, but you know that somebody will tell him, so let me hear that story now."

I took a deep breath. "You may think that this is a made-up story, but it is not. Everything happened just the way I'm going to tell you, but I don't know if anyone will believe me. It's going to be very hard to prove how I ended up with this baby... I don't know if I'd believe it either because it's so strange." And then I told her what had happened on the train.

"Oh! Krina it was so horrible. I thought I was dreaming; I didn't know what to do in that moment. It was just like a nightmare for me. Elsa didn't want to keep her. And if I hadn't taken the baby from her, she probably would have tried again. So that's how the baby is with us. She's only three months old. Where is she now?"

"Don't worry, she's in a small basin I found in the kitchen, with some blankets and a little bottle. That will do for now until you get to the city and buy more baby supplies. Look on your left, she's right there beside you."

"Oh, my little angel, you look so good, and look Krina, she's smiling... Thanks to Auntie Krina, everything is going to be all right. Well, I have to get ready to go to the city, and when I come back, I know that I have to report to Mr. Tekish and explain our newcomer. Please, Krina can you keep an eye on her until I come back?"

....

The bang on my door was so loud that it woke up the baby, and I knew right away that it was Mr. Tekish. Mr. Tekish was a big, mean, always drunk, and very scary-looking man. I was hoping that because Ramona was just a baby that he wouldn't mind her, but I was wrong.

He didn't even wait for me to answer the door; he just stormed in like a mad dog, which he was! Eyes bloodshot and mad as hell. None of that bothered me though. This time, I was ready to fight. Mr. Tekish and I went back a long way; almost five years. I knew his habits and his needs…I knew them all, so this time, I thought I would blackmail him.

I met him head-on. "Hello! If I may say so from the way you look, I presume you have heard the news that we have a new girl, and that this time, it's just a baby. I'm sure you're not so pleased with that, but we can sit down and talk about it. A good discussion will be useful for both of us."

"I want you in my office in half an hour, and I sure hope you have a good explanation for all of this."

"No problem Mr. Tekish. Would you like me to bring the little one with me?"

"Clara don't play with fire, you will burn, just like everyone else who has tried to destroy me, which no one has succeeded at yet. I am in charge, and I always will be." Slamming the door, he left.

I needed to find Krina; she would help me with Ramona while I was with Mr. Tekish.

On the first floor, I spotted twelve-year-old Tana, one of the orphans. "Tana, have you seen Krina? I can't find her anywhere. Can you look for her and tell her I need her right away?"

"Miss Clara, Krina left early this morning. She seemed like she was in a rush—never even said goodbye."

Krina hadn't said a word to me about leaving. "What did you just say?"

"She left this morning. I'm sorry Miss Clara, but all I know is that Mr. Tekish told her that her brother was here to take her home."

So, he is already giving me a hard time, I thought. *We will see about that.* "Okay, Tana. Can you stay with the baby until I come back? I won't be long, I'm just going over to see Mr. Tekish."

As I headed to Mr. Tekish's office, I knew there would be harsh words, but God help me he was not going to win this time. I practically ran into his office and I could tell he was a bit surprised, but his smile made me sick.

"Mr. Tekish, let me say this. Before we go any further I want to know why Krina left in a hurry."

"I'm not sure. Her brother came and said she had to go home with him—that their mother is very ill."

"You're busted. We both know Krina doesn't have a brother or a mother. You made her go, didn't you?"

"Look Clara. Do not start with me."

"I think she was threatening to expose all your secrets, and that is why you kicked her out. However, you'll see that is a big mistake. Trust me on that."

"I am sure that we will never hear from Krina again. She said goodbye to me, and Krina is not your business—we are here to discuss your newcomer."

"Mr. Tekish, you will not get away with this. Krina knows more about you than anyone else, and I think she left because of you. I am letting this go for now; I have a baby to take care of. Also, if you don't want to hear how I ended up with this baby, then we have nothing more to discuss.

"OK, then start talking, but make it short. I'm not interested in a long story."

"If you don't want to hear the whole thing, then it's like this. The baby's mother threw her baby in my arms and said she was mine, I could keep her. Then she ran away with another child, who was a boy. All she said was that the baby's name is Ramona, and she is three months old. Before I had a chance to stop her, she took the next train, and that is all I can tell you in a short sentence."

"Why did she keep a boy but not a girl? That is very strange... I don't know."

"Well, you said you wanted a short story. Why Elsa did that is a long story, but look at it this way—you like girls. Don't you, Mr. Tekish?"

"Get out of my office before I lose my temper."

"Nevertheless, Mr. Tekish, don't forget that I know your secrets, and I do know about your love for younger girls. I have always turned my head, but not anymore. You will accept this baby, and you will watch her grow. However, I promise you that if you ever touch her, I will kill you and I will tell everybody about you, and I will confess why I have never reported you. Therefore, this is all up to you."

"All right, you made your point. Get out of my office. Go to my sister and get the proper papers, so that I can send a report to City Hall."

"One more thing," I said. "She does have a mother, and you don't know the whole story because you are not interested—all you care about is money.

However, I will make sure that Ramona gets the proper papers for her sake. Since I don't know her last name we have to make one up."

Before I got to the registry office, I thought I should stop at the train station and ask some questions. I knew Milan, a train engineer, and I thought he might be able to help me, because we had been friends for many years now. It was a long shot, but you never know.

My next problem was whether that car we had would start. I knew Mr. Tekish wouldn't give me his car or drive me anywhere, so I went to the back of the orphanage to find Stefan, our handyman.

Good—he was there, cleaning up the garage. I hated to ask Stefan to do things for me; he was an old man, who had lived on this property since before it became the orphan village. But he was very nice and just like everybody else, he didn't like Mr. Tekish.

"Hello! Stefan, how are you? I need to go to town, and I was wondering whether that old car is still working. Walking will take me forever in this weather."

"Yes, Miss Clara, the car is all right. I checked it yesterday. I don't think it will go too fast, but I'm sure it can manage to town and back."

"Thanks, Stefan."

....

A clerk at the rail station looked at me with a smile and asked if she could help me with anything.

"Yes, please. May I talk to engineer Milan?"

"Yes, madam, of course. One moment please. He is in the back."

In just a few minutes, Milan came out with a big smile. "Oh look who's here! My friend Clara. How are you these days?"

"Not too bad Milan, except you know I always have to do things with my girls and never have much time for myself."

"I know. That's why I am still single, my dear."

"Ah Milan, stop playing with me. You know that is not the truth. We are friends and I'm sure if you wanted more than that, you wouldn't call me your dear. So my friend, I need your help, and I have a favour to ask you. Last night I came home on the 6:30 train, and on that train, I met a young woman with two children. When we got off she left something, and I think she was in trouble.

I did try to talk to her, but she took off on me. Also, on top that, she took off on a different train. I wasn't able to stop her, but I managed to remember some numbers of that train. Milan, I thought maybe you could help me to find out where that train went. When I spoke with her, she said she'd been on the train for three days. If she was on the train for three days why would she take another train back? You see my point. That train that we were on last night, would you be able to find out where it originally came from. I boarded it in Nis. If she'd been traveling three days, she must be from Bosnia.

"Milan, I know she needs help, I thought if I could contract her, maybe I could help her.

I know you will ask me questions; I can see it in your eyes. Milan, she dropped her baby in my arms, and I don't even know her last name… I don't know anything about her. I'm not sure who she is. She took off with another child, a little boy, maybe about four or five years old, but she just dropped the baby in my arms and said I could keep her; she didn't want her. Now you can see the problem that I have, and why I need to find her, which is where you come in. So you can see that I do need your help. I know this might take forever, but there'd be no harm in starting. You know where to find me if you find anything at all, and I will be grateful for your help."

"Clara! How grateful? Are you going to marry me then? Okay, I'm just kidding. I will see what I can do, and will let you know."

"Thanks, Milan, for everything. Oh yes, the number of the train that she took off was 78936980. I'm sure that's the right number."

The registration office in the city was not too far away, but I hated to go there. Mr. Tekish's sister, a nasty old woman, had worked for the City office for a long time. I was sure she and her brother were cheating the government with lots of lies and fake documents, but I had no choice but to talk to her.

"Hello Miss Helga. How are you?"

"Never mind the sweet talk, I know why you're here. My brother called me this morning, so you see I knew you were coming. So let's see what you have."

"I don't have papers if that's what you mean. Ramona's mom just left her at the train station. There was a little note attached to her blanket saying that her name is Ramona, and she was born on October ninth of this year. Since this is only December 28th, that makes her three months old. I have no other knowledge. So, to report a newborn to the government, I need proof of her birthplace and all the other documents. I'm sure you know how that goes, and that is where you come in."

"We have done this many times," she said. "So this will be very easy, but I sure hope it will be the last time."

"Don't worry, trust me, there will be no more babies or girls coming."

"I will make sure of that, and what kind of name is Ramona? Her mother must have hated this child."

I chose to ignore this remark. "As for her last name, we can choose something like Senich. So if you agree, let's name her Ramona Senich, born October 9th, 1948, in Vrnjac, Yugoslavia. I will come back tomorrow, and I hope that all the documents will be in order, because you know your brother likes money, and without proper documents there'll be no money."

"I know you don't like me, Clara, or my brother. However, my grandparents left us that building, and we, I mean me and my brother, we put our home to excellent use. Opening a place for orphans was good for everybody."

"Yes, I am sure of that, among other things." I gathered up my things. "I have one more stop and I have to get going; the little one will need bottles and some food."

....

Ramona did fine, and she quickly adjusted to her hew home. She didn't cry as much as before, and everybody in the house loved her.

Time flew, and before I knew it, Ramona was one year old. She was a happy toddler.

Spending time with her was happy too. Sometimes we all just watched her and the things that she tried to do. Walking was one of the funniest things. One day...I think she was almost two, she pulled me by my skirt, and she said, "Mama."

I will never forget that moment as long as I live. Tears came rolling down my face. No one had ever called me mama. In that moment, I knew that I would always be there for Ramona; she was all I had and all I loved.

I took her in my arms and gave her big hug and kiss. "Yes," I said. "I am your mama." But I was thinking, *For now*. I knew this relationship would end one day, but for now we were one.

It was almost three years before I heard from my friend Milan, and then one morning he came to see me. Because I was afraid someone would listen in on us, I asked Milan if we could go to a small coffee shop, which was across the street.

With a big apology for how long it had taken, he said that he had some news, though not much. He explained that tracking trains was a big job, and he'd been out of town almost for almost sixteen months, but had done the best he could.

"The train that she took back went to eight cities with its last stop in Dubrovnik, Croatia. It was a fast train that only stopped in a few cities. The train that you came home on was one of our slow trains. I mean it stopped almost in every town and every city, so you see she could be from anywhere. That train started in Slovenia, Bosnia, and went all the way to Subotica, Serbia. So you see Clara, you have a big job ahead of you."

"Well, this news was better than nothing. At least now I had almost ten cities to check out. The only thing I had going for me was the chief of police's last name. Even the fact that he had passed away was better than nothing. People always seem to remember those who have died.

I thanked Milan for his efforts, but I knew it would be a big job for me to find Ramona's mother.

The chief's name, Stanovic, was one of the most common last names in Bosnia, so I would start there and work my way up. To get information on a person who had passed away, I'd have to write to some government offices. I knew there would be a lot of questions about why I was looking for him, but I had to work my way around that. When the time came, I'd come up something. Right now was just the start. As for the train that she had taken back, I would start with a city close to us, because there was an orphan village for boys there. You never knew—maybe she didn't want Sasha either.

I knew a woman who worked at the orphan village there, so I thought I would send her a letter and start from there. It might be easier than looking for the town where Ramona's mother came from.

CHAPTER 3

Everything was running normally, and there were no complaints. Even Mr. Tekish had a lady friend, which we all noticed. She came every other day, and that made all of us happy, especially me. We were all seeing less of Mr. Tekish, and I thought perhaps he was over little girls and was ready for a relationship with a woman. (Little did I know how wrong I was.)

One day though, I was looking for Ramona and I saw one of the girls coming out of Mr. Tekish's office. She was crying.

With her hands over her face, she tried to pass me by, but I stopped her. One look at her, and I knew what had happened in Mr. Tekish's office. Apparently, his woman friend was just a cover-up for him. He wanted us to believe that he had changed.

I rushed to his office, mad as hell, and kicked the door open. It scared him. His face was red, and his eyes were bloodshot. I knew right away that he was drunk.

For a moment, he looked panicked, but then he started yelling, "What do you want? I didn't call you! Get out of my office if you know what's good for you. One word out of you, and you will be out of a job forever. Do you hear me?"

That hurt me so badly, because I knew I had no choice if I wanted to look after Ramona, and I'm sure that he knew that as well. I made the wrong decision. I wanted to go to the police to tell them everything that was happening. I know that I am just as much to blame as he was for not reporting him. All I knew was that I had to protect Ramona from that monster, so help me God.

As I was lying down in my room later and wondering what to do, I heard a knock on my door.

It was Ramona. "Mama, I wanted to see you. You have been crying, and I saw you running from Mr. Tekish's office. Why is that? Are you okay?"

"Yes, I am all right!"

"I went to see Mr. Tekish; he said that I am the most beautiful girl in here. He gives me some coloured pencils and many papers to draw on. He likes me to sit on his lap, and we play seesaw. I go up and down, and he likes that a lot. Then he puts his hands on me and likes to pretend that he is carrying me up in the air, and then he puts me in his lap with both hands on my bottom, so he said I wouldn't get hurt from his wicked boner. I don't know what that means, so we just play a lot of other games. Sometimes he is a doctor and I am a nurse, so we check out each other's bodies. He always likes to look inside of my panties and then I look into his. We touch each other pretending that something is wrong, and then because he is a doctor he looks to see if anything is wrong. We just play. We always play like that. Just a game we like. I like to be a nurse so I can check all his parts that hurt. He always has something he likes me to check in his underwear. Sometimes he tells me that is how his mother played with him, so we touch each other and that's all.

"Is there anything wrong, Mother? I think he is a very nice man. He told me I could come and play with him anytime, and I like that. For me to come and see him every day, I said I have to ask you first. But he said that I don't have to ask you for everything—that he is the boss of this place and that you only work here."

My heart was pounding. "Oh my dear Ramona, I'm glad you told me that, but listen to me. As of now, you will not go to see Mr. Tekish at all. Please try to understand when I ask you not to go and see him anymore at all. Do you understand me?"

"Yes, Mommy, I do, but why? Why can't I see him? He likes me, not like the girls in here."

"What do you mean, girls in here?"

"They make fun of me. Some girls are saying that you found me in a box, and one day my turn will come with Mr. Tekish, which I don't understand what that means!"

"Look, Ramona. Don't you listen to those girls. Some of them are mean, but I don't think they will be like that all the time. To most of them it's just a game."

"Okay Mama. Can I go now?"

"Ramona, go to the kitchen and wait for me. I won't be long, and then we can go and play with the other girls."

Now I knew he was after Ramona, which gave me no choice but to start looking for Ramona's mother. I had to get her out of this place, and that meant I had to find her mom. I knew I couldn't keep an eye on her all the time. That old bastard was always looking for his prey, and I was getting tired of him. I had to put some more time into finding Elsa. I hoped that she had forgotten what happened to her a long time ago, and that she'd be happy to see Ramona. Maybe then I could prevail on her to take Ramona under her wing, because I didn't know what else to do to keep that monster away from her.

First, I thought I'd go to the boys' orphan village in the next town. If I remembered correctly, there was a teacher in charge, whose name was Vera. I also was going to write a letter to the government in Sarajevo where I thought Ramona's mother might be from, or in the small town near there. They would supply me with Chief Stanovic's address and then I would take action.

I had to do it that night because I was going to town the next day and I could mail it before things got out of hand. I wanted to save Ramona from bad memories later on in life, and I hoped it wasn't already too late.

From then on, I had to be more careful when I left Ramona by herself. That monster would find her as soon as he saw that I was gone. I was busy with the other girls too. After all, I was a teacher and my time was spent all over the place; I couldn't be with Ramona all the time.

All Tekish did was sit by the window and watch his prey.

Now that Ramona was five years old, she was his favourite, but she thought it was all just play. Mr. Tekish and his games were so tricky for little girls to understand. Ramona was going to grade one next year, so at least I'd know she was safe while in school, but meanwhile, I had my hands full. Also, the problem was that Ramona was too young to understand what I was trying to tell her, and Mr. Tekish was taking advantage of that.

I did have one more option to save Ramona and get her out of there. There was one very wealthy woman in town, Miss Blechingwood, who always wanted us to give her one of our girls to be with her. I took Ramona there a couple of times, and they both liked each other. Ramona was always a happy child. She loved to play with cats and dogs and we didn't have any animals in the orphan village, which was a good selling point. But I thought Ramona was too young for Miss Blechingwood; she needed some help as well, so she was looking for an older girl. We had talked about that, and she was willing to wait a year or so.

I had told her Ramona's story and she was touched and sad. After that, she wanted Ramona and promised not to use her as a worker but as her child. For that, she knew that she had to adopt Ramona before Ramona could come to stay with her. Unfortunately, that decision was not only mine. It also had to come from the Social Services office in the city, and that would take a long time. Meanwhile, Ramona could go to Miss Blechingwood's house after school every day, and stay with her until suppertime.

That was just one of my options, but if I found Ramona's mother that would be my first choice. I thought maybe she had changed and would be happy to see Ramona, but deep inside me, I knew that was only my wish. If Ramona's mother had wanted her, she could have come to see her a long time ago, and she had not. So that told me there was not much of a chance. Still, I thought I'd try—you never know.

I had thoughts about a lot of other things too, like why didn't I adopt Ramona?

I was as guilty as Mr. Tekish was. I had let him get away with this all this time and for what? For my selfishness, so that is why I could not adopt Ramona. I had to find her mother or beg Social Services to let Miss Blechingwood adopt her.

For now, I thought I would wait to see if I got some replies to my mail. If not, then I had to take some action. For I knew I couldn't watch Ramona all the time, and that was breaking my heart...

School was starting next week, and Ramona was so happy that she could go out just like other girls and jump on a bus. She always was interested in going to the city and the bus was her favourite way to go, because she knew she could go far on a bus.

It might seem funny to us, but to a little kid, going to school for the first time without parents was something big. So, Ramona was thrilled about all that, and I was relieved, knowing she would be safe at school for least few hours. That gave me more time to concentrate on other issues.

Days went by, and I was getting worried that I wouldn't get any mail. But my worries were ended two weeks after Ramona started school, when mail arrived from my long-time friend Vera, at the orphan village for boys. My hands were shaking, as I wondered what the news would be.

Vera wrote me that she remembered Social Services bringing a boy about six years old. His name was Sasha. They had told her that his mother had said she couldn't look after him for now, and that if they found him a home for maybe a year, she would come back for him as soon as she found a place to live and a job. But the mother didn't return for a long time, and she never called or came to visit.

Vera wrote:

However, he is not with us anymore. His mother eventually came and took him home. There was a question of where she had been all these years, and apparently, she was in a hospital, which is so strange to me. You know Clara as well as me; they don't care about these kids. Before she left, I did have a chance to talk to her. The boy was so friendly and always happy-go-lucky; never cried or complained, I liked him.

I asked her where she came from and she said her name was Elsa Jakic, and she came from Bosnia. To me, that was fishy. How did she end up all the way here? She wouldn't talk much, took the boy, and didn't give an address, even when I insisted; she just said she had a job in Novisad, and that was where she was going. To tell you the truth I didn't believe a word she said. Sasha didn't want to go (I know). He was with us almost five years. and I will not be surprised if he runs away. Also, I'm sure I'll see him again. I had that feeling, especially when Sasha gave me a dark look and had a hard time letting go of my hand.

However, I remember when he first came, he asked about his sister. At first, I was not sure what he was talking about, and I left at that. A couple of weeks after he settled in I did ask him what he meant by "my sister." He looked sad and confused and never answered me, just walked away with tears in his eyes. Therefore, I never asked him again, and when you wrote me a letter, I was surprised that you were asking about this boy, and now I think you have met them both. I am sorry for not trying hard enough to get more from Elsa, but she was not a person that likes to talk.

You know Clara, just between us; I don't think that Elsa is all there. My feeling is that she is in trouble and needs help. I sure hope Sasha will be okay.

I had also explained to Vera what Elsa had done six years before, and the reason I was looking for her. Hoping that she could give me some more information, I thanked her, hoping to hear from her soon with maybe some more info that might help me. Now that she knew why I was looking for Elsa I was sure she would write sooner this time.

I had to go to the post office to mail a letter, but I worried that Mr. Tekish might get suspicious about why I was going to the city so often. So I decided

I'd better keep an eye out for the mail carrier, and give him my letter. He came almost every day. That way no one would notice what was I doing.

....

Ramona ran in looking so happy and excited. In her hand, she had a picture she'd drawn of me at school. "Mama, Mama, this is for you!"

My tears ran down. Like before, no one ever called me Mama, much less making a picture of me. I was so touched and said I would keep this photo forever and Ramona smiled and said there would be a lot more.

"I love you, Mama," she said.

The days were going well, and there were no complaints from anybody. I went to Ramona's school, to see how she was doing in classes, and the report was positive. She was an excellent student and always wanted to learn more.

Soon she was in grade three, and nine years old. I noticed that she was not talking much, like before. It bothered me and I wondered if Mr. Tekish had anything to do with it. So, I decided to have a good talk with her.

Right after school when she came home, I asked her to come to see me. She had stopped going to see Miss Blechingwood, because Miss Blechingwood got very ill. They had to take her to the hospital, and no one knew if she would make it. Ramona was sad about that.

"Hello Mammy, you wanted to talk to me!"

"Yes, I do. Have you seen Mr. Tekish lately… and the truth now."

"Yes! Now and then. No harm in that, is there Mommy?"

"No, but I am surprised because I remember telling you not to see Mr. Tekish at all, and you did promise you would not see him. Then tell me, what is the reason, that you go now and then to his office?"

"Nothing. Now I have to go. Please Mommy, let me go. I have lots of homework to do. Mommy, there is no reason, in my opinion, for you to worry so much. There is no harm done. Please just stop these questions all the time. If I have anything to tell you I will."

I knew there was something wrong, but for now, I had to go and concentrate on other things. What worried me was that I had never heard from Sarajevo about Chief Stanovic. Maybe he was not from that area. I decided I would wait another month or so and then try other cities, Ramona's mother had to come from somewhere, but the big question was, from where.

Ramona:

I do have a lot of homework, but I feel ashamed not telling Mommy the truth; that Mr. Tekish has called on me a lot. He always seems to find time for me when Mom is out. It's like he has a spy telling him what is going on, (maybe he has someone), and he is asking me to do things that I don't like anymore. It was okay when I was little, sitting on his knees, jumping up and down, but he is playing little rougher now.

I can't tell this to Mom because according to him, this place is his, and one word out of me, he will kick Mommy and me out. He knows that I'm scared, and that's why he is making me do all those crazy things. I will get even with him one day.

I am only ten now, but the time will come. This I promise to myself. A situation like mine is not possible to explain…the pain I carry in my heart every day. Sometimes I wish I could just die. My revenge will come soon.

CHAPTER 4

Clara:
Ramona was approaching her eleventh year with us, and that was a long time for one person to be in the orphanage. Most girls stayed with us seven years—top, but Ramona had been there since she was a baby. I thought it was time for me to tell her the truth. I knew that this would be hard for both of us, but if I didn't tell her now, a letter would be even worse. She might hear gossip here and there, and I didn't want that to happen. I decided to-day was the day.

As I was far away with my thoughts, a knock on my door made me jump. In a small voice, I said, "Come in."

There was Ramona, standing and holding a letter in her hand. My heart was going so fast, I thought it would jump out. Where had she found that? The first thing that came to my head was, *She knows!* I had to pull myself together before I said anything.

"Mom, you got mail," she said. "This one is from Sarajevo. I didn't know you had anybody in Sarajevo."

It took me a second to calm down. "No honey, I'm not sure anybody in Sarajevo knows me. Must be a mistake, or maybe my long-lost relatives." I was trying to be a little funny, but I knew that letter was from influential people in Sarajevo…or at least, I was hoping. It had taken them almost six years to answer me. I was so happy, hoping to hear some good news.

Ramona left with a question in her eyes; she was suspicious.

My hands were shaking when I started to read; the news was something that I had been waiting for, for a long time.

Dear Miss Clara Slavich,
Please accept my apology for not answering you sooner. Everything has changed after the war. I am surprised that your mail reached me, because I am the one you are looking to for help.

I am in charge of records for deaths from 1943 to now. Also, when I saw your letter, I was wondering what possible connection you had with Chief Nenad Stanovic, since he was from Bosnia and you live in Kosin Banat and are a teacher at an orphan village. That got my attention. I have read about Stanovic, but that was a long time ago. If my memories serve me right, he died in 1949, in a car crash, and his wife was with him at that time. I'm not sure if you knew how he died, but I hope to tell you in a way that will not disturb you. I am telling you this just in case you don't know. You see, Stanovic was one of a kind. He was one of the biggest communist leaders we had in Bosnia. He helped many soldiers that came home with broken hearts, and he was just a good man until this awful thing happened. Someone or maybe some mad person, we don't know and probably will never know, has killed his son. The boy was 15 years old. He was very smart, and if you ask me too bright. What I mean by that is that he had kind of a big mouth. He fell in with some bad boys, and got in trouble with the law; he was a troubled kid. On many occasions, he called people names and made fun of other children and a lot more. His father did try to work with him, to stop that kind of behaviour, but sometimes it was hard. Then one day, the boy was found dead. There was a message on his shirt; simple words that said, "You got what you deserved, smart-ass!"

Nenad Stanovic was so heartbroken and devastated. He started drinking and committing grave sins in the city. That went on for quite a while until one day, the chief of police was struggling with him. He was so drunk, and it was impossible to make him better, and nothing worked. Nearly everybody in town was fed up with him, so the police put him in jail for two days. When he got sober, the police told him that the best solution for him was to pack up and move somewhere else. It was felt that this would help him ease the pain. Nevertheless, to alleviate the pain of a dead child... that is too much to ask. He agreed to move to a small village not too far from Sarajevo, where his brother was mayor of the surrounding communities. His brother made him the offer to be the chief of a police station in the area. We all thought that was a good idea, because then his brother could look out for him. (So everybody thought.)

We heard he was doing well until one day he started drinking again. What caused him to start drinking again I don't know, but that is why I am giving you the address of that village, in case you need some more answers that I cannot provide you.

I sure hope this will give you some closure, if that is what you were looking for. If I ever hear anything, I will let you know, Miss Clara. And just in case you'd like to come and find out more about Chief Stanovic, he lived in a small village called Bukovina, not too far from Sarajevo.

It was my pleasure to serve you, and sorry for such a long delay.
Take care of yourself, Miss Slavich.
Tomé Kruic.
Director of the population in Sarajevo

I sat there staring at the letter. Was I happy? Yes! I was happy because there was some truth in what Elsa had told me; that she was from Bosnia. Therefore, I knew I had to talk to Ramona right away. Because I wanted to go to Bosnia, where Elsa came from, to find some more information. But leaving Ramona along with that monster would be a big mistake. I knew she would not be alone.

However, I learned that all the older girls had other plans. That meant Ramona would not be looked after while I was gone. First thing I had to do now was find Ramona and have a good talk with her.

It was going to be so hard for me and far more difficult for Ramona, because I had been lying to her all this time. If she got upset, I would understand. My only hope was that I could get her to understand me, so she might see why I had done all this for her.

"Tana, do you know where Ramona is? I am having trouble finding her."

"No Miss Clara, I was in study room almost all day and haven't seen her. Try Mr. Tekish's office. I know her; she goes there quite a bit."

"What did you say? Never mind, thank you." I ran there, and yes, she was there, talking to him. I saw a smirk on his face, and I grabbed her hand and pulled her out. I was so mad at her, but I didn't show her that I was upset about her being there. I needed her now more than ever, and both of us would have to get through this.

She looked at me somewhat sadly. "What's wrong, Mom? Why are you so upset? We weren't doing anything. I just went there to ask him some questions about summer break. There is a girl in school, we're friends, and she asked me if I would like to spend the summer at her grandmother's farm. She knows that I don't have anybody but you, and you need a little break. That was all. Please don't worry so much about me. I'm older now and a little wiser. Even if you don't trust him—believe me. You can believe me, everything is okay. I can handle Mr. Tekish; we know each other well now. We don't play nurse and doctor anymore, we do other things; some things that I don't like all the time, but then some are okay. What was the big rush to find me? Is anything wrong?"

"Oh! Dear Ramona! I don't know how to start. Yes or no, let's go to my office so we can be alone."

Once in my office, I firmly closed the door. "First of all Ramona, you don't have to go to Mr. Tekish for anything; I can do all the signing of papers from now on. I haven't told this to anybody yet, but Mr. Tekish is under investigation. Do you remember, Slava and Dian, those two girls that left us in May?"

"Yes Mom, I do. Why are you asking me that? Moreover, what do you mean Mr. Tekish is under investigation?"

"Ramona, listen to me. Those two girls went to the police and told them everything that Mr. Tekish has done to them and to many other girls, including you. He will be going to court. I think the orphan village won't be open in a year or two, so this is why we have to talk, and I need you to understand. Ramona, it's crucial that you understand everything that I am going to say. Everything I have done was to protect you. I know that I haven't done a good job, and I am so sorry about that."

"Mom, you're scaring me. I knew that Slava and Dian were going to the police. They told me because both girls knew that Mr. Tekish was sexually in contact with me many times, even though I told him to stop. I never wanted to say anything to you, because he said that if I did, he would throw us both out. I knew he was quite capable of doing that. I kept my mouth shut, but Slava and Dian knew all about it. Sometimes one of them would comfort me, but sometimes I just hide and cry by myself. If Mr. Tekish is going to jail or this place will be closed, what is going to happen to us, or you and the rest of the staff?"

"Well is why I want to talk to you. I don't know how to start, but I have to tell you. You remember when you told me that some girls were making fun of you, telling you that we found you in a box? Ramona, I was the one who found you, or how to put it? I was the one who saved your life. I'm not your birth mother. but I have looked after you since you were three months old.But I have looked after you since you were three months old, and I love you as much as any mother could.

You see I met your mother on a train when I was coming back from a holiday. She was on the same train, and that is how we met. Oh! Dear God, how can say this? She was holding you and crying. I knew something was wrong. She was going to jump, or was planning to throw you out; I didn't know what to believe. I grabbed her and saved both of you. On top of that, she had another child sitting with her, and I was not going to let her destroy all that.

"Yes, Ramona, you have a brother, but right now, I don't know where he is. I am trying to find your mother first and we'll see about the rest."

Ramona was crying, and I thought maybe I should stop talking, but she had to know all. "Why are you trying to find her now? What gives you the right to keep this secret so long? Don't call her my mother, which she is not. You are my only mother, or so I thought, but now I'm not so sure what to believe. If I have a brother maybe you can find him, but not her. Why are you doing this? Are you trying to get rid of me? Why? What is going on? Why did you never tell me all this before? Many times I have thought about what those girls said to me. It makes sense now. You never talk about my father; your husband.

"There are no photos of me as a newborn or of where I was born. If I look at you and me, we don't even look alike, so I thought that maybe I look like my father, but deep inside I knew there was another explanation. Mr. Tekish always had a sly smile when I said 'my mother,' meaning you. Did he know all about this, and did everybody know except me?"

"No, Ramona, no one knew about it except Mr. Tekish and me. I had to go to a registration office to register you, because I didn't know your last name or where your birthplace was. We had to make one up. No one in here knows, because most of you girls have a similar story. All that is kept confidential.

"Ramona if Mr. Tekish is going to court, I am sure I will too. You see, I know about all those things that he has done to them. I have not reported it to the police, which I should have done, but I didn't. Consequently, lots of this is my fault, and I will not be able to take care of you, because I will not be around. Most of the time I will be in court and maybe jail. Also, you don't need to see that, so that is why I want to find your mother, so she can take you from here when Social Services takes over. They might give you to a farmer, or to factories that need light work. In a year or two, orphan villages will be closed. Also, if I don't find your mother you won't have much choice but to go to some farmers or God knows where. It's not because I don't love you, it is because I do love you. Maybe your mother has changed, and she will be glad to see you or have you."

"Mother, why haven't you tried to find her before? Why? If you knew all that, then why haven't you reported Mr. Tekish to the police? What stopped you for all these years? You had to have had a chance to tell everything that was going on, but you didn'thing. Are you telling me everything now? Mom, I would like to know, because that is so bad and maybe you could have stopped all of this! Why Mother? Why didn't you stop any of that?"

"That is a long story Ramona. Right now, I would like to see if we can find your mother."

"I told you, don't call her my mom, and I have lots of time, so let me hear the whole story, and I mean now, Mother!"

"Ramona, this is difficult for me, and I'm not so sure you'll understand. You are still a child."

"Yes, I am a kid. I'm a kid that had to grow up fast and get to know things that girls my age should not know. So, don't worry about me, just tell me why."

"All right, if that is what you want. Then sit right beside me and listen very carefully, and then you can judge. Just sit and listen.

"I came to the orphan village a long time ago. I was about twenty-five or so. Mr. Tekish had just opened this place. He needed a teacher who could look after about seventeen girls then. He offered excellent pay and all living expenses, and he was young himself and good looking. Like all young women, I fell for him right away, and I am sure he knew it and so he gave me the job with no problem.

"Seven of the girls that we had at that time were all between four and seven years old. Most of them had been brought here from the Social Services office, which is how our orphan village got started. Mr. Tekish and his sister had this place to themselves and they said that they wanted to do something good, but I think it was more about the government paying lots of money.

"So I started working for Mr. Tekish, and we got pretty close to each other. Then one day, he asked me if I would like to move in with him, and maybe one day we would get married. In those days you didn't that because that was a big shame. I was polite and told him that we had lots of time to get to know each other, and then maybe we could get married…but living together, I didn't want.

"In the beginning everything was good. I had my girls, and Mr. Tekish was always polite to everybody. We even got three more girls from Social Services, which agreed that we were doing a good job. I saw Mr. Tekish on a regular basis, but the plan to get married never came up again, and then I came to learn that he was not the man I thought he was. He changed and started to drink and was acting very strangely around the girls, which made me scared.

"Many times, I would ask him what was wrong, but he never wanted to talk to me. I wasn't sure what I had done wrong, so I just ignored him, concentrated on my job, and tried to stay away from him. Then one day, my worst nightmare came. I went to see Mr. Tekish for something, and like always, I knocked on his door. His response was, 'Not now, come back later, I'm busy.'

"To me, that was strange. What could Mr. Tekish be working with? So I ignored his answer, and I opened the door. Then I froze. He was playing with one of the girls, and I mean she was almost naked. His eyes were bloodshot, and he yelled at me to get out.

I was so scared. Mr. Tekish was a madman. He was going to rape her like I had been raped as a child, and no one knew how bad this was, but I did. I was in pain all the time. Oh God help us!

"What a dirty, disturbed man. I was so wrong about him. What could I do now? Report him? I just didn't know what to do in that moment. Two or three minutes after that, I saw the same girl coming out of Mr. Tekish's office. She wasn't crying or anything, but I stopped her and asked her, 'Is this first time you have done this, or are there any others like you?'

She looked at me and said, 'No this is not the first time, Miss Clara. We all thought you knew about this. He is a monster, and you, what are you doing with a man like that?'

I didn't know what to say to her. Kicking the office door open, I stormed in. 'Look, you dirty, mad man, what you are doing? I will go to the police and report you if you don't stop, and I mean as of now!'

We stood there looking at each other, and then he said, 'I am sorry. This will never happen again. Please forgive me, Clara. I promise I won't do this anymore.'

I believed him and took a long walk to think about all that. I knew this had been going on right under my nose. I knew it had been going on always. I always forgave him, until I found out he was after you, and you kept all that a secret. Why Ramona?

Why didn't you tell me this before? So now, you know why I am trying to find your mother. This all happened a long time ago, and right now I don't understand how I am going to deal with all that."

"Yes Mom, I can see all that, but you should have stopped it. If my mother… well if she wanted to see me or wondered about me, why hasn't she come to see me, or why hasn't she looked for me? All these years have passed by, and you think she will see me now? Even if she does want me, I don't want her. You don't even know where she is. That letter from Sarajevo, is it from her?"

"No Ramona, that letter was my starting point to find her. Now I know where she came from, we are going to see a place where she lived a long time ago, and to see what else we can find out. Your mother told me about many things that had happened to her, and why she didn't want to keep you. Your father raped her; she was a very young woman. Also, after that, she became a very ill person. She had an awful vision of life when she wanted to give you away. I see your point; why she never tried to find me I don't know! However, let's see how this will go. I'd like to ask you to go with me. It would be a nice trip away from here, and you and I or both may find what we are looking for.

"Yes Mom, I'd like to go with you, but not for the same reason. I'd like to get out for a while to see other places, and maybe I would like the place where I was born. But looking for my mother is your responsibility, and I don't care if you find her or not. It won't make any difference to me."

"Right now, I'd like to be alone, and I'm happy that you told me the whole story. But remember this; she's not my mother—you are. I love you no matter what happened, even if lots of this is your fault, which I'll try to understand one day. You made many mistakes a long time ago, and I'll try to forgive you for that, but deep inside me, I don't think I can let this go."

We both started to cry; hugging and kissing. I knew that Ramona was strong, but I wondered if she was strong enough to face this new fact of her life. Somehow, I had a feeling that it might take a while, so I kissed her, and then she left.

One thing I was glad about was that she wanted to go with me. I knew Mr. Tekish would say okay, but that he would not give me any more money for a trip. I had saved quite a bit, though, and it would be enough for both of us. I had to book a bus to Beograd, and from there we would take a train to Sarajevo.

I was looking forward to this trip. Maybe Ramona and I would get even closer, and we could help each other. I just hoped that she could take all of the surprises she would face when we got to Bosnia, because there was a lot more that I hadn't told her yet. Nevertheless, I would be there for her when the struggle came. I would try to help Ramona face the truth and the pain.

Before I went to tell Mr. Tekish about my trip, I thought I'd just pop up to see Ramona. When I got to her room, she was under the blankets, and I could hear her crying. I thought it was best if I left her alone for now, and that I'd check on her later.

When I got to his office, Tekish was sitting there asleep, but I knew better, he was drunk as always. When he saw me, he looked at me and said, "Can I help you?"

He was so drunk he could barely stand up, and his pants were so messy he looked disgusting, but I kept my mouth shut about it. "Yes, Mr. Tekish," I said. "I'd like to let you know that since school is out for the summer, next week I'd like to take a trip to Bosnia to see some of my old relatives. I want to take Ramona with me. I'll pay for all of her transportation, because I'm sure you need every penny you have. At first, I was going to leave her here, but knowing you, I changed my mind."

"What the hell do you mean by that?"

"Well, I know that you are under investigation. Also, you and I are both in trouble, more so you than me, but I don't want to talk to you about that now. I'll come and see you when I come back from the trip, because we do have lots to talk about. I'll be leaving on Monday, so make sure the other teachers are staying put. We're going for fifteen days. We both know that Ramona needs some new scenery, and I have lots to think about.

CHAPTER 5

THE BUS TRIP to Beograd was fun. I could see that Ramona was very excited; she looked everywhere at everything, and she said that she thought Beograd was the most liberal city. She said, "Mom, one day, I'm going to come and live here."

I never said anything; my thoughts were on the trip to Sarajevo.

The train was leaving in about four hours, so we had some time to look around, and see how the city looked. Some buildings were still under construction, but there were many restaurants, and people were walking everywhere going into many stores. Ramona was amazed to see all that. So was I.

The last time I'd been in Beograd was in 1944, when it was not a beautiful picture. Beograd was building up so fast, and I was sure that in few years it was going to be the biggest city.

Finally, we both got tired of walking, and the train for Sarajevo was due in thirty minutes. There were so many people at the bus station waiting for buses to arrive. But we did manage to get through okay. The trip to Sarajevo took about two days, so I booked us a sleeping car. I wanted Ramona to experience the best, and I was right. She was so amazed about everything. Watching her made me cry, and those were happy tears.

Ramona didn't notice my tears and I was glad. I told her that those were happy tears, and she just smiled. We got settled down in our sleeping car, and we were on the way to Sarajevo. Because we were both tired by now, it didn't take us long to fall asleep. The train was moving nice and smooth. I got up once to check on Ramona, but she was sound asleep, just like a little angel. Looking at her, I asked myself, *What I have done?* Why did I let that monster ever touch my Ramona? Why did I not report him? However, right then I didn't have an answer. My guilt would haunt me for the rest of my life. I didn't deserve any peace at all. I had Mr. Tekish in my hands, and I did nothing. All I hoped for now was that Ramona would forgive me one day.

By now it was a beautiful summer morning in Bosnia, and what a place. So many mountains, rivers, and fields full of corn; just a perfect picture. Ramona woke up a little bit confused about where she was until she remembered that she was on the train.

I opened up some sandwiches and some milk that was still good. Eating and looking out the window, we both had our minds somewhere else. As we were thinking and eating, a knock on the door kind of made us jump. A conductor told me that we would be in Sarajevo soon, and that we would have to take a bus to Bukovina, which was about forty-five minutes from Sarajevo.

I thanked him and we started to pack. Ramona was not talking much, and I didn't batter her with questions. I let her just go on with her thinking, but I could tell she was excited about all of this—so was I. I wasn't sure what we were going to find in Bukovina.

When we arrived in Sarajevo it was almost lunchtime. Fresh food and water were what we needed. Like Belgrade, Sarajevo had many restaurant and little cafes, and I noticed many new bakeries. The city was incredible; different from everywhere else I'd been. Ramona just loved everything she saw. She noticed some people were dressed differently and got a question in her eyes. I told her that Sarajevo was the most international city, which meant lots of different people and different religions. Her nod answered, *Okay*.

We found a little restaurant near the bus station. Lunch was superb, and that baklava was something else. Time just moved by so fast, and our bus to Bukovina was right on schedule. I was excited and a little bit scared, wondering what we were going to find out about Ramona in Bukovina! The road to the countryside was a bit rough, but that was not unusual. After the war there were a lot of rough roads between towns; there was so much more to be done, and roads were the number-one job.

The bus driver said it would take forty-five minutes, but it was longer because he had to drive more carefully when it started to rain. I was not happy about the rain because once we got off the bus, I was not so sure what to do first. There were no hotels in the village or taxis, so we'd have to walk to the police station. Luckily it wasn't too far, but we still got wet.

The police station was a small, simple place. When we walked in, a smell of fresh coffee hit me. I wished I could have one; it was the first thing on my mind. I was getting tired, and I needed a break. A police officer was very friendly, and he greeted us very politely; "My name is Officer Branko. May I offer you fresh coffee?"

I think he was reading my mind. "Thank you, Officer Branko, my name is Miss Clara Slavich, and this is Ramona. We came from Vojvodina, and we are quite tired. I just wonder if anybody in this village has a room to rent for maybe two or three days."

"Yes, Miss Slavich, I think I can help you there. May I ask what is your reason for visiting our village? You see we don't have many people that stay for few days, that's why we don't have a hotel. However, I think we will have one soon. We have a lake not too far from here that is hot all year round; some people like to be in that water for a long time and it gives them some relief. Some of our elders are saying that is holy water, but no one knows. So, that one big company from Sarajevo is having a look around here. However, for now, we have one person who offers a room with a meal, and I can say you will love it because she is the best cook in town. Now let us get back to my question. Why are you here? Is there a problem/ I see you have a little girl with you, and that is my concern.

"I came to talk to Nikola Stanovic's brother—it's critical," I answered.

"You want to speak to Mr. Stanovic's brother! Yes, you have the right place, but his brother died two years ago, and now I'm in charge. May I ask you, Miss Slavich, what those two brothers have to do with you?"

"Let me explain from the beginning. I'm looking for a woman; her name is Elsa. I don't know her last name and that is part of my search, or you may call it a problem. I met Elsa almost eleven years ago. She left her daughter in my care, and I thought that she would be back, but she never came back. You see, I work in an orphan village in Vrnjac. It's a small city, but very nice. We look after girls that have been abandoned and don't have anyone to take care of them. How I met Elsa is a long story, but it was lucky for Ramona that I was there at exactly the right moment. Elsa never came back to see her daughter, not once in eleven years, but now we are in the process of closing the orphanage and that's why I'm trying to find her.

"The only one thing I have to start with was the name of Chief Nenad Stanovic, who lived in Sarajevo and then moved here to your village. Elsa told me quite a sad story about how Chief Nenad raped her, and lots more... other things that happened to her. On top of that, she had a little boy as well, and I have no idea what happened to him or what happened to Elsa either. I was lucky to find this village because I had Chief Nenad's last name. There are not too many Chief Stanovics in your area and it narrowed down the search, so I wrote letters to every major city that might have any information about him.

I know he died in a car accident, so the news was in the file, and it happened to be in Sarajevo. The man in charge of deaths knew him. Also, to tell you the truth, it was not pleasant to hear that Chief Nenad had a drinking problem, and his problem led him to your village, and I guess to Elsa as well. I'm trying to find out more about her.

"I know she was married, and I would like to know what happened to her husband and how Nenad fits in all this. I just can't understand what happened to Elsa that she left such a beautiful village and never came back, or never wanted her daughter. I'm having a very hard time understanding all this. Is there any way you can help me with all this, Officer Branko?"

"Miss Clara, may I use your first name?"

"Yes, of course."

"Why don't we go to Mrs. Sofia Besih's, which is the place where you will be sleeping or staying as long as you like? We all call her Aunt Sofia. How you approach her is up to you. After you settle down and get some rest, I'll come back, and we can continue our talk about Elsa."

"Thank you, Officer Branko. I can see that Ramona is exhausted, and we do need a good rest; our trip was very long. I'm looking forward to talking to you again."

Ramona and I met Aunt Sofia and loved her at once. She was very friendly and polite, and the room that she gave us was so good and clean and fresh. The blankets were old fashioned, all made by hand. I wished I could have a blanket like that back home.

Aunt Sofia told us to rest, and that she would prepare an excellent supper for us. I told her that Officer Branko would come back to take us out, but she wanted to make dinner. I thought that maybe I'd leave Ramona with her, and I'd go with Officer Branko by myself. That way we could talk about Elsa openly without making Ramona sad or mad. She hadn't said much, and that worried me, but I'd have to find out all I could, with Ramona or not.

We both needed a good wash up, and then we went to the guest room to rest. I must have been much more tired than I realized because as soon I lay down I was out.

I don't know how long I was sleeping, but I heard Ramona calling me to get up; that it was almost seven o'clock and she was hungry. That word "hungry" made me jump, thinking of that little boy on the train eleven years ago. Then I realized I was with Ramona in the guest room. It took me a second or two, but then I was back to myself.

Ramona was all lovely and clean, and I saw a happy face, which made me think she liked it there, or that maybe Aunt Sofia had promised her something… about which I was right.

"Mom, Aunt Sofia made cheese pita, and she has a fresh goat yogurt, which we don't have back home. She made some apple strudel as well, so let's go, and have a good supper."

"Okay Ramona, but I promised Officer Branko that I would go out for dinner with him. I told him that you wouldn't mind if I went. You could stay here and perhaps you will meet some girls in the village, and have fun. Aunt Sofia knows many people, and I'm sure she will keep you occupied. I hope you don't mind."

"No, I don't mind, I'm glad. Aunt Sofia told me that she would show me where I was born, and there are girls that I'd like to meet. Go and have fun, and I sure hope you find what you're looking for."

"Okay then, but make sure you listen to Aunt Sofia, and we'll talk tomorrow. It's possible we could stay for a couple of days longer, we'll see. Don't stay up too late because I don't know what time I'll be back."

As arranged, Officer Branko knocked on the door at 7:30 sharp. "Good evening, Clara," he said. "How's your room, and what do you think of Aunt Sofia?"

"The room is fantastic, and to tell you the truth I have an eye on one of Aunt Sofia's blankets, which I'm going to ask her to sell to me. Aunt Sofia is a great person; I like her and it looks like Ramona has fallen in love with her. Maybe it is a grandmother's love that she was looking for and found in Aunt Sofia."

"Okay then, let's go. I'm sorry I don't have a car, but the restaurant is just around the corner. We have two restaurants, and about four coffee and cake shops, and then about two bars. They're all on the same street. We have a few small stores, and that's all.

A family runs the restaurant where we're going; they've been open for business in our village for almost one hundred and ten years. It's difficult to believe but it's true. One of the old Yugoslavian kings once came for dinner. You'll see everything on the wall; it's fascinating. Most tourists that come here just love this place, and I'm sure you will enjoy it as well. Once we settle down and order our dinner, we can talk about Elsa. I do have lots to tell you, because I can see you have no idea where she is from, but I do."

Thank you Officer Branko. You're right, this is a beautiful place. I'd be glad that I took this trip even if I didn't get any answers about Elsa; the trip alone has been worth going this far. I just love this place. It's so different from ours, so friendly. I could go on and on, but let's talk about the subject at hand."

"Clara, I don't know where to start—there is so much to tell you about Elsa, and her life here."

"Branko! Can I just call you by the first name? I'd feel much comfortable that way. calling you Officer is business-like, and makes me feel strange."

"Yes of course. So, let's see where we were. Oh! Yes, we were talking about Elsa. Let me pull myself together because the story is very long, and it's a little bit sad for me to go back to the good old days with Elsa and Peter.

"Elsa and I had known each other for only five years before she disappeared, but those five years were the best that friends could have. Peter was her husband, which I'm sure you didn't know. Peter and I grew up together in this village, and we were friends until he died. We met Elsa on the same day in the same place. You see, we were in the army together, and our first station was the on border between Yugoslavia and Hungary; the big friendly city called Subotica. That was 1942. I'll never forget that day; the bombs and the fighting in that area weren't too bad. We got a day off, so we went to the city for a drink and we were hoping to meet some girls for fun, but that fun became real for both of us, especially for Peter. Then there she was."

....

Branko

"Two young army men having a drink alone is not fun. You think we can join you?"

Both Peter and I jumped, we were so startled we practically just stared at them. Peter was the first to respond.

To make a long story a little shorter, let me skip our stupidity and go back to the women. One of the lady's names was Rada, and the other's was Elsa. I saw Peter's eyes on Elsa right away, and I got the message that Elsa was his. So, that is how it all started. Because of the war, we didn't have much time to see Rada or Elsa that often.

Elsa was working nearby, though, so she came often. The love between Peter and Elsa was getting stronger and stronger, and war was the only thing that kept them apart. Time was flying and before I realized it, they were talking about marriage. The talking didn't last long. Accordingly, in March 1943, those two got married in a middle of a war. They were so much in love that bombs and gun noises didn't bother those two.

The captain of our outfit let them see each other quite often. Even though Peter and Elsa were married, there was no place for a woman in our bunkers, and on top of that, it was dangerous for her to be there. One day during a bombing, Peter was hurt very badly; which meant the war was over for him. He got discharged, and he was going home.

Just before they were going to leave Peter told me that Elsa was going to have a baby somewhere around December. The news was great, because the war in Bosnia was much heavier than it was here.

I was happy to hear that they were going to stay with Elsa's sister, who lived not too far from Subotica. That way I could come and see them. In some many ways, I was happy for them, but I was worried as well. The war was getting worse and Peter was a stranger in this part of the country, but knowing Elsa made me feel little better. She was a person that could do just about anything she put her mind to. When they left, I was lonely and sad.

The girl that I was seeing stopped coming often, and one day she told me she was not coming back. I didn't ask many questions because I was okay with that. We never actually clicked that well, certainly not anything like Peter and Elsa had.

I went to see them a couple of times, but it was dangerous for me to travel back and forth because the war was still going on. Nevertheless, all I wanted was to see Peter and Elsa; I was getting so lonely and sad. Peter was very concerned about me traveling so much, and he told me to stop coming that often—it was too dangerous. I took his advice and went to see them every other month or so. Both Peter and Elsa looked great, and Elsa was getting big. She was so happy that Peter was with her.

CHAPTER 6

ELSA'S SISTER JANA was very kind to them. She gave them a little cottage at the back of her house so they could have privacy. The place was charming and cozy. Elsa learned a lot from Jana and Peter got along splendidly with Stefan, Jana's husband. He liked hunting, and fishing but hunting was not such a good deal at that time because of the war. They spent some time fishing, but most of the time they stayed at home.

Stefan hadn't been able to join the army because of a heart problem, and it made him very upset to stay home while others were fighting for their country. Peter and Stefan would play cards or just talk; there was not much to do. The war was getting little worse, and everybody was scared. The food was getting low, and life was very depressing at that time.

Not hearing from them for a long time was very scary for me, and then during the holidays on December 28th, I got a letter from Peter. I was so happy and hoping for good news, because I knew that Elsa should have had her baby by now. And I was right, she had given birth to a baby boy on December 15th.

They named him Sasha after Peter's father, which was very nice since his father had died a long time ago. After that news, I didn't hear from them for a long time. I didn't have a chance go to them often as I would have liked because it was just too dangerous because of the war, and I was all over the place anyway.

There was a time that I was so scared and drained because of the war and its never-ending battles. When winter came it was even worse—so cold and no food for days. There were times that I wished I were dead, but thinking of Peter and Elsa gave me a little more courage to go on. By now, it was 1944 and springtime, which is the most beautiful time of year, but not for soldiers like me. The war was still on. There was talk that the Americans might be coming to help, but help how we didn't know? However, what worried me the most was that I had not heard from Peter for a long time.

I knew there had been significant bombing in Novisad, which is not too far from The Banovobrdo, where Peter was.

I always said to myself that no news was good news, and I was right. Then in late spring, I got a letter from Peter telling me that he wanted to go home. I knew Peter was lonely without his friends—he didn't have much of a family, but his mother was still alive, so he had that. I wrote him back, but I knew he would do whatever he liked. To travel with a little child at this time was not a good idea, but he did.

It was late September when I heard from Peter. I was pleased to hear that he'd gotten his little family home okay. He said the trip was long and quite scary because of the war. Whenever soldiers stopped them it was especially scary, but when they looked at them, they knew they were just a family trying to go home, so no one gave them any problem. The trip was very hard and took them almost a whole month because there were not many buses or trains; they travelled on foot, or somebody would offer them a lift. Coming home was the best thing for him until he found out that his mother had passed away the year before. No one except me knew where he was, to tell him about his mother, so the shock was very painful. He wanted his mother to meet Elsa and her grandson, so coming home was sad.

Time was going quickly and before we all realized it, it was winter again and almost 1945. There was news again that the enemy was pulling back, and I was wondering... pulling back from what country? Hitler was all over Europe, and we all suffered because of him—one man, how bad is that and so sad. I was the lucky one that never got hurt, and was hoping to get home soon.

Then one day in May, my captain came and held out a letter with a big smile on his face. I knew there was a letter for me, but there was more than a letter. Yes, one letter was from Peter and the other was from the army head office, saying that we could all go home in early July.

That moment I was not sure whether I should I kiss him or whether I should cry. The news was the best. Finally, I was going home after three years of this awful war. It was May when I wrote to Peter to tell him the good news. I was hoping he'd get this letter before I arrived, but to me it was all the same. After all, it was a war that had just ended and everything was moving very slowly.

Homecoming was one of the best times in my life. No one knew I was arriving that day; you should have seen their faces when I showed up. Peter thought he was seeing a ghost, and Elsa just stood there and stared at me. But my mother, who was there for some reason, she jumped up and started to cry about how happy she was. We all hugged each other for a long time, and we knew that our lives were not going to be the same as before the war.

Peter and Elsa looked good and Sasha was a happy little boy. We all agreed to get together after I got some rest. There was a lot to talk about; past and future. We were all finally free and happy.

A few days went by and I got a good rest, so I was very anxious to see all my friends. My mother told me that three of our boys didn't make it, and the big news in the village was that we had a full-time chief of police on duty. I was surprised at that. We were a small village and to have a chief of police was strange, but I just left it like that, figuring I would hear about it soon. However, I did have to wonder what a well-known chief of police was doing in a small place like ours.

Peter and I met in our little bar, just to catch up on everything that was going on, and the topic was the chief of police. I asked Peter what he knew about him. The story was somewhat strange but made sense to me. If thief was suffering from the loss of his child and wanted to ease his pain, I figured this place was good as any. However, Peter said that there was something strange about the man. Chief Nenad, which was his name, liked to drink, and he always had eyes on every woman he met.

Elsa told me that a couple of times he had asked her if she was happy living in this lost village on earth. I don't think she liked him, and you know what else? She was not the only one who felt that way. He was good at what he did, but as for his personality, I don't think he was likable. That is my opinion but quite a lot more people around here think the same, and you will find out soon why.

Peter was right, I didn'tice that something was odd about that Nenad, but I just ignored it for now. Peter and I, we talked about our dreams for a long time. He told me about an idea he had, and I was not surprised; he was always ahead of everything. Because it was winter, Peter asked me to help him made his dream come true. He hoped that he and I could be partners.

Peter wanted to build a large barn and raise pigs and chickens. He had sold some land and had enough money to buy new supplies for a shelter. Peter was so wrapped up in his project that he spent every minute building from the bottom up, and in spring, he planned to put on a roof. You see he knew that raising pigs and chickens was a good idea.

Because of that long war, many of our animals were gone. Feeding the army on both sides had left people without anything, and pigs and chickens were in demand. I liked his dream, but I had to tell him that it was his dream, not mine.

My dream was to be a police officer. I didn't like to work in the fields or with animals; I had a weak heart when it came to animals. He just laughed at me, but I told him that I would give him a hand in building the roof, and we just laughed about that and had a real good time. Winter was a bit long, but we managed to do a lot. The roof was next, and Peter was exhausted from working day and night.

Many people in town came to help, and his dream was coming along. As soon as all the snow went, Peter went to the store to pick up his supplies. He wanted everything running by summer; he already both small piglets and chickens were next. He always said, "So far so good."

This is the part that I wanted to forget but I can't, and that now I'm telling you going over all this is almost making me sick. You see that day… it was early May when Peter had almost completed his barn and was so exhausted. Standing on top of the roof, he was calling Elsa to come and see his final touches. I don't know, and we'll never know how it happened, but Peter slid down from the roof right on top of a sharp rake that was in the barn, and the rake went through his lungs.

I was just going to see him when I heard that awful scream; the one I will never forget. And I'll never forget that look on Elsa's face as long as I live either. I ran as fast as if my life was in danger. When I got there and saw what I saw, I almost threw up. I hadn't seen something like that, not even in the war.

Elsa was holding Peter halfway up, and there was so much blood, so much screaming. Not only was Elsa was going crazy, but Sasha was yelling, "Daddy! Daddy!"

I grabbed Sasha and threw him to Aunt Sofia; she was there like almost everybody in town. Elsa was screaming so loud it was heard all over town. The doctor came, but there was nothing anybody could do; we couldn't stop the bleeding.

Running out of blood, Peter didn't suffer too long, but it was long enough for Elsa to go insane. She was holding him and would not let go. The doctor pulled her over and gave her something to relax her. She didn't look right; she sounded like some zombie, there were strange looks that she was giving and she was mumbling something. The doctor said that was normal and would pass, but trust me, Clara, she didn't move on, by any means. Elsa was gone; her mind was not there anymore.

She never even asked where Sasha was; she just didn't care—entirely gone. I went home and cried like a baby. I didn't know what to do next; I was so scared for Elsa and Sasha, because deep inside I knew Elsa would never be the same.

I'm not so sure when Chief Nenad came into Elsa's life but right after Peter's, death, he was there every day. I didn't like that—Elsa was always speechless and numb, there were no feelings on her face at all. The chief worked his way in, and I thought he must have said something right, because she let him come quite often. Even Sasha had adjusted to him coming all the time, and they became close. Everybody in the village noticed, and many folks wondered what was going on, because as I told you he was married, and in a small village like this, that was strange.

I talked to Elsa about that, and her response was that I should mind my own business. I even spoke to my police commander about it, and his reply was shocking. He told me that if I wanted to keep my job, I'd have to look away when it came to the chief.

I knew that was wrong, but as a young officer I had no choice, and I didn't bother Elsa about the chief anymore. Deep inside me, I knew that was wrong too; I watched him using Elsa all the time. One day I noticed she had a black eye. I asked her what had happened and she said that Sasha had opened a door on her face. Right there I knew she was in trouble, but to my shame, I have to tell you I did nothing. That was going on all summer and fall. Moreover, one day just before New Year's we had a big party in the village, and everybody was there, even the chief with his wife and his favorite, Elsa as well.

Everything went well until Chief Stanovic got too drunk. He grabbed Elsa and start kissing her in front of everybody. That didn't look good. His wife caught Elsa and called her all sort of names. Elsa ran out, and so did the chief. What happened that night no one knew then, but after nine months we all knew what had happened.

Yes, Elsa was having a baby, there was no question about that, and the baby was the chief's. When Elsa was about six months pregnant, she came to see me. I was very surprised because she had been ignoring everybody in the village except Aunt Sofia. She came to tell me that the baby was Nenad's, and she wanted me to tell him that and about the responsibility that he would have.

I was in shock that she thought that I didn't know who the father was, but I played along. I promised her that I would talk to Nenad and get back to her.

After a week or so I saw Elsa again, and this time she was almost black and blue, which I know because she showed me all the bruises… done by the chief. I was so sad for Elsa, it made me want to go and kill that bastard. Nevertheless, I knew couldn't do that. The only comfort I could give her was to talk to her about the good old days, but then she would cry, so that was not such a good idea. In the meantime I did talk to the chief.

He told me to go to hell and mind my own business if I knew what was good for me. I was too green to know who was in charge in this village. He also said that if I didn't like him I could get another job. I knew that was a threat, so again I backed off… another one of my big mistakes.

Then sometime in late July of 1947, the chief was coming home with his wife from a party. However, he was so drunk, he lost control of his car and smashed right into a tree. The car was pretty old, and the big crash caused the car to explode. Both the chief and his wife died on the spot.

Soon, the news about the chief officer's death was all over the country, and I went to tell Elsa about it. She just stood there looking at me with no sign of sadness or happiness. I can say she was relieved, and to tell you the truth Clara, so was I. I hated that chief and his brother; both of those men were monsters in some ways.

Some people in the village were sad about losing a chief officer, but many were somewhat happy that he has gone. Among them was Aunt Sofia. She had never liked him; she was always saying that he was not a good man. She might have judged him harshly though, because I did find out he was not like that before. All his problems started when he lost his son. So I was wrong about him a little bit, but for the way he was treating Elsa I could have killed him many times. He was set to rest, and so was the rest of the village.

Then in the same year, on October 9th, Elsa gave birth to a baby girl. Aunt Sofia did an excellent job in delivering the baby; she helped Elsa a lot because she was Elsa's only friend who knew the truth.

After the baby's birth, Elsa went to Sarajevo many times. The baby and Sasha were always staying with Aunt Sofia. What she did in Sarajevo she would not tell me or Aunt Sofia. Then one day in early December, some new people showed up in the village, looking for Elsa. I was the one who met them first, so I asked them why they were looking for her. Well, I got a shock. She had sold all her properties to these people and was going back home. Then right at that moment, I knew I had failed Peter in helping Elsa. I had lost her forever until you came, and now it is an entirely new chapter of her life. If I were not married, I would go with you to find Elsa, because deep inside of me I know I still love her. But it is all over now, and I sure hope that Ramona will bring some comfort for Elsa.

Elsa's story is a tragedy, and maybe she is still confused and probably needs help, but no one knows about Elsa's problems. These are hard times nowadays, and there's not much help there for women, or mothers for that matter. Whatever, I hope you can find her and give her a second chance with Ramona.

....

Clara:

Our dinner was finished and so was Branko's story. "Thank you, Branko," I said, "for all that information. Now that I am aware of her whole story, perhaps I can help Elsa, and maybe Ramona will forgive her mother. So let's see what she has learned from Aunt Sofia. Knowing Ramona, I'm sure she had many questions, and I hope she found the kind of answers that she was looking for. It has been a long evening, and I must say most joyful, and I do thank you for all your help. I hope tomorrow will bring us a little more understanding about Elsa, as I am sure that Aunt Sofia knows more about what went in Elsa's house. We'll chat some more tomorrow, and maybe you can show me that lake and the rest of the village.

"Goodnight Clara," he said. "And I sure hope to see you both tomorrow. What time would you like me to pick you ladies up? I was thinking of bringing my horse buggy. I have two of the most gorgeous white horses; Ramona will fall in love with them. Then we can go to the lake and visit the rest of the village and some other small villages if you ladies wish.

"Oh Branko that would be lovely, and I think maybe around eleven will be just fine. That will give me some time to get a good rest, and I will ask Ramona about your plan. Either way, we'll see you at eleven a.m., and one more time thank you."

When I got to Aunt Sofia's house, it was already 10:30 p.m. I just went very slowly, trying not to wake up Ramona and Aunt Sofia, but Aunt Sofia was sitting in the kitchen, waiting for me.

I wasn't surprised at all. "Well hello, Aunt Sofia. Sorry for being so late, we just went on and on, and neither of us looked at the time. You should have gone to bed. How's Ramona? Has she asked you a lot of questions? I'm sure she did."

"Yes Clara, she did ask me a lot of questions. Some I answered for her, and some I have left just for your ears. I notice that Ramona is a sombre child; she doesn't like to talk much about her life in the orphan village, which is very strange to me since she has been there almost her whole life. I would like to talk to you some more, but now it is very late. Both of us need some rest, and we will talk tomorrow if that's okay with you.

I do have a lot to tell you, and I do have many questions that I need you to answer for me. Therefore, I will say good night for now, and I will get you girls up in the morning. Oh! One more thing I'd like to ask you. Have you and Branko made any plans for tomorrow? If yes, I will talk to you when you get back, and maybe I can give you a picnic basket so you and Ramona can have a good day, which I think that Ramona needs very badly. Did you ever notice that her eyes are full of questions and full of tears? In this short time that I've known Ramona, I think that she is one of the saddest kids I ever saw, I wonder why that is. Do you, Clara, know anything about that?"

"Yes, Aunt Sofia, I have noticed all that and trust me, I have tried my best. Are you accusing me of anything, Aunt Sofia? The best thing is to wait until tomorrow, and I will answer all the questions you may have. Also yes, Branko wants to take us with his two gorgeous white horses in a beautiful buggy for a tour of that mysterious lake and to see the rest of the village and some more. I think it will be good for Ramona to get to see the place where she was born. I will be more than happy to accept your picnic basket and thank you for your generosity, Aunt Sofia. You are so kind, and I have never met anyone like you. So, let us go for now, and we will see you in the morning."

I had a feeling that Aunt Sofia didn't like me; she had misjudged me, but why? I'd have to wait until tomorrow to find out.

I must have been exhausted because as soon as I lay down, I slept. My periods of rest were always short and messy, but this time I slept so well that I couldn't believe that Ramona had to wake me up again. It was almost ten o'clock when she came to get me. I jumped up so fast because I knew Branko was coming about eleven to take us on a ride and a picnic.

I remembered that I hadn't told Ramona about our date with Branko because she'd been asleep, so before I had a chance to dress, I called her to come back, because I had something to ask her.

"Yes Mother. What would you like?" The tone of her voice was biting—different from the one I knew. I wondered if Aunt Sofia had something to do with this.

"Ramona, you were asleep when I came in last night. I wanted to ask you if you would like to go with Officer Branko and me on a tour of this area. He has two big white horses and an old-fashioned buggy. What do you say about that?"

"I'd love to, and I have packed everything with Aunt S., which is what I call her. I like her, and we had a good talk yesterday. I have lots to tell you, but for now let us get ready. And breakfast is available; you should taste these eggs, so fresh and yummy. I am ready whenever you are."

"Okay Ramona. Give me five minutes, I'll be right there."

CHAPTER 7

Breakfast at Aunt Sofia's was very tense for me. I had a funny feeling that Aunt Sofia didn't like me, but I thought I would wait for a real talk with her when we came back from our day trip.

The trip to the lake and over all the other villages was superb; the weather was perfect, and the places we went were just hard to describe. It was very nice everywhere we went. People were just as friendly as everything in Bosnia was. I will never forget those moments as long as I live. Ramona was so happy and friendly with everybody we met. All in all, the trip was incredible.

We came back right after six in the afternoon. I could tell that Ramona was tired, and so was I. We said our thanks to Officer Branko, and I stated that I would like to see him again. I did have more questions, and he agreed with me and then left.

Aunt Sofia was waiting for us; more so for me. I knew she was looking for some answers, and I knew I'd have to be very careful with her. Let's face it; she was the only one who knew what happened in that house after Elsa's husband's death.

In addition to all that; knowing Elsa's relationship with Nikola Stanovic, she was the only one who helped Elsa bring Ramona into this world. However, if I didn't give her the answers she was looking for, I was afraid that she was going to be upset and she wouldn't like me at all. I was going to do my best.

As soon as we walked in in she said that supper was ready, and that after that Ramona could go to play with the animals, or she could go and have a rest. It was up to her.

Supper was a dream. I couldn't remember having had duck for very long time, and all those fresh vegetables, but everything was so good. After supper, Ramona said she would prefer to go and feed the animals and then she would rest. I could tell that Aunt Sofia just couldn't wait to talk to me. I offered to help in the kitchen, but she said to leave it for after, that she'd like to talk to me since we were leaving the next day.

She made the Turkish coffee that was popular all over the country, and with that, we started our talk. To my big surprise, she came right out and asked me. "Can I adopt Ramona? I loved her the day she was born, and I know I can take care of her."

Wow! I hadn't expected that. "Aunt Sofia, before we go any further, I have to tell you more about Ramona and her situation as of now. The reason I am looking for Elsa, Ramona's mother, is that she is the only one who can say that Ramona could be with you or me or anybody else. Elsa is the only one that can sign those documents. There's nothing I can do without Elsa's permission. That is the law. Many times I have thought that if Elsa won't sign the ‚documents there isn't anything I can do. We are in a different province, and each province has its own rules; it's not up to me at all.

"If I get in touch with her, I will tell her about you and maybe if she still remembers everything you have done for her, perhaps she will sign the document. After all, she never, ever came forward even to find Ramona. You might have a chance, we'll just have to wait and see for now."

"Clara, let me ask you another thing. Why didn't you adopt Ramona when you brought her to the orphan village? You had a chance…no one knew who Ramona was or where she came from except you. You had a clear run, so why not? Why have you let that monster destroy Ramona's life? Yes, I know everything. Ramona told me she was a toy for Mr. Tekish until she was about seven, and then he was more aggressive sexually with her. Why have you allowed that? Why? Can you explain that to me? Are you involved with that monster? All those horrible things he's done to those girls, you never even reported him. Why? Do you have an explanation for that? When Ramona told me those horrible stories, I was crying. Do you know that she promised him that one day she would come back and she would kill him? Can you imagine that an eleven-year-old girl is thinking of revenge? How sad is that? Oh Clara, what have you done?

"You did nothing to save Ramona or any other girl in there. I could just rip you apart, but for Ramona's sake I will play nice. I love that child and sure hope that I can adopt her. Just because we had this talk doesn't mean you have to go back and forget about me, because I will pursue this. I will ask Branko for help. That is all I have to say to you, and if you don't mind I am going out to find Ramona; it is time for bed soon. Tomorrow I'd like to show her the house where she was born. You can come with us or not, it is up to you. One more thing. Do you know why Elsa gave Ramona that name? I don't think so. I'll tell you why. She loved Peter so much and he always wanted a girl, so even though she didn't want Ramona, she gave her Peter's mother's name. So now you know. Elsa was a real woman and what happened to her is all our faults and yours as well."

"Well, Aunt Sofia, this is some accusation you have made against me. First, you don't even know me, so don't judge me before you know all the answers and the hell I went through to keep Ramona in the orphan village. Otherwise, she would be dead by now, or we both would be dead. I guess you didn't know. Elsa was going to throw Ramona off the train, or she was planning to jump. I don't know for sure, but if I hadn't stopped her there would not be a Ramona today, so don't tell me I'm not a fit human being. I will not go into all the details, but I want you to know that if I could have, I would have adopted Ramona a long time ago. I wasn't capable of that. That's another story you don't need to know for now. Aunt Sofia, you can think whatever you want of me, but as far as I can see, you and Branko failed Elsa and Ramona more than anyone did. You didn't help her when that Chief Nenad was raping her or when he was beating her, and you were just across the street. Couldn't you hear her crying? Or did you just pretend you didn't hear all that noise? Did you never hear Sasha calling for help? Tell me how you allowed all that to happen, and then look at me and tell me if I am not fit to be a human. Just remember that both of you failed Elsa more than anyone, and no wonder she didn't want Ramona. She is still probably depressed, and with no help. No one cares about women's troubles these days or before.

"Maybe in the future, it will be different, but for now those are the facts, and no one cares. So we are both responsible for someone; you for Elsa and me for Ramona. What happened to Ramona is going to haunt me for the rest of my life, and I know I will pay for my mistakes sooner or later. Now I am very upset that you and I didn't come to a good relationship, but I will go to bed now; I am so exhausted. I hope that we can work out something in the morning, so you won't think of me like that."

When I woke up next day, Ramona and Aunt Sofia were nowhere to be found. The first thing that came to my mind was that Sofia had taken Ramona off to a hiding place with her relatives. I was sure if that happened I would never see Ramona again. I panicked, just like that day when Elsa took off and left Ramona. I started to shake and cry...and then both of them walked in. God, what a relief—I almost fainted. "You two scared me. I woke up and nobody was home. Where were you?"

"Oh Clara don't be scared. You were sleeping and looked like you needed to rest, so Ramona and I went to the garden and picked some fresh vegetables so you can take them with you on your long trip back home. Tell me what you were so scared of. Did you think I would do something stupid? No, my dear Ramona loves you even though she knows your secrets; I would not do that to her. I am hoping that one day you will write me about Ramona and yourself."

"I am so sorry Aunt Sofia. I will do my best. When I woke up, I couldn't find either of you, and I just panicked. I knew that you wouldn't treat Ramona badly or do anything that would be painful for me. Now that we both know what we came for, I'd like to ask you one more favour. I have a couple of more questions to ask Officer Branko, and I won't stay too long. Our bus is living at seven p.m., so we still have some time to go and see the place where Ramona was born. You two can go without me; maybe that way will be more interesting to Ramona, instead of me asking questions all the time, which I think makes her sad. So, go ahead. I will see you shortly.

Officer Branko was just coming to see us, so I was glad to catch him; I preferred to talk to him in private. "Well! Good morning or afternoon, Aunt Sofia let me sleep longer, so now I am so rested and fresh. And let me tell you that Aunt Sofia is something else. We had our real talk; some good some bad, but we both know that everybody does make mistakes in their lives sooner or later. Mine and hers were sooner. At least we both agree to do what is best for Ramona for now, and we will see what happens after. That's why I need to talk to you and see what else I can do.

"When you and Peter were in the army and met Elsa, did you get to know what town she came? If you know, that will give me a start to look for her. Maybe she went home after running away from me that day."

"Oh yes," said Branko. "I'll never forget the day she invited us to come to her sister's house because that was where she was living. I think her parents went back to Hungary, but she never talked about them. She really loved her sister Jana—we all did. Jana had one boy then and I think she was expecting another baby, but I'm not so sure about that. She was always glad to see us and loved Peter right away.

"The town was very friendly, but you could tell that there were many different languages among the people there. Some of them I didn't understand a word they were saying. The name of the town was Vrba's or Vrshac, I'm not so sure. They both sound almost the same, but it's more likely it's Vrshac.

"There was a war going on. We were always taking a chance going there. Also, I never paid any attention to the name of the town, but Peter always said don't worry it would be okay, and I guess we were okay."

"Branko, would you have an address by any chance? I know this was a long time ago, but there's no harm in asking."

"No Clara. I never even knew the proper name of the street or town. We just knew the house, and we went. However, I think I can help you. Jana's last name is or was Jurik. Her husband's name was Stefan. I can write a note to the police station asking them to look into that, and I'm sure if they're still living in Vrshac, the police will find them. Most people these days do register when they move out or move in. I'm just not so sure where they live now."

"Well, I guess this is all that I needed for now. If you don't mind, I would like you to give me your address, so that I can tell you what's going on; that is, only if you want to know."

I don't mind. I've already done that, but I have one question for you. You see,

when my wife comes home from vacation, I would like to talk to her. I'm going to ask for her support, so we can come to your orphan village and take the proper action to adopt Ramona."

"Can I ask you why? Is there some guilt that has a hold on you?"

"Well, yes and no. I did make many mistakes then. I was young and afraid of my captain, and others that didn't care about Elsa. I know that I was wrong, and maybe things would be different if I'd helped her, but now I'll never know for sure."

"You see, Branko, Aunt Sofia asked me the same question. It looks like all three of us do have some guilt, but Branko you know better than that. To adopt someone, only the mother can sign the paper. The story would be different if Ramona didn't have anybody, but our central office knows that Ramona has a mother and just like me, they are looking for her. They have some information but not much. I have a better chance of finding her, and only then we can see what will happen. If the orphan village closes and Ramona's mother is still not found, then I will write you. However, you know you are in a different province, and that means different laws. If Elsa's sister finds out that Elsa had a daughter, I'm sure that she'll be interested in having her too. If not, then you might have a chance, but it is a long shot for now. Just don't lose your faith; I will let you know either way."

"Well then, Clara, I have to go now. It's my turn to look around the village for security. I will drop by and walk you to a bus station. Hope you have some more fun before you leave."

"Thank you, Branko. See you in a few hours."

Just as I was getting to Aunt Sofia's house, she was crossing the road towards it.

"Hello Aunt Sofia, where's Ramona? I thought she was with you."

"She was, but she's staying little longer with a girl just across the street—actually in the house where Ramona was born."

"How did she take it when you told her that's the house where she was born?"

"Not so bad, she never said much. The people that live there are very friendly. They have a daughter about Ramona's age, and they just got along good, like they knew each other for a long time, so I was glad to see that. She didn't ask many questions, but I saw a touch of sadness in her eyes. She wanted to see the rest of the house. I was surprised, wondering why, but the girl that lives there said she would take her all over, and I need not stay or worry about Ramona. I wasn't comfortable with that, but Mrs. Hasima, that is the woman, she told me don't worry she will be okay, so then I left.

"Tell me Clara, does Ramona knows anything about Elsa's first husband or her father? Seems to me she was looking for something there, as if she was trying to get some picture."

"I don't think so. I've never mentioned Elsa's first husband or her father, but you know she might have been listening to Branko and me. When I was talking to Branko, she went out, but now I wonder if she really went out, or if she was hiding and listening to what we were saying. To me, this is most likely, but knowing Ramona she will never admit it. She'd rather keep it to herself."

"What are your intentions? Are you ever going tell her about her father?"

"Honestly, Aunt Sofia, I don't know what to do. I'm very confused, and I just don't know what to do. Please, can you tell me, what would you do if you were me?"

"Clara, I always say the truth is the best medicine. However, in this situation, I would not tell Ramona anything about Sasha's father unless she asks. But if she does ask, I'd sit down with her and tell her the truth. She needs to know not only for herself, but because she might think differently of Elsa. As of now she just refuses to acknowledge that Elsa is her mother. That is my opinion, but you do whatever you think is right. Just make sure you pick the right time for it. It won't be easy to hear that your father was a drunk and a rapist. So, choose your words and time carefully."

"Thank you, Aunt Sofia, I think that is the best way, and I will try my best when the time comes..

But since Ramona is not an heir now, I'd like to ask you to forgive me if I stepped out of line yesterday. We were both under stress about Ramona, and I think you are the most honest and nicest woman I ever met. I'm very sorry if I hurt you—it will never happen again."

"My dear Clara, don't worry about that. I know I said a lot of things that I should not have said, so we're the same. You don't have to ask me for forgiveness—you have to forgive yourself. You have done nothing wrong in my book, but whatever happened before that is past, my dear. I wish you all the best. Whatever happens, I will always remember you and Ramona. I am grateful that you brought her into our lives, even it was for a short time, but that was good enough for me. I always wondered what happened to them; now you've given me some closure, and I sure hope to know what happens when the orphan village is closed. For that, I wish you would let me know either way… if the news is good or bad. That is all I am asking of you."

"Aunt Sofia, I promise that as soon I know anything, I will let you know. Branko gave me the address where Elsa's sister is from; where they met in the wartime. I sure hope that her sister still lives there, because from there it will be easier to locate Elsa. Look. Just in time," I said. "Ramona is coming back; I'm glad that we've finished our talk, and I'm hoping that Ramona had a really good time, with you and everybody that she met in Bosnia. We still have a few hours before we have to go. We'll pack up and then say our goodbyes."

"Before we say any goodbyes, we have to have a little snack," said Aunt Sofia. "I have made you our great pitas with cheese, and some goat yogurt. I noticed that Ramona loves it, and I've packed some for your trip.

I gave Ramona a hug. "Hi Ramona. Did you have fun at your new friend's house?"

"Yes Mom. Those people are very friendly, and I like them a lot. Some of them are a little bit different from us. By being different, I mean they eat and dress differently.

I have never seen people dress like that, and Bina is the girl that lives in that house. After seeing the look on my face she said that they're Muslims, which is why they dress different, but everything else is the same. I told her I don't care if you're a monkey, you are my friend just the same, and she laughed.

"But something strange happened to me while I was there. I went to the barn to see some new kittens, and an old man was sitting there. His eyes were so bright and he smiled so soft, and he had a face full of life. He took my hand and said to me, 'My child, don't turn your head to look back. Always look forward, there is a new day every day. What happened before was before—look to brighter days that are coming tomorrow or after tomorrow. There is always a new day!' I was stunned. He must have been about a hundred years old. For a second I turned to look at the kittens, and he was gone. Now I'm not so sure if I imagined him or what. I asked Bina, 'Who's that old man?' but she just looked at me and said, 'What old man?' I can't explain it. Do you think I imagined things in that barn? I don't know what to think but it's okay. I had fun after all, and the smell of Aunt S's burek makes me hungry. Do we still have time? Besides, after that, I'd like to go and say good-bye to my goat Dushan; I gave him that name because I like it."

I ruffled her hair. "Yes, we have about two hours, which gives us enough time to eat and pack. Branko will come to help us catch our bus for Belgrade and then we will switch buses and go home."

"You know, Mom, I'm glad that we're going back. Even if perhaps our home will not be our home for long, I still missed it, and I guess I always will because that is the only home I ever had.

When Ramona ran upstairs I lowered my voice and said, "Aunt Sofia, did you hear that? She named her goat, or your goat, Nenad. That was her father's name. Is it possible that she knows more than we think? I never told her anything, but it is possible that she was listening to you and me when we talked, or maybe the people across the street told her."

"Clara, don't worry. She'll come around when she's ready and then she will ask you lots of questions, and you'll answer them. For now, let it go."

My tears started rolling again. Ramona had seemed so sad when she was saying that about home. Deep inside I could tell that she would always miss her first home, and I would always miss her. Sometimes I thought that both of us knew that our mother-daughter relationship was coming to an end soon… but we hoped not too soon.

I noticed that Aunt Sofia was silent, and I saw her tears coming too. It made me sadder because we did have to say goodbye, but how do you say goodbye to someone like her? I knew it was going to be harder that I thought.

Once we finished packing, and Ramona ate it was time to say goodbye. Branko was waiting outside with a sad face, and that made it harder for me to handle. I saw Aunt Sofia sit down because of her emotions, so I told Ramona to go and give her a hug and many kisses, and that I would be right there.

Aunt Sofia was crying so hard that it made all of us do the same. I took her hand, and squeezing it I told her we would never forget her, and I promised that I would write to her. Letting go of her was like letting go of my own mother as I had long time ago. I was shaking and crying, and Branko had to come and pull us apart. Ramona was crying too, but she acted strangely. She told Aunt Sofia not to be so sad—that they would meet again, if not tomorrow, in time. I don't know what she meant by that; I just told her that we had to go before we missed our bus.

We got to the station just in time to get our bus, which was just as well for me because saying goodbye to another new friend was hard.

I looked into Branko's sad eyes, and we both just gave each other a big hug. I went inside to the bus while he was talking to Ramona, and they kissed and hugged, and that was it.

The bus driver was kind of in a hurry and mumbled something like, "It's about time," but I just ignored him. We were going home.

CHAPTER 8

SITTING ACROSS FROM Ramona on the train that was taking us back home, I wondered, *What is she thinking of all this?* I wondered if she was happy that we'd found some information about her mother, or if she was confused. Looking at her, it was hard for me to figure out if Ramona was happy or sad.

Most of the time she just looked out at the window, and there were no signs of whether she was sleeping or dreaming with her eyes open. I wanted to talk to her. But every time I looked at Ramona she gave me a funny expression more or less signalling that she wanted me not to bother her. So, I decided to let it go for now and would see how she felt later on. The trip going back would take us just as much as had going to Bosnia.

Since I'd have plenty of time to talk to Ramona later, I wanted to make one more stop before we went back to our place, but I wasn't so convinced that Ramona would like that.

"Ramona, are you hungry? Or tired?"

She didn't answer me, so I took the chance to ask her about an extended trip. "Look, Ramona, I would like to make one more stop before we return home, and I was wondering if you were up to that. It's crucial, but if you don't feel like continuing this trip, I understand and then we'll go home. You see your mother's sister is not too far from us, and I'm sure she can help us locate your mom."

"How many times have I told you not to call her my mother? Mothers don't do what she did."

"Yes, I know Ramona, but legally she is your mother, and as soon as you admit that, you will be all right. It's very hard to understand all this for now, but let's see first how can we find her and then you can judge her."

"I've been thinking about all this and to tell you the truth all I want is to go home. I'm not so sure that I want to continue this trip. The best thing is that we go back and then you can go by yourself if you wish to find Elsa, but I don't have any interest in that. I'm sorry, but that's how I feel right now, and I'm so tired of all this. I'm getting confused about who to believe and who to trust. Please let me be and let's just go home. Perhaps when we get home, and you've had your rest, maybe we can talk about what we've learned and how much more we want to know."

"I spoke to her soothingly. "Well, it's getting late, and if you'd like to go to sleep, it's fine with me. We can talk tomorrow or not. Just have a good rest, and I will do the same. We have one more day and then we'll be home."

Morning came so fast, or else I was so tired that I just didn't realize how stressful this all was. I just didn't want to drag Ramona along any longer. Perhaps the best thing would be to go by myself after we got home. Ramona wasn't interested in finding out about her mother. Sooner or later, though, she had to face the fact that Elsa was her mother... that is, if I ever found her.

We both had some leftover sandwiches, and there was some yogurt. We ate in silence. I could see that Ramona was avoiding my look, so I just ignored it and gave her some space. I knew she would come to me to talk when she was ready. In a couple of hours, we'd be home and what a relief. I hadn't felt like this for a long time. Something was telling me that things were not going to be good. I don't know why but there was something in Ramona's eyes as well. It was like she was crying without tears.

An hour or so passed by and then Ramona jumped up. With a big smile on her face she said, "Look, Mom, we're almost home. There's my school and the fields of apple trees, and we're home. I'm so glad because the trip took so much time and was too sad for me. I don't think that I ever want to go back to Bosnia."

Her happiness at being home and her not wanting to go back to Bosnia got me worried. I had been so sure that she'd enjoyed the trip and all the people she met, but I guess I was wrong. She had never been truly happy. Most of the time I think she was putting an act. All she wanted was to go home, and now I saw that it was going to be a big problem for her when the orphan village closed.

"Ramona," I said. "I thought that you liked all the places we went in Bosnia, and the village where you were born. What happened? Why didn't you tell me that while we were there? Why? What's going on?"

"Mom, do you want to know? I'll tell you why. I heard everything Officer Branko was telling you, and I heard everything you and Aunt Sofia talked about. While I was there, I just pretended that I liked it, but I didn't like it...

I don't want to hear about Bosnia—about that woman Elsa and her sad life. Does anyone care about my miserable life? No, so let's just get off the train and go home. It's the only home for me, and I love it. Despite what happened to me, it's my home."

By now the train had stopped and we got off and collected our things. I put my arm around Ramona. "Okay my dear, let's go back to our home. Do you want to walk back? Or maybe we can find someone going our way; walking will take us a long time, but if that's what you'd like, it's okay with me."

"I don't mind walking," she said. We were on the train for so long, and walking will do us both good, so let's go home."

"Do you want to talk about anything Ramona?"

"No mom, let's just walk."

"Ramona, there is one question I have to ask you. Since we have a long way to walk, I'd like to talk to you about you and me. As you know for sure that I'm not your mother, what are your intentions about addressing me in front of people? I won't mind if you call me Mom, but we both know that will sound funny since we're aware of the truth."

"I haven't thought about that yet. I know that you are not my mother, but you are the only mother I know. If you don't feel right about me calling you Mom, I will address you as Miss Slavich, just like the others do. You did many wrong things, but as far as your motherly instincts, I think they were there. I know you were not able to watch me all the time, and that monster knew that. So, don't worry about anything. I'll call you Miss Slavich, but in my heart, you'll be Mom."

"Oh my dear child, you make cry. I have never loved anyone the way I love you. I want you to know that in future no matter what happens, you will always be loved by me, and I will carry you in my heart forever."

"Mom, I don't like it when you talk like that, and when you use words like "in future." You and I will always be together no matter where we are. If by some miracle you find Elsa, and if I have to go and live with her, I will always write to you. Also, when I get old enough, I will come to live with you."

I persisted, "I hope everything is going to be all right, but if not I want you to be strong always, and never forget that I love you."

"Mom, I don't like it when you talk like that. Let's just get home and see what's going on. You know it's been almost ten days, and hey, you never know what's going on in there. For all we know, the rumours that our house is closing are just rumours, and that's all."

"Oh! Look, Ramona, we're almost there. Listen, someone is running towards us.

My God! That can't be her—that's that old woman from the kitchen—Tina. I wonder what's going on. Why is she running? And look, the gates are open. I know that Stefan always keeps the doors closed. Something is wrong."

Tina was waving frantically and shouting, "Miss Clara wait! Don't go in, Miss Clara wait...wait...wait I have to tell you something! Don't go in!

"Oh dear," I said. "Something is definitely wrong."

Ramona slowed down. "Let's wait until she gets closer to us. Tina never leaves her kitchen, and to see her running like that … something is not right."

At last Tina reached us. "Miss Clara, please let me catch my breath first. No one saw me coming out; I used a back door. I saw you coming from my window and had to get out and warn you. There are police and social workers and people from the city; they are all there waiting for you."

"Okay, slow down Tina. How did they know I was coming back today?"

"I'm not sure Miss Clara, but they came every day, to see if you and Ramona were back."

"Why Tina? What is going on? Tina?"

"Miss Clara, I don't know what you've done, but last week police arrested Mr. Tekish, and he's in prison. Rumours were that he was accusing you of something; something that nobody likes to talk about. All I know is that police are waiting for you, and I just wanted you to know. Please, be careful Miss Clara. We all love you, and if we lose you it's going to be horrible for us, but don't worry about what's going to happen to Ramona. We all are going to look after her."

"Tina, nothing is going to happen to me. I thank you for the warning, so now please just go back, and let me see what's going on. Don't worry; everything is okay."

I turned to the frightened Ramona. "Well, Ramona, let's just go. Please act like as if we don't know anything. You just go to your room and let me talk to them. Also, remember what I told you before. Keep your head up and don't worry. I will always love you no matter where I am or where you are. Now my dear, no tears, just stand by me nicely and come. They don't know that we have been warned about visitors. Just walk as if nothing is going on and let me do all the talking."

CHAPTER 9

"OH, WELL LOOK who is finally coming back from holidays. I sure hope, Miss Slavich, that you had a lovely time on your vacation because trust me that was your last one."

"Excuse me, Officer? I'm not sure, are you speaking to me?"

"You know damn well that I'm talking to you. We have waited for you for a long time, and personally, I never liked you. So yes, I was talking to you, and trust me, that was your last holiday for a long, long, long time. Where you are going there is no sun or blue sky; all you are going to see is your four by four walls. Also, you can get pictures in your head of all the girls that you could have saved from that monster, but you didn't, so yes, I'm talking to you."

My knees were shaking but I kept my voice strong. "Officer, you have no right talking to me like that. Can't you see that a child is standing right beside me? She doesn't need to listen to your accusations against me; we can continue talking when I get settled and take Ramona upstairs. In the meantime, mind your manners; you are not in charge of this place. If you have anything else to tell me, you may wait for me in our office. I hope I've made myself clear."

"Yes, Miss Clara you've made yourself clear, but let me tell you one more thing. You might as well say good-bye to your girls and your pet Ramona, because this is probably the last time you will see them all. You will end up in state prison just like Mr. Tekish. And his sister is in a holding cell for now, and that's all I have to say. I will be in your office, and please, I'm expecting you downstairs in about an hour or so. Please don't make me come up to get you, because that won't be a lovely sight for the girls to see."

"All right, Officer. There's no need to be like that. I will be in my office as soon as I talk to my staff and the girls."

"You have no staff, Miss Clara. There is a social worker and staff from the city; they are in charge of this place for now. You don't need to talk to anyone from the team, but you can tell them goodbye. My orders are to take you in, and that is what I'm going to do. Since you just got home, I'm giving you an hour, like I said before, and then we have to go."

"Officer, I realize that you have orders, but you have to give me more than an hour. I'm not going to run away or anything else that you might be thinking; I will come down as soon as possible."

"Okay Miss Clara, but remember I'm in your office and do not try anything funny. I know you have lots of friends in this place, but I will be on the lookout for you. Consequently, do not even try to run away."

It was clear that the man hated me. I thought I'd better get Ramona and tell her about my notebook and other things before he came looking for me. I had many regrets, and perhaps things were impossible to fix. I'd have to be careful what I said and did. When I spotted Krina I asked her to look for Ramona. I didn't trust her too much, but I didn't have much choice.

Krina's look was unfriendly. "Miss Clara, you know why this is all happening and to tell you the truth I don't feel sorry for you, but I do feel sorry for Ramona. You have been brainwashing that girl; she thinks you are her mother and look what's happened. I will bring Ramona to see you, and I hope that it will be the last time for you to put lies in her head. When I came to work here, I did like you, until I noticed funny things going on between you and that monster. Many times, I thought I was just jealous of you, but now I know the tragedy you put those girls through...and poor Ramona. I just can't be bothered to talk to you anymore. I will go and get Ramona and I hope I will not have to talk to or see you again."

"Thank you, Krina, and please forgive me if you can. The law will be punishing me for my mistakes, and I sincerely regret what I have done."

In about ten minutes or so Ramona was running toward me, tears all over her small face. I could tell she knew what was going on. I'm not so sure how much she knew.

We went to my room and closing the door I told her to sit down and listen very carefully because this possibly would be the last time we could be together. Ramona was a smart girl, and we'd had a talk about this before, so she was ready. We looked at each other and hugged and cried. I knew this is the end of us together, so I went right to the point.

"Ramona, you are my beautiful child, and you always are in my mind and heart. I have something for you, something that I was keeping for the right time to give you. I was hoping that this time would never come, but tragedies do happen and this is one of them. You and I have talked about things that I have done and things that I should have not done. Well, the time has come for me to face my mistakes. I know that my dark side is impossible to fix. Ramona, I have this notebook for you, and what is in this notebook is a very moving but true story. The story is about you. I have written in this journal nearly every day; I know that one day you will have to know the truth about your mother. When you start to read this book, some of it will be hard for you to understand, but in time, you will eventually see what your mother went through. You will realize the wrong things she has made, but at the same time, you will be heartbroken knowing that I have made some mistakes as well. I'd like you to be careful about trying to understand all this, but Ramona, do not read this notebook now. Just put it in a safe place, and when all this scandal goes away then find a quiet place and read it.

"I know Mr. Tekish abused you, but I'm the one who is asking you to forgive me. Try not to be so disappointed about the love that I have for you. I don't know why I didn't look for your mother right away; I just don't know. I wanted you for myself, knowing that she didn't want you, but Ramona, please forgive me, I never meant any harm to come to you. I'm looking forward to my punishment because I know that I do deserve it, but all I wish is for you is to try to forgive me one day.

"Ramona, I can hear the officer is coming. Give me the biggest hug ever, and please don't cry. Ramona, we will meet again one day."

A loud bang on a door shook us both. I knew this was the end.

"Goodbye, my dear, and please forgive me if you can."

The door swung open. "Are you ready to go, Miss Slavich? I have to go now, so let's go. Little girl, you go to your room, and we will talk to you later. Stop crying like a baby. You know Miss Slavich is guilty. She's not as nice a person as you thought, so get going."

"Look Officer, you don't have to yell at her, she is only a little child."

"Yes, she was a kid, perhaps ten years ago. Don't pretend to be so innocent, just run to your room, and I mean now!"

Ramona clung to the door frame. "Goodbye Miss Clara, you will be my mother forever. I will come and look for you when I grow up. Please take care of yourself."

Okay, enough of that," growled the officer impatiently. "Get out, and go to your room. I won't ask again."

"Goodbye Miss Clara! Goodbye my mother! Goodbye!"

CHAPTER 10

Ramona:
I never thought this would happen so soon. I knew that one day the truth about Mr. Tekish and his behaviour and abuses towards us was going to come out. It was just a matter of time. Now that Mr. Tekish was in jail we were safer there, but knowing that Miss Clara would be prosecuted in an open court scared me. I wished I could help her. However, I could tell by the officer's tone that she had no chance.

Even the social workers who had known Miss Clara for years; who knew the work she had done... I mean a good job—even they were looking at her as the biggest criminal or something like that. She wasn't crying when she left with the officer, but I could tell that deep inside of her, she wouldn't be able to take all this.

She was a lovely person caught up in the web of a monster who took advantage of innocents. I needed to be strong for her. I knew they would be asking me many questions, and I wasn't afraid to tell the truth.

I decided I would tell them how Mr. Tekish had treated me, and that he'd said if I were to tell what happened in his office to anyone that he would destroy Miss Clara. Perhaps my truth will help. I had to try to help Miss Clara.

All I had was a notebook to remember her, but I wished I could do something. I held onto the notebook, planning to read it in my darkest moment, but for then, I had to be patient and see what was next.

I just wanted to hide and run, run, run forever.

Sitting in my bed, thinking of Miss Clara, my mind was far away. Then I heard someone calling me. I had no desire to listen to anyone, so I just ignored the call. I was just about to go to my locker to get a notebook when a loud bang on my door scared me. It was Lela, another orphan who was a few years older than me. I was the youngest girl there.

"Lela, what is wrong with you? Why all that rush? Please slow down. You're scaring me. Did anything happen?"

"Yes. Yes, Ramona. I've been calling you, and you didn't answer, but I've got to warn you. There is a man from the city. He's asking questions, and we were all interviewed, and now he is looking for you. Please, Ramona, don't hide anything. That will make it worse for Miss Clara. Tell the truth. I did, but we all know that you know more than any of us. Please come downstairs with me."

"Lela, what kind of questions are they asking?"

"Well, I don't know about the others, but they asked me about Mr. Tekish and Miss Clara's relationship in this place."

"What do you mean, relationship? They never liked each other—he was just as bad and mean to her as he was to us."

"I don't know, Ramona. I told them that Mr. Tekish is a sick man and about everything that he did to me. I don't know what he did to you; it's up to you to tell them, and the truth will be the best. I'm pretty sure they know all about Mr. Tekish, but you might even help Miss Clara with your story."

"Lela, what he did to me is not a story, it's a horrible truth."

"Yes, I know Ramona. I'm sorry; we have to go downstairs before that little social worker comes up. You know I hate that woman."

"Lela, I hate that woman too, but right now, we have no choice but to pretend that we're happy. Soon we are all going to be gone somewhere; I hope that I don't go with my mother and I hope that they never find her."

"Ramona, last week I overheard them talking about your mom. They may have found her. I'm not so sure about all the details, but it seems like they are pretty close to finding her."

"What do you mean close to finding her? Don't they know where she is? No one said anything to me. Also, why haven't you told me about this before?"

"I don't know. I know you don't want to go with your mother, so I was kind of hoping they wouldn't find her."

"I sure hope that too. Elsa never cared for me, before so why would she bother now? I hope they won't find her for a long time. I won't stay with her; the first chance I get, I will run away from her."

"Ramona, I don't think that your mother has a choice. She has to come for you. You see most of us are like you in this place; we all have to go, but some of us have a parent, and some have none. Maybe you are lucky if they find your mother."

"Lela, you can have my luck. I don't care about my mother now, nor will I care in future. She never wanted me in the first place, so I don't want her in my life at all. I know I don't have the power to control what is going on, but I can tell you this: Mark my words, as soon as I can I will leave her. You see Lela, I do have a plan. When I'm eighteen I can do whatever I like, and that is when my revenge will come. I will find Mr. Tekish and then I will deal with him my way. I know this is a long wait, but I don't care how long I've got to hold on, the right time will come. You know what? Why don't you go, and I'll come down in a minute. I've got something to do."

"Okay Ramona, but I've warned you."

I wanted to read that notebook before I went downstairs. I needed to know how I ended up with Elsa. Miss Clara was hiding something from me, and I thought that was why she gave me the notebook. There was something in that notebook that she never wanted me to know.

She never expected that the orphan village was going to be close one day, and that is why she never told me the truth. I knew some information about my mother, but there must be worse then I thought; that is why she never told me, and that is why she wanted me to read this notebook. But as I got out the book I heard someone coming. I hid the journal until I found some other time to read.

It was the man from the city. "Listen little one; I'm so tired of waiting for you. Get downstairs right now. I don't have all day."

"I'm sorry," I said. "I was just packing some of my stuff, so I can be ready to go when the time comes. I didn't mean to keep you waiting."

When we got to the office, he closed the door. "All right Ramona, let's sit down and have a real talk. Do you know who I am?"

"Yes sir, I do. You are a very important man, and I'm pleased to meet you. If I may say, you look like a very nice man, and I'm sure you will do your best for us."

"Well then, can you tell me about Mr. Tekish and his behaviour towards you, and everything he did to you for as long as you can remember? Don't be afraid to tell me everything; some of the facts we know but I'd like to hear them from you. As you know Ramona, Mr. Tekish is in prison and he cannot harm you anymore, or threaten you or anybody else. As for Miss Clara, she is in jail as well, but there's a chance she can be judged lightly for her mistakes. So Ramona, you're free to tell me all and don't worry about anything."

"Sir, can I ask you something? If I tell you everything, is it going to help Miss Clara? She is not as bad as some people say she is. Miss Clara tried to protect us all; not only me. But she couldn't watch us all the time. Most of this tragedy with Mr. Tekish happened when she couldn't be there."

"Ramona, I can see you are stalling for time, but you have to tell me about Mr. Tekish and his behaviour towards you. Your story will help us to put him away for the rest of his life."

"Sir, I don't have a story, what I have has been a genuine tragedy for me and some other girls. I would not say that those are stories. No sir; stories are what you read in some newspapers. What I've got is the dark side of my younger years and yes, I will tell you everything. Sir, what is your name? I don't like to keep saying, sir."

"Okay Ramona, my name is Mr. Zoran Nemic, and now that you know, please let's start."

"Mr. Nemic, I don't know where to start, but I will do my best. I'm twelve years old now but I think I must have been about four or so when Mr. Tekish called me to come to his office for the first time. You see, we were not allowed to go there unless he called us. Otherwise, you got into trouble. When I went there the first time, I remember he was so kind to me. Indeed, I thought what a pleasant man he was. He got me many different pencils that were all different colors; I'd never seen anything like that and I was so excited I didn't care what he wanted me to do.

"In the beginning, I would always sit on his lap and play, while he was so kind and so happy. Sometimes he would be bouncing me up and down. I thought he was just playing games with me until I got older and then I noticed his games changed. I didn't like them; him putting his hand in my underwear was not what I expected as a game. And his request that I put my hand in his trousers... all that made me sick. His finger was hurting me sometimes, and many other things that I cannot explain because they're too personal and I'm so ashamed of them."

"Ramona, did you report all that to Miss Clara?"

"No, because he said if I talked about what we did in his office to anybody that he would throw us all out, together with Miss Clara. We all knew that he controlled the orphan village, and we didn't know who we could tell or call for help. As I was getting older, I tried to avoid him as much as possible, but sometimes I had no choice. One day, he hurt me, I'm too embarrassed to tell you how, but I came running out and that is how Miss Clara caught me. Until then she had not a clue that he had molested me all that time. I didn't have to tell her what happened—she knew, and she said that she would report him to the police. I don't know what happen then, all I know is that she did not go to the police, but she had a good talk with me."

"After that, Ramona, did Mr. Tekish still ask you to come to his office?"

"Yes sir, but I didn't go. One day Miss Clara went to town, and Mr. Tekish knew that. And so he sent one of the girls to get me to go to his office right away. I knew what it all was about, and I promised myself that I would be strong and fight back. When I walked in, right away I could tell that he was drunk, and I noticed that his pants were almost off. My first instinct was to run, but before I had a chance to do that he locked the door. He grabbed me, threw me on the floor, and he was just about to rape me. But that's when Miss Clara broke down the door and helped me out. That was the last time he ever tried to touch me, but then I was about eleven... old enough to know what he wanted. I never went back, and if I ever see him again, I think I will kill him."

"Now, now, Ramona slow down. Let's take a rest."

"Mr. Nemic, I'm all right, don't worry. Me killing him is just a figure of speech. I'm sure that the police have enough evidence against Mr. Tekish that he will end up in prison for a long time. I know that I'm not the only girl that he raped; but I know that I was his favourite because he was getting even with Miss Clara on my account. Also, thanks to those two girls who reported him, everything is in the open now and over for us."

"Yes, Ramona, Mr. Tekish will be in prison for a long, long time. I'm only sorry that no one ever reported him to us, especially Miss Clara. She knew what was going on, but then she kept all under the rug. You know, Ramona, that she will go to prison as well. I sure hope not for a very long time, but you did help us understand her. Still, she should have come and spoken to us right away; all this could have easily been stopped a long time ago. I'm sorry for all you girls and hope that one day you can have a better life."

"Mr. Nemic, there was some talk in the city that Mr. Tekish was a strange man. I've been in the orphan village since I was a four-month-old baby, so this was my home, and growing up in here I always knew that Mr. Tekish was different. Sometimes when I was in his office, for what he would call 'play time,' he'd push me off his lap, and then he'd scream, 'No Mother! Not like that!' and he would push me into a corner and cry. I was so young at that time and I didn't understand. I would ask him what was wrong, and then he would yell at me to get out. Later in my life, I realized that he had a problem. So, I think all that talk in town that he was a very disturbed man was right."

"Yes, to answer your question, but tell me one more thing. Why did no one cry for help from outside of these walls?"

"We did, but no one cared. It looks like no one told you what happened a long time ago. I'm not so sure; I must have been about seven or eight. One day he was so drunk and confused. He came outside where we were playing, and he was carrying a gun and was holding a cat. That cat was mine. Then he fired some shots in the air and then he screamed at us to look at what would happen to us if we talked to anybody about him. He took the cat and shot her in the head. I will never forget that moment. I went toward him not knowing what I would do, but Miss Clara stopped me. So you see why we never told anybody about him. We were all so scared, and no one cared anyway. After he fired those shots police did come to see what was going on, and they did nothing. One of the cops laughed at us and told us just to behave, and they left with smiles on their faces. Mr. Tekish had a good laugh—he got warned about using a gun, and that was all.

"After that incident, he never used a gun again, but we were all so scared every time he got drunk, that's why no one cried for help. We were trying to save each other that was all. To save each other we did what he wanted, and was like that all the time."

"Now I can see how difficult it was for you girls, but that's all over now. I know you cannot forget all this, but time will heal. Ramona before you go, I'd like to ask you one more thing. Miss Clara has given you a notebook…please don't say 'What book?' she told us about it. You see we have a little problem and that notebook can help us and perhaps will do some good for Miss Clara as well."

"Why do you need that notebook? I haven't even read it yet and don't know if I'd like to part with the only one thing I have from her."

"Ramona, we will return that notebook back to you as soon as we see if there is something in it that we can use to track your mother."

"Mr. Nemic, do you think that I would like you to find my mom? I'll tell you what. I hope you never find her, and as for the notebook, I will read it first and then we can talk about it. I know you cannot make me give it to you, but I will hand over the notebook as long as it will help Miss Clara, not for helping you to find that woman that you call my mother. My real mother is in your prison."

"All right then, I will be back in about two days, and hope that by then you will be kind enough to give me that notebook. Moreover, you have my promise that I will return that notebook to you. So, do we have a deal, Ramona?"

"Okay then Mr. Nemic, see you in a couple of days."

CHAPTER II

THE NEXT DAY was Saturday, so I had lots of time to read Miss Clara's notebook. There were not many of us left somehow; it was very sad. We had all known each other for a long time and now it was like we never existed. It was so quiet, so sad, and very lonely.

I had been thinking that maybe Mr. Nemic would help Miss Clara; he seemed involved, not like the others. He cared. I had one more thing to tell him, but I had to go help in the kitchen since we all had to share the work now. We didn't have the full staff anymore; most of them had left, except the woman who cooked, and now she helped in cleaning as well. There were only six of us girls left.

Two more girls were leaving on Monday and it looked like I would be the last one to get out this place, just like I had been the last new girl who arrived. It was now 1960, and I was thirteen years old.

It was sad. This place would have been perfect if not for Mr. Tekish. We had everything; good food, good clothes, and a good education, but like everything that is so good, there is always something wrong as well. I know I will never forget this place, but my childhood is like a sad story. There was no choice but to try to go on, with my mother or without, but I preferred without her.

It looked like everybody had gone home, or to their rooms. I decided I would do the same and the next day I would start reading that notebook. I was almost afraid to know what was inside of it; something told me that this notebook was not meant to be read by anybody; including me. I think Miss Clara had been writing it for herself.

No one from the orphan village would be near to each other now, and there were so many young girls living on the streets, but because of Mr. Tekish, the whole thing had fallen apart.

Right after breakfast next day, I ran upstairs and made myself comfortable. I had the notebook in my hands, ready to see what Miss Clara did not want anybody but me to know. It was a bit nerve wracking wondering what I was going to find in this journal, but I had to do it, so I might as well start.

As I expected, the notes she wrote were dedicated to me, with the words so sad that they made me cry right away. Reading page by page forced me to realize how much I didn't know about myself, and soon, shaking and crying out loud, I had to stop. There were so many tears they were starting to destroy the pages.

The saddest thing was that she had lied to me how she found me. I remember asking her if it was true that she found me in a box at the train station, and she told me many times that it was not the truth. Nevertheless, finding out that my birth mother wanted to throw me off a train was the worst thing that any child could learn, and not only that but Miss Clara had met my mom before. She had been lying to me all these years, pretending that now she was looking for my mom. I just couldn't understand why she did that. I had so many questions now; it was worse than before. My whole life in the orphan village had been lies, lies, nothing but lies.

Crying and looking at the wet pages made me think about my so-called brother from a different father. I wondered if he'd been left just like me, or what he was doing now. I wondered if perhaps one day my brother and I would meet. Time would tell. Thanks to Miss Clara I had found more than I was expecting.

I had to make a decision about the notebook. I knew there is some information in there that Mr. Nemic needed, and if I didn't give him the book it might make things worse for Miss Clara. But I was now wondering if she deserved my help. After all, she had kept me as a prisoner, not knowing the truth about myself. Why had she done that? What was the reason for it? She had mentally abused me, and that was wrong—even I knew that. I planned to ask Mr. Nemic if I could talk to Miss Clara. I had lots of questions for her as my disappointment grew bigger and bigger.

I read the rest of the book but I was familiar with most of the other stories in it. Mr. Nemic could have the notebook, and I didn't want it back when he was finished taking the information that he needed. I had learned what I needed to know. Finding my mother should not be hard for them now.

I figured I'd better go downstairs before they thought I was hiding (though lots of times I had done that).

I was just coming down when I heard one of the girls calling me. Right on time, I thought. "Yes, what is all that noise all about?"

"Ramona, please come down. Hurry, there is bad news for all of us, especially for you."

"Calm down Lela, why you are so upset? Have you been crying? What is going on? Come on Lela tell me."

"Ramona, please come to the dining room. We've all been told to be there right away. I think it's bad news."

"Lela, bad news, or good? If you don't know, why you are crying? You are not telling everything, are you?"

"Please, Ramona, just let's go."

Mr. Nemic was waiting for us in the dining room. "Quiet everybody, please. I have sad news to tell you all. It is about Miss Clara."

My heart almost stopped when he said Miss Clara. Something went right through me, like a cold January wind; cold but hot at the same time. I knew all eyes were on me. I was sure they all knew the news, but were keeping it from me. I had to be strong, to not let Miss Clara down. She always told me to keep my head up and look straight, but it was not so easy now.

I couldn't hear all the words, but "she is dead" struck me like a knife in my back. I had been mad at her, and said she wasn't my mother anymore but for her to be dead, no, no that couldn't be true. It had to be a mistake.

I don't remember anything else. I woke up on the sofa, white as a ghost. Lela, Korina, and Tina were all there trying to talk to me. All I could say was, "No, no, this not right."

Lela grabbed me by my shoulders and shut me up. "Ramona, wake up, wake up Ramona. We are all here for you. Come on, let's have a big hug."

With a tiny voice, I managed to ask, "Was I dreaming or is it true that Miss Clara is dead?"

"Yes, Ramona, Miss Clara is no longer with us. It's not a dream."

"But how, and why is she dead?"

"Ramona, do you remember Mr. Nemic? He is here and wants to talk to you. Do you think you can manage or would you like us to come with you?"

"I think it will be okay to be alone with Mr. Nemic. He is a kind man, and I do trust him. Thank you, but let me deal with this on my own."

My hands were shaking, and my feet were just dragging to go and to hear the worst news in my life. One thinks, *I cannot understand why. Why is she dead?*

Miss Clara was always a healthy person, and she taught us how to take care of ourselves. I remember she said that we were going to be lovely women one day, and to accomplish that you have to take care of yourself. She cared for all of us, not only me.

I stood in front of the door, and my hand just froze. I could not bring it up to knock, but Mr. Nemic must've had a sense that I was there because he opened the door.

With a soft voice, he asked me to set down and take a deep breath. He offered me juice but he knew that all I wanted was the answers to my questions. How did Miss Clara die and why?

"Ramona, you know why you're here, so I will come out and tell you the truth about Miss Clara's death. Everybody knows that she died, but so far, no one in the orphan village knows how she died so before rumours get people talking I will explain it to you. She did leave a note for you and a big letter for me. I have not opened your message, and if you don't want me to know what is in that letter I won't ask. It's up to you. However, in my letter, she did explain everything; how she found you and why she kept all that a secret. Therefore, you don't have to give me her notebook. I have my answers about your mother, and will talk about that in a minute, but let us go back to Miss Clara's death.

"You see Ramona no one knew that she was suicidal, so no one bothered to check on her. If we only had known, it could have been prevented but unfortunately no one knew. Miss Clara was always so quiet and kept to herself, and there were no signs that she was planning anything. Ramona, I'm not so sure how to say it. You are a child, and it's very hard for me to tell you this."

"Mr. Nemic you think because of my age that I am a kid, but I stopped being a child a long time ago. Don't worry, I can take anything you have to tell me. My life is so full of sorrows to add one more will be just another bad thing. Miss Clara will always stay in my heart as a beautiful person, and I will never forget her, so no matter what you say, she will be my beautiful lady who saved my life."

"Ramona, Miss Clara has hung herself."

"She did what? How's that possible? How, how, how? Where did she find a rope or whatever she used? Why did she do that? Why?"

"She used her stockings and her bed sheets. I am so sorry Ramona, and why she did it must be in your letter."

I just sat there like a zombie, not hearing any other words that Mr. Nemic was saying. I wasn't even crying, but my heart had just broken in half. I had lost the only person that I loved, and now, now what? Go to my mother? God please no, not her! Why couldn't she have hung herself, not Miss Clara?

"Ramona, are you all right? Ramona, look at me."

"Mr. Nemic, yes, I'm okay. Can I be excused and go to my room? I'm not feeling good; I'd just like to be alone for a moment, and maybe we can continue our talk later."

"Okay Ramona, I will be back tomorrow, so take your time and please talk to the other girls if you need to or go to Miss Tina, I know you like her. Talk to somebody, though. Don't just go to your room and get isolated, Please Ramona."

"Don't worry Mr. Nemic, I'll see you tomorrow."

"Ramona, can you tell Lela to come in, please?"

Going up to my room, I imagined that all the rest of the staff was wondering what was going on. Well, maybe Lela would update them since she would learn the rest of the bad news.

I knew that reading Miss Clara's letter was not going to make me feel any better, but she might have told me why she hung herself. I just couldn't believe that she ever did that, but I guess it shows you that one person can take only so much, and that's it. All I knew was that I would miss her forever.

My Dearest Ramona

If you are reading this letter, then you know that I am gone. Before I explain to you why I did this, I'd like to ask you one last favour. When you read this letter, please don't cry, Ramona.

If you are reading this letter, then you know that I am gone. These words were the first ones I spoke to you when your mother left you in my arms—actually the same words. You always cried and I always said, "Please don't cry, Ramona."

Ramona, I did this is because everybody is pointing the finger at me and using ugly words, calling me a child abuser and a child molester. If they ever let me out, I know that someone somewhere would do me wrong; call me names, or treat me like a criminal. I am not strong enough to take that. I have done some things wrong, but I know I am not a child molester or child abuser.

Ramona, you are still a child, and it is hard for me to explain everything, but please try to go on with your life, and I will be with you all the time in your heart.

Attempt to listen to your mother and try to find the brother, which by now you know you have. That's one of the things I made a mistake in not telling you. I cannot fix my mistakes, but you can.

Ramona, Mr. Nemic is a nice man, and you can trust him. I have told him everything, so the notebook that I have written all these years is yours to keep if you wish. If not, I will understand.

Now, my dear I am saying good-bye for the last time. Please don't cry, Ramona.
Love, you forever,
Miss Clara (your mom).

I held the letter to my breast and sobbed. "Oh, my Miss Clara why did you do that? Why? I was going to come back for you one day, and we would live together the rest of our lives. I will do what you ask me to do; that is if I can. I will try to forgive my birth mother and will find my half-brother. I promise you that, but for me not to cry, you know I can't do that. I can't even see because my tears are just rolling down.

"One thing I will do is I will write a book about you, about me, and about all of our lives in the orphan village, and I will dedicate the book to all women that are treated poorly by men like Mr. Tekish. He is the worst person that exists on this planet."

(Little did I know that he was not the only most dangerous man.)

A knock on the door kind of staggered me. I grabbed my letter, put it under my pillow, and pretended I was sleeping. I hoped whoever it was would go away if I didn't move. I wasn't looking for company. Lela came in anyway; she knew I wouldn't speak to her, she just sat on the edge of my bed, took my hand and placed on hers, and didn't say anything.

We both knew that Miss Clara's death hit me harder than it did anybody else; she was like a mother to me, a mother that I never had. After a few hours, I noticed Lela was not there. I must have dozed off and she left in my peace. I knew that there was nothing else to do but go on with my life, and try to ease the pain that I was suffering.

The rest of a week went fast. No one asked me too many questions, and I was glad for that, but I did notice that Lela was following me a lot. It was getting a bit annoying, so I asked her to stop. She said that Mr. Nemic had asked her to look after me, just in case I got sick. I know she meant right, but I told her I wasn't going to do anything stupid, and to stop following me.

Friday came very quickly, it seemed to me because I was so excited to find out what Mr. Nemic had to tell me. I bet it was about my mother. Perhaps he could not find her, and he'd found a new home for me. That was my dream, but it probably wasn't likely. So as soon as I heard the main gate open, I ran downstairs to meet Mr. Nemic just as he was coming in. He saw my worried look, and I think he knew that the news he had for me was not happy.

"Hello Mr. Nemic. I am dying to find out why you need to see me. Is it about my mother or is it anything else about Miss Clara?"

"Well, Ramona, I have good news and bad news. It is news about both."

I was hoping that his words would be, *We could not find your mother...* but they weren't

"Miss Clara was laid to rest last Monday and the good news is I have found your mother."

I stood there with a cold look and didn't know whether to cry because of Miss Clara or because he'd found my mom. Deep in my heart, I had known that one day they would find her, so I had no choice but live with that.

"Ramona, I know this is not the news you were looking for, but you knew that one day we were going to find your mother. I went to see her; she lives in Novisad and has a beautiful place, but she promised to look for a bigger one so you and she can live comfortably. She is here in town right now, waiting in a hotel room, so I could come and talk to you first. Meeting your mother for the first time is going to be very hard for both of you, but I will be here with you, so don't be scared, and let's see what happens.

"She's not talking much; I have no idea why, but let's give her a chance and see what we can accomplish here. She will be here tomorrow, and I have a little suitcase for you, so you can put all your belongings in there and be ready when she comes. I know how hard this must be for you, but Ramona she is your mother and let's give her a chance. You have been through a lot, and perhaps your life will get better."

"Mr. Nemic, I have been in this orphan village for thirteen years and not once has she looked for me, not even once. How can my life be better with her? I know I don't have a choice, but let me tell you one thing, as soon I turn eighteen, I am going to leave her. I am coming back here. I will be going to school and becoming a teacher one day, and my dream is to help other children like me. So don't worry, I have a plan, and she is not in it. And now Mr. Nemic, I'm going to get ready for tomorrow, but I'd like you to know that I'm not looking forward to it."

I didn't think I'd sleep at all. My mind was on Elsa. How was I going to face a person called my mother, when she had never been there for me? What was I going to call her? I didn't think I had an ounce love for her; therefore, she would be Elsa for me.

As I walked down the hallway towards the main lobby, I heard Mr. Nemic telling Elsa that everything was going to be okay She was crying, but this would not have happened if she had wanted me—she just left me with a stranger at a rail station. As for me, I was little nervous, but I just told myself it wouldn't be for long.

I knocked on the door, and Mr. Nemic opened it with sadness in his eyes. I wasn't sure why, but I think Mr. Nemic knew that this woman who called herself my mother did not deserve to have me. I just looked at him and said, "It's going to be okay, Mr. Nemic. Don't worry."

Then he gave me a little smile, and that made me feel better.

She was standing there with one hand wiping her eyes. I looked at her and the first thing that came to my mind was, *Why are you crying now? It's too late for that.* I walked towards her very slowly, hoping that she would make the first move, but no, all she did was stand there and cry. I took one more look at the room, knowing that it was the last time I'd be in the orphan village. I saw her standing there like a piece of furniture, and I had no feelings. All I wanted was to stay in the orphan village or go somewhere else, but not with her.

Finally, she took me in her arms and cried loudly, calling my name. Yes, it would have looked sad to a person who didn't know her, but I just stood there without any emotion of love or care. The first thing I said to her was, "So you are my mother who ever cared for me all these years!"

My first words to her must have surprised her. She looked at me and simply said, "Get your things and let's go, we have a bus to catch."

I was angry now. "Did you say a bus?! Maybe you would like to go on the train with me again? Why bus? I heard you like trains."

I saw the shock on Mr. Nemic's face. The first meeting with my mother and me was going horribly. "Ramona stop that," he said. "Be a good girl; she's all you've got for now."

He took me in his arms, and speaking softly he said, "I am so sorry Ramona, I had no way of knowing that she's that cold. I know now that I made a mistake, but Ramona this is my address and if you ever need anything just write me. Please take care and be strong, and as your real mother, Miss Clara said, 'Look up and walk straight, be your own person, don't give up, and please don't cry.'"

The time had come to say good-bye to everyone. Everybody who was still there come to say goodbye. My life in the orphan village had ended, and with tears in my eyes, I tried to be brave, but inside, I was dying. I took Lela's hand and said, "Don't forget me, promise we'll write to each other," and that was the end. I took my suitcase and walked away. The year was 1960.

CHAPTER 12
Mother and Daughter (1960-1963)

Out on the road in front of the orphan village, I turned to Elsa. "Now that we're alone, can I ask you one thing? What should I call you, Mother or Elsa?"

"Well, since you ask me, let me tell you one thing, and I will not repeat this again, ever. I don't care what you call me. In public you may call me Mother, but other than that I don't care. Get this through your head. I never wanted you before, and I don't want you now. The difference is that now I have no choice but to take you to live with me, and as soon as you turn eighteen, you're on your own. I'm not a mother that you're looking to have."

Her iciness shocked me. "I didn't expect to hear this from you, I actually thought that maybe we could work out what happened before and give us a chance to get to know each other."

"Hurry up. We're catching a bus."

"But why don't we take a train? Are you uneasy with trains? Maybe the train station reminds you of what you did thirteen years ago."

"I haven't a clue what you're talking about, so let's just go. We'll have lots of time later on to talk, but right now I don't feel like talking or I don't want to listen to you."

"That's fine with me right now, but soon or later you will have to know everything. I'm pretty sure you fooled them, but you know what you did with me, when you left me in the cold winter of 1947."

For the rest of walk we were like two strangers; we didn't talk or look at each other. Deep inside me, I was hurting. I honestly had been hoping that she might mellow and at least try to be my mother, but I was so wrong, so wrong. It was like having a nightmare in the middle of the afternoon. The tension between us was so thick you could cut it with a knife. She was ice cold—not an ounce of love in her.

After even more silence I began to wonder if she was okay, or if maybe she was a dangerous person, but then out of the blue, she said, "Are you getting tired? We can take a five-minute break. The bus is fifteen minutes away."

I looked at her and thought to myself, *Is this woman insane? On the other hand, maybe she just doesn't know how to be nice, or something is stopping her from getting closer to me.*

I thought perhaps that she had turned cold towards everybody when her husband died; she must have had a shock and never got over it, and in those days, no one cared about a woman's troubles that much. Perhaps she needed help, and she never got it. In any case, I was determined to be a good girl for now, and all I said was, "Sure, fine with me."

We sat on a log that was on beside the road, and we never spoke. I kept looking at her, trying to go deep inside of her soul, but she was just hard to understand. I realized that talking to her then would be a mistake, so I just sat there quietly. She was just staring into space as if a person lost forever. I felt sorry for her. She was not a bad looking woman; she must have been only about thirty-six years old, if that.

She looked at me and in a small voice came out hushed question. "I see you're quiet, no more comments."

"Well, I'm just tired, but I do have many questions for you. I just don't think it's time for that now. We're both tired so let's walk in peace. We will have plenty of time to talk."

"Okay then. Let's continue our voyage and perhaps when the time is right, we'll speak."

My suitcase was getting heavy for me, so I asked her to help me a bit. The look she gave me almost scared me. All I could think was that this woman was not healthy and that I was in danger, but to whom was I to tell that? No one cared.

She grabbed my suitcase, threw it far ahead of us, and started to laugh. "Now your bag is ahead of you. Take a rest, and get it for yourself. I'm not your keeper so that you can ask me to do things for you. If your bag is too heavy for you to carry, then why don't you throw away some of the things that you have in there? Maybe then your bag won't weigh so much."

I ran to get my bag, and I started to cry. "You're the meanest the person I ever saw, and wish you hadn't given birth to me. A mother like you does not deserve to have children. You're nothing to me but a person that I have to live with, and trust me, as soon as I can I will leave you forever. And what kind of name did you give me? Ramona? What is that? You must have hated me the day I was born."

"No need to scare me, Ramona, I don't want you to stay with me a minute longer than you have to. You're with me now, but that was not my choice, so we can live together for a few years, or you can get out of my way now. I don't care."

Just to make sure of one thing Elsa, I don't want to be with you either. Don't act like you're doing me a favour. To tell you the truth, I was hoping that Social Services never found you. My worst nightmare was when they said you're coming, so now you know how I feel, and now let's go—the bus station is right over there. I'm so tired of everything."

I didn't tell her, but I wished I were dead, and with tears in my eyes we continued walking in silence. As we approached the bus station, I was very angry with her, so out of the blue, I again asked her. "Why are we taking a bus? Isn't the train your favourite? On the other hand, perhaps because I'm not a baby any more, it wouldn't be easy for you to handle me."

For a second or two, I was somewhat sorry for saying that, but she turned around and gave me such a hard slap on my face that I fell, and my nose was bleeding. I was shocked. Then she bent down and whispered in my ear so no one could hear, "I have been thinking about that."

I looked at her and saw the monster in front of me. Was this woman my mother? Or had I met a devil? I thought Mr. Tekish was a demon, but this woman must been his double.

I sat on the ground crying and looking for help. Many people were standing there and there was even a police officer close by, but no one came to help me. Then I saw the police officer talking to Elsa, and she kind of smiled. He approached me and with a warning tone said that I'd better listen to my mother, or he would punish me.

I knew that if I couldn't get any help from an officer than I was on my own.

Elsa grabbed me and threw me on the bus. I could tell the bus driver wasn't pleased with all that. He offered me a Kleenex and gave me a small smile.

As the bus driver closed the door, I said good-bye to the only home that I'd ever had. Tears were coming, and I noticed that Elsa was looking at me, but she never said anything. I thought that just as well, otherwise we would say harsh words again, and I was not up to that. I saw the bus driver looking at us in the mirror, and I gave him a sign that I was okay.

Though I was crying I must have slept, but not for long. She grabbed my arm and shook me, saying, "Wake up, we're almost there." Finally, I realized I was far away from my home, and my new life with a mother was going to start at the next stop. That scared me a lot.

CHAPTER 13

THE BUS CAME to a full stop, and I heard the driver saying, "This is a dead end." I looked at Elsa like, *What now?*

In a cold voice, she said, "Let's go home."

To me, that was the strangest word; I'd never had a home. Getting off the bus, I looked at the bus driver and gave him a small smile, just to say thank you, and I'm sure he knew what I meant.

As we started to walk, I told her that I was hungry and exhausted and asked if it would be possible to stop in a small cafe and have a sandwich and water. She looked at me for a second and with a smirk on her face asked me if I had any money to pay for a sandwich.

"I don't think that's funny. I'm tired and hungry, and no I don't have money. You call yourself my mom so you should provide me with all I need. You're supposed to feed me and look after me."

"Oh! Yes, I will take care of you. As soon as we get home, I'll give you a sandwich and water or maybe you would like something special? I have roast beef, I have fried chicken, and some good salami, just choose whatever you like."

"You don't have to make fun of me, one sandwich and glass of water will do me just fine."

"Glad to hear that, because we have at least another fifteen minutes to walk, so if you can walk a little faster, maybe we can be home sooner. When we get there try not be too disappointed. I don't have much but it's mine and you can share it with me for now."

I felt like we were walking on the moon—I was getting so tired, and my feet were killing me. I had never walked so much. In the orphan village the walk to school was ten minutes every day and I'd thought that was a lot, but this was way too much.

We passed some beautiful buildings. It seemed as if the city was so friendly, and much more prominent than the one I'd come from. I didn't think I got the name right, so to make some conversation I asked her the name.

She looked at me funny again, and her darkish look was there. "Well, well, Miss Know-it-all doesn't know the name of the city where she is going to live. How nice of your Mr. Nemic to tell you. If you must know, because you should be aware, the city is called Novisad, and it's one of the biggest and loveliest towns in this part of the country. I have lived here for a long time, but it's home for now."

As we walked, she said, "There, at the next corner we turn right, and that is our street. In a minute or two, we'll be home."

Inwardly I thanked God. I was completely exhausted and so hungry. Breakfast was the last thing we'd eaten, and that had been in the orphan village early that morning. It was five p.m. by now. All I needed was a glass of water if nothing else was there.

As we turned the corner, she pointed out a store and said, "This is where you get milk and bread, and some fruit, and right over here is our place."

From where we were, the small house looked immaculate and friendly, so I thought that it wasn't bad at all. My shock came after we went inside of the courtyard and she pointed out our place.

"Before we get to our apartment, I'd like you to know your neighbours. You may meet them tomorrow, but right now I'll tell you a little bit about them. These two doors on the main house are only for the owners. On the left side of the courtyard is the first apartment. Two men live there. The second apartment is on the right side. It belongs to a family with a little boy. They're shy people considering they have a four-year-old boy.

Next to them are a mother and a son. He is about sixteen years old and very sweet; maybe you can be friends with him. His mother is okay; I don't often see much of them. We all mind our business, and I expect to you to behave yourself. No one has ever made any trouble in here, and we'd like it to stay that way.

"The old woman that I pay rent to, she is a bit strict and sometimes mean when it comes to the kids, so try to stay away from her. So now, let me show you our place."

She opened the door, and with that playful smile on her face, she said, "Welcome to your new home."

I froze; there was one bed, one small table, and one chair. It was a place that looked to me like where you put the stuff you don't typically need in a house; more like a large locker. There was a small stove and one little closet that had only one small shelf for clothes, food, and just about everything.

"Wow! Are you kidding me, Mother?" (I figured I might as well get used to calling her that, since I was going to call her that in public.) "What is this? Is this just for me or for both of us? You can't be serious that we're going to live here together. Look at this room. There's barely big enough to move. I hope you're joking with me—I can't take it anymore. Please let's go in. I'm so tired I need some rest, and for now I just don't care what kind of place it is, big or small."

"No, Ramona, I'm not joking. This is all that I have, and now you can share with me, like it or not."

I just stood there not knowing what to do, to cry or to laugh loud. This couldn't be true. She'd told Mr. Nemic that she had two rooms big enough for both of us, but this place was not decent even for a cat.

If this was all then I'm even less happy to be with my mother. What was I going to do? *Oh dear God, please help me.*

I was so scared and confused, standing in front of the door that she just pushed me in and said, "Jump up on the bed. Your suitcase will be under the bed, and I have some bread and butter. Let me show you where you get your water, and where the washroom is before you get too comfortable."

I'd forgotten all about water, and had never thought about the toilet until she mentioned it. I hoped I wasn't in for another shock and wondered if there were there any other things even more nerve racking.

She took a small pitcher for water, and showed me that in the middle of the courtyard, there was a pump. I knew right away what it was because we had one in the orphan village. We drew water for horses and other animals, but I was shocked when she said, "This is where you get your drinks, and you can wash in here in summer, but in winter, you can bring the water in." Then she headed back across the courtyard. "Now let me show you the toilet."

I noticed she didn't say washroom because there wasn't any such thing there. Another shock. The toilet was at the back of the house and had just one seat, no flushing water, and no paper. I had known toilets like this did exist, but I had never had one or seen one, so you understand my shock again. I was sad and confused about many things.

Looking at her with tears in my eyes, I was speechless and even more mad, so I asked her, "Mother, why did you lie to Mr. Nemic? If he knew about this, I'm sure he wouldn't have let me go with you."

"Why did I lie to him? Well, to tell you the truth I don't know. Maybe I wanted to meet you, and to lie to him was the only way to assure him that I have a safe place for you and me. However, I can see that you're very disappointed, and there is nothing I can do. You can write Mr. Nemic and tell him about your new place, but honey trust me, he does not care as much as you think. The orphan village was closing, and they were glad to get rid of all you girls, no matter with whom. So, if I were you I would be grateful to have a place to sleep, but if you can find a better place then go right ahead. This is all I can say for now.

"So, let's go in and have something to eat. As I said before, I only have some bread and butter, but if you'd like to go to a store and buy something, go—get some canned food, or whatever you like. I don't have much money, but here is ten dinars—that should be enough, or if you don't feel like going to a store, help yourself to bread and butter, it's up you. I have to go to bed, because I work the night shift, and I'm exhausted as well, just let me rest for a while."

"Are you planning to leave me here all night by myself? I have never been by myself. I'll be scared. Do you have to go on our first night? Please can you stay? I won't bother you. I just don't think I can be by myself, not tonight, no way. Please, stay home this evening."

"I'm sorry, but I can't stay. You're a big girl now, and this place is very safe. The neighbours are kind, so don't be a crybaby. I have to go to work, and that is the end of the story."

I couldn't believe it. "You know I have tried many times to be kind to you, but every time I try, you turn out to be a cruel person. I can see that you don't care about me at all, so go, go to your work, and just leave me be. I have lost all intentions to be kind to you or to forgive you. You show me nothing but bad feelings, and I'm sure that I will never forgive you."

"Ramona, I don't care what you think. I'm your mother, you will do what I tell you to do, and that is the end of the story. Go to the store or go out and play, I need to rest."

I slammed the door and left without knowing where to go. I thought I might as well go and meet my neighbours, maybe I could kill a couple of hours that way, since she needed to sleep. The first door I knocked was the owner's. I was a bit scared, but all they could really do was to tell me to go away.

At my knock, an old woman come out with questions in her eyes. She was just an old lady and I thought, *Well this can't be so bad.*

She looked at me and I looked at her. Like a stupid kid I was just standing there without any words.

The old woman said, "Well, are you going to talk or are we just going to stare at each other?"

For a moment, I didn't say anything, so to make it easy she spoke first. "Okay, I know who you are. Well I'm not quite sure, but I saw you with Elsa, so you must be Ramona, Elsa's daughter. I knew you were coming. So are you going to talk or are you mute?"

I finally found my tongue. "Yes, yes, I'm very sorry. I'm Ramona, Elsa's daughter. We arrived about an hour ago or so, and Elsa, that's my mother, she has to go to work, and she went to sleep for a couple of hours. Since I don't know anybody for the moment I thought I should to start to meet my neighbours. So here, I am...And so, hello, and, how are you?"

CHAPTER 14

"ALL RIGHT RAMONA, would you like to come in? Or are you planning to stay on the front porch like a salesperson?"

"No, of course. I'm sorry. Thank you. I don't remember you telling me your name. Since you know mine, I'd like to address you by your name."

"Well, well what a pleasant girl. Don't have many of that kind of kids these days; friendly and polite. My name is Miss Selka Tomic, but you may call me Miss Selka. Now that we know each other's names, we can go to the kitchen and have a neighbourly, friendly talk. Perhaps you would like a warm milk and some freshly made pita. You look exhausted and I'm here by myself, so you don't have to worry that someone will be disturbed by us."

"Yes, thank you, Miss Selka. I'm famished and tired, and warm milk and pita sound heavenly."

"Ramona, before you start to eat, have you washed your hands since you came?"

"No, I'm sorry."

"Where are you going?"

"Out to the pump to wash my hands. Isn't that what you want?"

"Yes, my dear, but I've a bathroom inside. The people that live in the courtyard, my tenants, don't have indoor plumbing, but I do. Go ahead, don't worry it's okay with me if you need to use the toilet as well. Just make sure you flush."

With a sense of surprise, I found myself wishing this old woman was my grandmother. I thanked her and was so glad to have a good wash and to relieve myself. As I wandered to the kitchen, I smelled fresh pita and warm milk. I ate all the pita and drank the milk in seconds; I was starving, and that was the first food I'd had since I'd left the orphan village.

Miss Selka asked me when was the last time I'd had something to eat. When she heard, she went and got me some fruit; an apple and a pear, and again I was so surprised that this old woman was an acutely beautiful person, even though my mother had told me she didn't like kids. She might have been like that in front of them, but deep inside I thought she might be a very lonely person, and I was so glad that I had knocked on her door first.

Once I finished all my food, we went to her sitting room and she said she wanted to tell me all about her tenants and a little about herself. She said that the people next door to her were quite wealthy. He was a tailor downtown, and she was a school principal, possibly at the school where I'd be going. "They don't have any children," she continued, "and they very much keep to themselves. Her name is Vida, and his name is Sava. In the courtyard, in the first apartment are two young men. Both are working all day and are very nice; their names are Nikola and Kicha. The second apartment has a couple with a little four-year-old boy. I think they're Albanians, and he is a very religious man. Sometimes I feel sorry for his wife. His name is Alia and hers is Havana and the little boy is Ahmet. In the third apartment are a mother and son. I like both of them. The boy's name is Slavko, and the mother's name is Rosa. Slavko always offers me help, and his mom is a beautiful woman. And my fourth apartment is now you and your mother. Your mom is somehow a very strange person. I don't see her often, and she's never home. I think she works in a hospital in the laundry room at night, but in the daytime, she will sleep or just go out.

I don't know if you are aware that you have a brother. I only saw him twice— a very, very nice young man, but I think he has a drinking problem. He came and stayed with her one week, and because of his drinking, she threw him out. That young man needed help, and he was not getting it from her. You know he painted all our buildings in this place, inside and out. He's an excellent painter, everybody in the neighbourhood was asking for him, but unfortunately he likes the bottle better. I always wondered what happened to Sasha. He was so young to have a drinking problem. I wonder was he abused as a child. Sasha (that is your brother's name, just in case you don't know), never came back after they had the big argument, and that was last year or so. All the people that knew him always ask about him. When he left, your mother told me not to let him in, if he ever came back, but he never did."

"Yes, Miss Selka I learned about my brother not too long ago. I'm not sure how much you know about me, but I was in an orphan village for thirteen years, and that was the only home I ever knew. Most of my life I had no idea that the woman who was working there was not my mother. But all that changed when the orphan village was closing and everything came out. I learned that I've got a mother and a brother, but knowing that my mom knew where I was and never came to look me up was a shock to me. Even now, the things she does aren't exactly motherly love. I know she just can't stand me. It's a long story, but for now, I'd better go and see if she is sleep. Maybe I can clean up the place and get a good night's sleep or don't be surprised if I knock your door. You see Miss Selka, I've never been alone before. All my life I was in the orphan village, and there you always have someone. That's why I'm so scared. I just don't understand her. Why can't she take one night off, knowing that it's my first time at home with her? I just don't understand her at all."

"Ramona, give her time and be patient with your mother. Eventually, she will change, and everything is going to be beautiful and calm."

"Thank you, I will give it my best."

Going to my apartment made me so sad. I asked myself, "Why me? Why can't I have a sweet mother and father? How many children in this world are like me?" As I opened the door, I got a surprise. My mom was gone. She never even bothered to see if I was around. She left a short note:

Ramona, I'm gone to work, don't know where you went, but stay in and lock the door. I will be back in the morning.

What now? I thought perhaps I could do some cleaning, and later on I could read a book. Talking to myself was getting weird, but I had no one else. I missed my friends from the orphan village, and I missed just about everything. I didn't know how I was going to survive all this.

Thinking about all these new things that were happening to me I must have dozed off. I must have slept deeply, due to the long trip, and next thing I saw was my mom, standing beside the bed and making her coffee. She said good morning but didn't offer me anything to eat. I just studied her questioningly and then I asked, "I don't know, do I have to make my tea or my breakfast all by myself, or what?"

I put my blouse on and went out to wash. Wondering if she had something for me to eat, I rushed back, but I was not surprised at all. She had gone to bed. All she said was that she was tired and needed some sleep, and that I could feed myself.

At least now I knew I had to do everything by myself if I wanted something or if I was going to survive. Going and begging for food from Miss Selka was not going to happen. I remembered Miss Clara's, words. "Head up, walk straight, and do your thing. Don't be too scared, you are a survivor." I grabbed the ten dinars Elsa had left me the night before, and I went out.

I had been planning to go see the city, so this was my chance. There was no one to stop me and no one who cared what I did or where I went. With a paper and a pen in my pocket, I closed the door, and without any words, I left making sure to write the name of my street and the apartment number, so I wouldn't get lost.

Having ten dinars in my pocket and an empty stomach, it seemed like a good idea to get some food, but where? The corner store sold everything, but all in large quantities. All I wanted was maybe a little cocoa and a sandwich. As I walked towards the main street, I saw a group of young girls standing by one small store.

I looked carefully and noticed they were gypsies. I truly liked gypsies; I had known a couple back in my school, so I approached them with a shy smile and said hello.

Because I was wearing a lovely dress I'm sure they thought I was a sweet girl, but I was far from that. One of the girls came closer to me and asked me what I wanted. I gave her a friendly look and told her that I was new in the city, and I was looking for a restaurant or a store for a little food.

I could tell she was puzzled. Why would a girl like me be looking for food? I took a chance and told her that all I had was ten dinars, and that I wasn't sure what I could buy for that. With a laugh, one of the other girls said, "Where do you come from if you don't know what you can buy for ten dinars?"

I did feel stupid, but I was being honest. I told them I had been in an orphan village all my life, and that now I was with my mother, who didn't care much about me.

You see, most people back then thought that gypsies were evil, but not me—I wasn't scared at all. One of the girls, I think she was older than I was, took my hand and walked me to a small restaurant, and to my surprise she told me to sit there and that she'd be right back.

I offered her my money, without knowing what ten dinars was good for, but she just put it back in my hand and walked away. In about five minutes she was back with a hot chocolate milk and a fresh bagel with egg.

I looked at her and said thank you, and I know I had tears in my eyes. My mother was home sleeping, and a stranger was feeding me. How sad is that?

She sat beside me and said that she would show me something, but in the meanwhile, she told me to eat.

"First, what is your name?" she asked. "My name is Karla, and those two girls are my sisters. We have been orphans for a long time, but we've taught ourselves how to survive. Yes, we are gypsies, but we don't care what other people think. You look like you like gypsies, and I wonder why. So now tell me your name."

"Yes, thank you. My name is Ramona, and I can't tell you how happy I am to be with you. I don't know anybody in this city, and I'm so glad to meet you, and would love to stay with you girls."

"No, Ramona, you can't be with me, but I will show you how to survive. First, never offer your money to anybody, because you cannot trust many people and it's dangerous. You see this? It's called a menu, and I'm sure you can read. If you'd like to buy something you have to look at the price, and then you can decide if you can afford it or not. Ten dinars is not that much, but you can buy this breakfast that you are eating now for three dinars. Some restaurants are very expensive, but if you go to small ones like this one, you can have three breakfasts in here. For ten dinars, you can also buy a loaf of bread and a little bag of milk. Also, maybe an apple and one or two candies. Every store will have a price on each product, but if they don't have a price always ask before you buy. You see, because we are gypsies we wait till stores are going to close and we get the leftovers, and let me tell you there is nothing wrong with leftovers.

"I don't know why your mother let you go out like this by yourself, but Ramona be careful. There are a lot of strange men that would love to take you, and that is not a good. I will sit with you for now, and then we'll show you the city, and then please go home. Maybe your mother needs time to get to know you. At least you have a mother. We don't have any parent at all, and most of our cousins have lots of children, so there is no room for us, but we're okay for now."

I didn't like the thought of going home. "Karla, can I ask you something? You see, my mother doesn't care about me or want me. Can't I join you and your sisters and be with you? We can sell some of my good dresses, and then I can wear a dress like the one you have. I'd love to be with you. I'm so scared to be home alone, and she says she works at night, so I don't think she cares if I'm home or not. Please, Karla, I won't give you any problems."

"No, Ramona. I can't do that. We are on the streets because we have no choice, but you don't have to be. Give your mother a chance. You said you were in the orphan village all your life, so you see, it's all new to her as well. All these years she never had to take care of you, and now you came along, and I think she is just as scared as you are. You can come and walk with us whenever you like, but you must go home as well. Maybe if you can try to talk to your mother to tell her how you feel...or tell your mom you love her!"

"Karla that will not happen, because I don't like her. She left me at the train station thirteen years ago and never looked back. How I can love someone that I don't even know?"

"That is sad, but you both need time to get to know each other, and time will tell. Trust me, you are going to be all right. You strike me as an active person, not a crybaby."

"Okay Karla, I'll try, but no promises. I hope to see you girls again. I live about three blocks from here. This is my address so that you can come, and I will show you my place."

"We're always going be on this corner. You see, we gypsies have our spots, and this one is mine. Go home now Ramona, and try to be open with your mother. Keep those ten dinars for next time, and we'll see you later."

I rushed home hoping my mom was at home so that I could talk to her. Like Karla said, the best way would be to talk it over, and maybe I as a child should be a bit easier on my mother. I was going to try, even though my heart said, *Don't bother, she will leave you again.* Little did I know my heart was right.

With big hope, I opened the door, and to my surprise, she was home. I said, "Hi, glad to see you at home, and I'd like to talk to you if you have time. Mom, this is critical, we have to talk, please. Looking at her, I sensed that she wanted to speak to me as well. She put her hot milk on the table and said, "Let's hear what's on your mind."

I was stunned, thinking, *What's on my soul, Mother, you will know now.* But what I said was, "Well, it's like this. I'm going to be fourteen in September, and that means you have to look after me for at least four more years. So let's start fresh. If you don't like talking about your past, then that's okay with me, and I won't tell you anything about my thirteen years in the orphan village. The only one thing I'd like to know is where my brother is. I know we came from different fathers, but he is the only brother I've got and I would love to know something about him. But as I said, if it's too painful for you, we could skip that as well. Maybe down the road one day you can tell me."

"Ramona, I know and I do feel that you don't care about me, but that is all my fault. We are not going to point fingers at who's wrong, and who's right. We can try to put the past behind us because I did. To take you back into my life, I'm forced to think back to my past, which is making me very uncomfortable and sorrowful. You are too young to understand, and it's very hard for me to explain it all to you. Perhaps one day when you get older we can sit down like mature adults, and I will tell you all about it, but for now, we have to try to work out how we're going to be a mother and a daughter. As for your brother, all I can tell you is that he is not a good boy or man. He is eighteen years old, and I tried to be a good mother to him but it did not work out. Therefore, you don't need to care about him at all."

"Yes, I understand, but I wish I could meet him."

"Possibly you may; he drops by sometimes. Now let me talk to you about your time at home alone. You see the summer is long, and I cannot leave my job to be with you, so I've got a friend ... well not a friend really. It's more like I was working for her.

She is the only woman in our country that is a captain of cargo ships. She is by herself these days because her daughter is in the hospital and will be there for some time. I've talked to her, and she is willing to take you with her for the summer. You will have a room right beside hers on a ship, and you will have a really good time. Sometimes she may ask you to help her load in small jobs in return, and you can stay with her until school starts. I don't think this is a bad idea and sure hope you'll like it."

"She is your friend, but to me she's just a stranger. How can you just leave me with a stranger again?"

"Ramona, I'm almost a stranger to you as well, and you are willing to stay with me."

"That's different. You're my mother, and honestly I didn't have a choice and neither did you. But going on a ship with a bunch of people I don't know, to me that is very heartbreaking."

"Well, you have a choice. Stay home by yourself or go and have a good summer on a ship. The choice is yours."

"If I choose to go on the ship, when do I go? Tomorrow or next week?

"Well, I will take you to her house before I go to work today, and then she'll bring you to the ship with her tomorrow, or whenever she wants to go. I bought you some summer shorts and blouses; the dresses you have are too fancy for a ship. Then when you come back from summer, we'll go shopping for new clothes for school. I know this is the best solution for both of us. Leaving you home alone every night is not what I want, and I would have to worry all night. So take your bag and put this in and the sandals as well, and let's go."

I looked at her and wondered if she had any feelings for me. I had lived with her for only two days, and here we went again, she was dropping me with a stranger once more. I just looked at her with sad eyes and agreed to go.

We have one big store in the city, and it's not too far from her house," said Elsa. "We're going to make a stop, and then once I drop you off I've got to go to work."

Funny, she hadn't even told me the woman's name. Oh God! Where was I going? Did I have to be afraid of my mother? All this was so fishy to me. Like always, I didn't have a choice, but I could run away! But maybe that captain woman did exist. Perhaps I was wrong, so I decided to go see.

As we walked and walked, I saw a big river, and I thought it must be Dunav River, one of the biggest rivers in Europe. There were beautiful houses all around. It was so lovely; I thought perhaps this was the place where she lived.

As we approached the river my mother pointed out; "There is the house. Don't forget to be nice to her, she is old fashioned and doesn't like kids that much."

"Mother, if she doesn't like kids, then why are you taking me to live with her?"

"She'll like you. It's only kids with big mouths that she hates, so try to behave yourself. Okay here we are. Remember to be beautifully polite."

"Mother, I will be friendly and polite, but it'd be good to know her name so that I can address her by name."

"Uh! You are getting on my nerves. I thought that I told you her name. Her name is Basic Vera; you may call her Aunt Vera, which is what she likes. Any more questions before we go in"

"Nope, let's go."

After we rang the bell, a lovely woman came out. To my surprise, she did look friendly, and she must have been about fifty or so. Her eyes and mine met, and there was a warm welcome in hers. I knew in that moment that I was going to be okay. Then my mother and Aunt Vera had a few words, and my mother was ready to go. She gave me one look, and then said, "I'll be back in about six weeks. Be a good girl and don't give Auntie Vera any trouble if you know what is good for you."

Auntie Vera heard what she said, and she told my mother that harsh words weren't necessary, and then with a strange look, my mother left. I was glad that she was gone, and I asked Auntie Vera if she'd like me to do anything for her before night came.

She gave me a warm smile. "Because it's summer and the weather is so sweet, we have lots of time before we have to go to sleep. So let's go down to the river and let me show you my ship. And Ramona, you don't have to try so hard with me. I can tell you're a good kid, and I'm sure we'll be friends. The river isn't too far—follow me."

When we got to the river, there were many ships, but one stood right out. The name on its side was, "I'm a Woman." I knew right away that it was Auntie Vera's. She struck me as an independent woman, and that ship was telling everyone that by its name. I smiled and pointed it out to her with a smile. "Aunt Vera, is this your ship? I know because your name is all over it."

"Yes, Ramona, that is my ship, and you and I will have fun all summer. You remind me of my daughter. She was like you in some ways."

"Why are you saying, 'was'? What's wrong? Did she pass away? My mother never said much of anything to me about you or your daughter, so I'm sorry if I'm asking you a wrong question."

"That's okay Ramona. You see my little girl is very ill. She has cancer in her bones, and we all know that she will not last long. She used to come with me on the ship all summer when she was young, and that is why you remind me of her. But let's not get mushy. I sure hope you're happy with me."

After that, we went home, and she gave me a pillow and a blanket and showed me a nice bed right beside a stove. Before I went to bed, I thanked her for her hospitality and promised that I would to do my best to help her any way I could. With that, I went to bed. I saw tears come down her cheeks, and again I thought, *Why can't my mother be like this?*

Morning came so fast, and the smell of cocoa and French toast woke me up. Aunt Vera was sitting outside on the porch, and as I went to see her she was just wiping her eyes. I could tell she was crying, and that made me sad. I wanted to make her happy, so I gave her a big hug and a kiss and just a plain old thank you. I wanted to go on the ship, and she was looking forward to that as well.

We packed a few things; most of the stuff we needed she had on the ship. All I brought was my sandals and swimsuit and one pair of shorts with a top.

We were ready, and I could see that my summer was going to be the best of my life so far.

CHAPTER 15

I WASN'T WRONG. THE summer of 1960 was the best time of my life. I had never been so happy and worry-free; all thanks to Aunt Vera. As long as I live, I won't forget Aunt Vera. She taught me a lot.

Most of all she always said, "Ramona don't hate, always forgive. You don't have to forget because time will do that. Never look back on what was—always try and go for new things. If you want something, don't give up. You try and try again until you have it."

She taught me how to use money, how to love, and how to cook, and she's the one who taught me how to fish. I liked catching fish, and she always laughed when I brought a fresh one into the kitchen. I could go on and on, but there is not enough paper for all the good words I have for her.

She always told me not to use words like "I wish," but I couldn't help it, I wished she was my mother.

Aunt Vera knew all of my secrets about what had happened in the orphan village and all about that monster Mr. Tekish. I also told her all about Miss Clara, and she said not to cry over Miss Clara so much because she was so selfish. She said Miss Clara could have stopped Mr. Tekish, but she didn't, all because of a poor excuse. If she had reported him on time, even before I came to the orphan village, none of that would have happened, and I would not have been severely damaged, hurt, and scarred for life.

Aunt Vera felt that Miss Clara was as much a part of the problem as Mr. Tekish was. If those two girls had enough courage to report him, why had she not done the same?

I thought about what she said, and I was sure she was right, but I couldn't forget Miss Clara that easily. Like Aunt Vera said before, time would tell, and eventually, it would fade away.

At the end of the summer, it occurred to me that I had never asked Aunt Vera how she knew my mother.

She was busy in the kitchen when I approached, but she looked at me and asked me if there was anything wrong.

"Oh no, Aunt Vera, I just have one more question to ask you. How did you meet my mother?"

"Really Ramona? I thought that I told you that she used to come and do some cleaning for us, but most of the time she was looking after my mother. She was with us about seven years, and then my mother passed, so your mom decided to stop coming. She and my mom were so very close and it was hard on her when my mom died."

"So, in all those seven years, did she ever mention my brother or me?"

"No Ramona, I'm sorry, I never heard of you until last year when she came asking me what do. I was shocked at what she'd done with you and your brother. I told her to get out of my house and that I didn't want to see her at all. After that, she didn't come back for a couple of weeks, and then she told me that she was going to bring you home to live with her. Although she did say it was not her idea—she had no choice. To me it sounded like she just didn't care. I told her that when you came, I'd like to see you, and she was glad to hear that. I don't know much about your brother, she didn't talk about him at all. So that is how we all know each other, and I hope to be your friend as long as you need me."

Knowing that made me sad again. Elsa had never cared until she needed help. I just went to get my stuff to get ready to go back to her. As I was packing my bag, trying to get ready for the next day, I noticed Aunt Vera on top of the ship's bridge, sitting and crying. That made me cry as well, but I knew that I had to be strong and healthy for her because that is what she taught me. I went up with a big smile, pretending that I hadn't noticed her wet eyes, and I joked being captain one day. She laughed and took me in her arms, and again she started to cry.

Seeing those sad eyes, I told her not to cry, that only babies cried because they are not sure why they are crying. We hugged each other, and finally, she stopped crying which made me feel a little better.

She took my hand, and she gave me an envelope. I asked her what it was, but with a big smile, she just laughed and said, "That is your pay, for all the hard work you've done all summer."

I knew it was not for that, but without opening the envelope, I put it in my bag and said thank you. With that, I went downstairs to pick up my bag, but mostly to have a good cry. Something was telling me that this was the last time I would have a talk with Aunt Vera. Something was telling me this was a real goodbye. That night, I cried myself to sleep.

Next morning, I got up with a touch of sadness in my heart, because this was our last day. My mother was going to be there in about an hour or so. I could smell hot cocoa and fresh eggs, and I knew Aunt Vera was making me a good breakfast, but she also made it clear that this was good-bye, and no more tears.

As I washed downstairs, I saw her looking at the pictures of her daughter Olivera. That made me sad again, because Olivera was dying, and there was nothing I could do. Aunt Vera saw me, and with dark eyes, she said, "Let's have a good breakfast. Just you and me and blue Dunav." She was trying hard not to cry, but I said that it was okay if she had to, because I couldn't hold my tears back any longer. Again, we hugged and cried.

As we sat down to eat breakfast, I asked Aunt Vera if I could ask her a personal question. She was surprised by my request, and with puzzled eyes, she said, "Yes of course you can ask me."

I thought about it for a moment, and then I told her that I had seen papers on the table that said the ship was for sale.

"I was going to tell you after breakfast," she said. "But since you'd like to know, I will tell you now. As you know, Olivera is very ill, and according to the doctors, she may only have six to eight months to live, maybe more or less. I would like to spend my time with her, and having a ship or working I cannot do both. Olivera is more important to me than any ship or money, so that is why I'm selling it."

I didn't say anything, I just gave her a big kiss, and I whispered in her ear, "I love you forever." She looked at me and smiled.

A knock on the door interrupted our hugs and kisses, as Aunt Vera opened the door I saw my mother. Without any hi or hug, she just asked if I had been a good girl.

Looking at Aunt Vera, I whispered, "You see, she doesn't care, but I will try to do right." With that, I took my bag, gave Aunt Vera one more look, and left with my mother.

As we walked home, I was wondering what she was going to do with me now when school started. I would be by myself all night. I was already scared but never told her that. To my surprise, she said that as of September 10th she would be working day shift, so that would mean only a couple of weeks that I would be alone at night. That news was unexpected to me, so I said, "Thank you. I'm so happy."

She didn't say anything else until we got to a big store. With a questioning tone, she asked me if Aunt Vera had given me any money. Unclear on what her game was, I said, "Yes."

"I won't ask you how much she gave you but I hope it's enough for you to buy yourself some real clothes and other things that you'll need in school, because I don't have much money, and I know she was going to help. The choice is yours if you like; we can go to this store and get what you need. I'm pretty sure you know what you'll need for school and what you like to wear."

I decided to tell her that I only had 200 dinars, and that I wasn't sure how much I could buy for that. She looked at me carefully, and with a funny smile she said that I was the biggest liar that she'd ever known.

Watching her, I was convinced she was just fishing, so I just laughed as well. "If you like I can show you the money," I said, (but I was hoping she would say no).

In a calm voice, she said, "Never mind; we can buy the most important things, and next month I will get you the rest of the stuff you need."

I was very surprised, but I actually didn't know how much money Aunt Vera had given me. I hadn't opened the envelope, and that kind of scared me. What if there weren't 200 dinars in there? My mother would probably think I'd lied. I thought I'd ask her to stop at a restaurant because I needed to go to the washroom, and then I could check and see what was in the envelope.

Amazingly, she said okay, and that we could have a pita and milk. Again, I was shocked; this person changed like the weather. One minute she was nice…well not that nice, and then the next minute she acted like she would like to kill me.

When I got to the washroom I carefully opened my envelope, and the shock was so large. There was a note saying:

Happy 14th birthday, Ramona
I know this is a lot of money, but I want you to have it. Buy yourself anything you like. Now you know the value of a dinar, so spend it and keep some for other days. You don't have to tell your mother about this. I'm sure she will ask you, but just tell her I gave you 200 dinars, and she will live you alone.

There was so much money, I was shaking. There were 3000 dinars in there. So much money. I wanted to cry, but if did she'd ask me what was wrong, so I took out 200 dinars, and the rest of it I put in my shoes, just in case she took my bag.

As I approached the table, she looked at me as if she knew something was wrong, but before she had a chance to say anything I gave her the money.

"There are 200 dinars," I said, "and you can do whatever you like with it. I think that's enough to buy me all the necessary stuff for school."

She took the money, and with a funny face, she mumbled almost to herself, "Aunt Vera could have given you more, but she was always so cheap. Her mother was always good to me; well I guess this is better than nothing."

After we ate we got some school supplies and we went home, if you can call one room home. It was getting late and she had to go to work later, so she went to bed and said not to bother her for a least an hour or two. Well, that was my cue to get out. With all that money in my shoes, I wondered what I could do with it. I was miles away in my mind until I felt a hand on my shoulder. I looked up and saw a boy staring at me. Because we were in the courtyard, I knew right away that he must be Slavko, the boy next door.

I just said, "Hi, my name is Ramona and please don't tell me…you are Slavko, am I right?"

"Yes, you are right. I have heard about you but you just disappeared all summer. My mother told me that you came in early July, but no one knew where you were. Now that you're here I'm pleased to meet you."

"Well, well, well, aren't you a nice one. Most boys are rude and mean, but you're different. I think we're going to get along just fine. I'm glad to see you because I was going to ask you about the school. I have to go and register, and I have no idea where it is. My mother told me to go and ask Slavko. I will be going to grade six. What grade are you in?"

"Well, first I will show you where the school is. It's not open until September first. It's just one block from us. As for me, this year will be my last one. I'm going into the eighth grade, and after that, I'd like to join the army and learn to fly big airplanes. So how old are you Ramona? I'm seventeen and a half, but next May I'll turn eighteen."

"I'll be fourteen on October 9th."

"Again, I'm glad to meet you Ramona, but now I have to go to help my mother in the city. You see, she has a newspaper booth, and sometimes I go and give her a break. So you and I will talk again, and perhaps on your birthday I can take you for an ice cream. I know a great cafe."

Slavko left, and I knew I'd met a good friend. The old woman had said that he was a nice person, and she was right.

On the street I went to look for my gypsy friend Karla. I went to the same place she always stood, but she wasn't there. No one was there, so I was sad and went back home. I knew my mother was asleep, she would be sleeping for another hour, so I knocked at the Alias and Havilas' doors, but there were no answers.

I was wondering what to do, and then I heard an answer from the Alias door. She asked me what I wanted, but she never came out. I said that I was Elsa's daughter, and that I had just moved in and wanted to meet all my neighbours. There was no answer, so I left. Wondering what to do next, I went out on the streets trying to find my new school.

Slavko was right; the school was not far at all. It looked beautiful and big. There was no one there, so I left and walked around, exploring my neighbourhood.

I went to the corner store, got a bag of candy and a carton of milk, and decided to go home and wait until Elsa got up. I didn't have to wait for long; she opened the door and said, "Come in, you don't have to sit outside the door like a dog if I'm asleep, just come in quietly and read a book or something."

She got ready for work and before she left she told me not to open the door for anyone, and that if I had to go to the toilet to use a bucket.

I looked at her and smiled. "You think that I'm going to use a bucket?" You are too funny. Listen Mother, I'm not a baby, so don't worry—just go." There was a small radio, so I took a book and listened to the songs, and eventually I fell into sleep and never heard her coming in.

That day we had a lot to do. After breakfast, we had to go to school to register, and after that we went to the store to buy books, and then she surprised me with a kind word. They were the first kind words I had heard from her since we met. "Ramona, I know that tomorrow is your birthday, so I'm going to take you to a circus that is opening the same day. I don't have much to give you, but I guess you deserve a happy birthday.

Now we'll go home, and I'll make something to eat. I don't have to go to work tomorrow so we can just relax at home."

I looked at her and wondered again if I'd misjudged her. Perhaps she had a heart.

My birthday came and went and it was time for school. I was a bit nervous about the new school, and how I would cope with it all. I went out into the courtyard to wait for Slavko, and I saw his mother as well. She was a lovely woman and made me feel welcome, telling me not to be afraid. I thanked her, and we went.

Slavko had his friends, but he knew I was new, so he stayed with me until I got to my class. Everything was almost the same as at my old school, except for the kids. I noticed right away that there were two groups in this category; that is, rich kids and not so rich like me. But I just didn't care. I sat beside one girl that looked about average—not rich but not poor either. She told me to get lost; that the seat was for her friend.

I looked at her and said. "To bad that you're waiting for a friend, I don't see any coming your way." Then I went and sat with a boy in the last row. He was very shy and gave me a small smile.

My school days went fast. I tried to do the best I could, not to please my mother but to be the best for me. I knew if I was going to make it in the world I'd have to do my best, not just try.

There were lots of handsome boys at school, but one stood out, and I could tell by the way he dressed that he was a wealthy kid. Every girl there did exactly what he asked.

However, to his surprise, I always ignored him, and that drove him crazy. I was happy about that. My experiences with boys or men were significant. I had promised myself that no man was going to make my life miserable again, so that kid didn't know what was coming to him if he tried to touch me.

As the days went by my mother and I were still somehow strangers—nothing had changed. She would go to work in the morning, and in the evening after supper she went out too, but where I have not a clue.

I did ask her one day, and she told me to mind my business, so I backed off. We never talked, so I was not so sure if she knew anything about my childhood in the orphan village, so I just kept it all to myself.

The New Year was approaching that 1961 and we had a dance in school, so Slavko asked to take his girlfriend and me. First, I thought it was strange that he would do that, but his girlfriend was a beautiful girl, so I went with them.

I had never danced before with a boy, or been to a prom at all, so when one boy came and asked me to dance, I said in a friendly and polite way, "No thank you." Then a wealthy boy came and told me to dance with him. I just looked at him and said, "No thank you, I don't dance with rich kids. I don't think they know how."

I could tell he was pissed, but I got my laugh. Then it was getting late and I couldn't find Slavko, so I headed home by myself. As I turned the corner, I felt a hand on my shoulder, and then a hard push against the wall. I couldn't move and was so scared, but when I turned around, I saw that gorgeous boy that I had called rich because he was. His name was Boban.

I looked at him and asked him what he wanted. He grabbed me by my arms and was pushing me against the wall. I told him to let me go and stop hurting me. He just laughed at me and pulled my dress up. I knew right away what was next, so I lifted my leg and hit him so hard between his legs that he actually fell on the ground holding his hand between his feet and crying.

I said to him, "I told you before I don't play or dance, and I don't like boys like you. So you see this will be a lesson not to be so smart if a girl says no, which means no. You're not the only one Boban, lots of boys and men just don't listen at all. I'm sorry that you had to learn like that. Sure hope you feel better in a couple of days."

Then I ran home, had a little mischievous laugh, and then went to bed happy. As I lay down, I wished Happy New Year to myself. My mother was out, and there was no one to wish me a Happy New Year, but I didn't care much about that—it was just another day for me. So now, we were going into 1961.

Winter was cold, and there was not much to do. Quite often, I would go to Slavko's and we would play cards or just listen to the radio. One day after school, I was doing my homework, but there was one math problem that I had been trying to solve with no luck. So I went to Slavko for help. He was home, but not alone. His girlfriend was there. I asked him if he could help me with the problem. She was a sweet girl and had no problem with me coming; she offered to help me as well. She said she was good in math and that she often helped many kids. I was happy about that. As we were busy working on my math papers, there was a knock on my door across the courtyard.

All three of us just looked up and wondered how that could be, especially since I didn't know anybody in this city, and my mother had never told me anything about her friends. I stood up to go see who it was, but Slavko stopped me.

"Ramona, let me go first. You never know who's out there, and at least I'm a guy."

"Slavko I'm not afraid, and you using words like only men can be strong, you make me sick. Do you think a girl can't take care of herself?"

"Ramona, I'm sorry. I just wanted to help."

"Slavko, next time use proper words, but thank you."

Yeah okay, no problem, and don't be so touchy. Remember we're friends and don't worry so much."

Both his girlfriend and I just smiled and he went out. I heard him saying hello to someone, but then nothing. I wanted to run out, but then in a loud voice, we heard him saying, "Is that you Sasha?"

I looked at Tara, (that was Slavko's girlfriend's name), and asked her if she knew anybody by that name. She just shook her head, meaning no. Then we heard Slavko asking Sasha to come in.

As he walked in, we both just looked at each other and said hi. Not knowing who he was, I didn't know what to say. Nevertheless, there was something about him that drew me closer to him. Our eyes met, and we knew that there was a significant connection—a connection that scared me. The first thing that came to my mind was, *Is this my brother?*

All four of us stood there without any words for a moment, and then Slavko spoke up. "Tara and Ramona, this is Sasha. Ramona, I believe this is your brother, the one you were looking for and hoping that one day you would find. So there he is, my friend; Sasha, your big brother. "

We just looked at each other and then started hugging and crying. Sasha took me in his arms, and while crying he kept asking, "Is this you? Oh, my dear sister, I've been waiting for this moment all my life. As a little boy of five, I knew you were real. Lots of people were telling me that I was imagining having a sister. I can see it clearly, but I do remember that day when our mother gave you away to a stranger. I was crying and crying, begging her to take you back, but later when I was older, I too was thinking I imagined all that. But look! Here you are. Thank you, Slavko, for making this happen for us. I'm glad I gave you my address, you are a good friend, and writing me about her was the best gift you could give me.

"I tell you what," he continued. "Slavko, do you mind if I go with Ramona to our apartment and have a talk before our mother comes home? I'm only here because of your letter. As you know, my mom and I don't speak. Tomorrow I'm going into the army for two years, and this is just the best time to see Ramona and all my other friends. Thank you, Slavko one more time."

All the time he spoke, I was just looking at him and trying to find any resemblance that would tell me that we were brother and sister, but there wasn't any.

Perhaps it was because we had different fathers, but we didn't look like siblings at all, which made me sad. But he was my brother, so I didn't care if we looked alike or not. Once inside my mother's room we just sat there for a moment, and then Sasha started to cry a lot. I took his hand in mine and with a soft voice, I told him, "Sasha, please don't cry. We have finally found each other. Let's talk. I'd like to know everything about you; what happened to you and where you were all these years. Did you live with our mom or where did you grow up? As for me, I'm sure you know that I was in an orphan village all these years."

"No Ramona, I didn't have any idea where that woman took you. I was too young to remember everything that happened, but I will never forget that moment. Believe it or not, it is always right in front of me, watching our mother just throwing you to that stranger at the train station. That's why many times I go to the train station with a bottle of rum, drinking to kill my pain and hoping to find you. I've asked Mother many times about you, but she always denied that you exist. Were you in an orphan village all this time?"

"Yes, Sasha— that was the only home I knew. I went there as a baby of three months. The stranger that Mother gave me to was a teacher in that orphan village. She was just going back to work when she and Mom met. She kept a diary of everything about me, and it is quite a story. I had good times and bad times in there. All that I'll tell you some other time, but when the orphan village was closing they had to find my mother. Actually they were able to find her because when you were a little boy, you told one of your teachers that you had a sister, but no one believed you then. As it happened, you weren't too far from me. Mother had put you in an orphan village for boys, and there was a teacher who remembered you and our mom. It's a great story, and that is how they had a chance to find her.

"Everything was so confused, and there were so many details and sorrows, so many our mother's secrets that she won't talk about. I think I know more about you and Mom, but both of you don't know anything about me. Even to this day, Mom refuses to listen to me when I ask her to talk about her, you, and me. She won't say anything, but I know almost everything. Sasha, do you remember Officer Branko and Aunt Sonia from Bosnia? Do you recall a man named Mr. Stanovic? He used to come to our house and wanted to be with Mom, and by the way, he was my father."

"I remember some of my life in Bosnia," he said, "mostly my dad and Aunt Sofia; she was always nice to us, but I don't remember much about anyone else."

"You see Sasha, I had an adopted mother, Miss Clara, but before I found out that she wasn't my mom I actually thought that she was, but the truth came out when a notice came that the orphan village is closing down. Miss Clara told me everything. She and I went to the place where I was born in Bosnia, and that's where so many secrets came out. I even know how your father died, so sorry about that. Sasha, do you remember your dad at all, and how he died? Do you remember anything from your life in Bosnia?"

"Ramona, you sure know a lot about my past, but you don't know about my life with Mother. She bounced me back and forth between orphan villages and living with her, then living with a relative and back to her. I had a terrible childhood, and it hasn't changed. I'm drunk almost every day because I'm trying to forget my sorrow. Many times I wanted to end my life, but finding you was my goal and it looks like now I've achieved it. We have found each other, but right now I have to get to the army. I won't be able to save you, or keep you from her. Ramona, our mother is ill. She needs a lot of help, and no one cares. Mom was once a good person; that's what I heard, but after my father died and you came after that, she broke down. She turned into a person without a soul; she doesn't care about anything, not only you or me. Look around you. Is this a place to live and raise a family? However, she thinks it's an ideal location. To her it's take it or leave it. That's why I left her. I live with some friends in a different city, and I do sometimes come to look in on her. Many times I have no idea where she is. You see, I honestly think you were better off than I was. All these years that you stayed in the orphan village most of that time I was on streets or with somebody else, barely ever with Mother. I have spent days and days crying, and it came to me one day I was going to end my life, but thinking of you I knew that was wrong. Ramona, it's getting late, I better go before she comes home, but I'll drop by to tell Mom that I'm going into the army for two years. She has a right to know, even though she probably won't care. You can tell her I dropped by to see you all. There's not enough room for all three of us, so I'll see you later. Tell Slavko that I need to talk to him before I leave.

Ramona, now that we've found each another everything is going to be all right, you'll see."

When Sasha left, I cried and didn't even heard the door when my mother came home. Looking at her face I saw a big question, but before she said anything, I told her that Sasha had been there; my brother that she wouldn't talk about, and that it was so sad that I met the only brother that I have like that. She had never wanted me to meet Sasha, so she was kind of shocked.

"Mother, why wouldn't you let me meet my brother? Why do you hate us so much? It's not our fault what happened—what happened to you happened to us as well. Why can't you get some help and let us live a normal life like most families do?"

"Ah so now, I'm not normal! Is that what that drunken boy is saying now?"

"No Mother, that's not what he was saying, and he wasn't drunk. He was so happy to meet me finally, and he came to tell you that he got his papers for the army for the next two years. All he wanted was to say goodbye for now and to let you know where he'll be. That's all. He's very sorry for everything; I can tell he cares for you very much."

The next day was a Saturday, no school, but I got up early. I wanted to get the place nice and clean for when my mother came home from work, and Sasha came to said goodbye. I wanted everything to be as perfect as it possibly could be.

Mother came home with a cake. (That was a shocker for me.) I was happy. I thought that maybe she would be different since both of her children would be home with her. We were really happy, and Mom made some goulash for supper.

I was so excited that we were going to be together, and then six o'clock came, and then eight o'clock came and went, but no Sasha. I was scared to look at my mother. She was getting more restless by the minute, and then she grabbed a piece of cake, opened the door, and shouted, "This is your cake, you no good son of mine!" She grabbed her coat and left.

I sat there crying and wondering what happened. Why had Sasha not come?

Slavko must have heard my mother slamming the door and me crying, and he came over wondering what had happened.

I just stood there saying, "He never came. He never came. Why? Why Slavko? Can you tell me why?"

Slavko didn't have the answer, and how could he? Sasha had promised he was going to come, but he never did.

After that day, I never saw my brother any more. Later on, Slavko told me that he was in jail because he got to the army late to register; which was a wrong thing to do. Because of that, he got three years of service and I never heard from him, not even a letter. Many times, I wondered if it was something that I'd done, or if maybe he was like our mother and they both needed lots of help. I was stuck right in the middle.

After that, Mother and I never talked about Sasha. Life was like before; Mom went to work, and I went to school—the same old, sad life that I'd had.

Winter was almost over, and I wondered what was in a store for me for summer this year!

CHAPTER 16

MY GRADE SIX for the year 1961 was coming to an end very fast, and summer was just around the corner. I was wondering where she was going to send me this year. I knew that being home alone was out of the question even though I was fourteen.

Slavko's mom invited me to go on a trip with them for two weeks, and to me that sounded grand. That night, I planned to ask my mother. I thought that if she was in a good mood she'd probably say yes, but the first thing she'd ask would be who's going to pay for it... that she didn't have money for my vacation.

That is what exactly happened. "There is no money for that, but I'm going to take you to your aunt, my sister. I know I haven't told you about her, but she's my younger sister, and she lives in a town named Branovbrdo. Her name is Jana, and your uncle's name is Stefan. They have two boys; Zoran is about your age and Milan is about Sasha's age. They don't know about you. I'll be going there on Saturday, and you will stay with Aunt Vera. She's in town for the next two weeks or so, and I'm sure you two have a lot to talk about."

Before she went on and on, I told her she wouldn't have to pay anything at all for the two weeks with Slavko and his mother. To my mother money was always an issue, but I had offered Slavko's mother money for the trip, and she wouldn't heard of it. She said that going with them would make Slavko happy, because this was his last year of grade school. In September, he would be going to start trade school, and this was his wish.

I thought about it for a long time, and I thought that Sasha might have had something to do with this. Slavko and Sasha had kept in touch sometimes, but I wondered why he wouldn't write me and tell me why he never showed up that day. Slavko was always very careful about what he said whenever I mentioned my brother. I was sure there was more to everything, but I let it go for now.

I told Mother that money didn't have to be an issue all the time, and that Slavko and his mom were okay with the expense for me. "You probably don't know," I said, "but they had a farm, and when Slavko's dad died, a farm was too much to handle, so they sold it. They live a very decent life here, and I like them both. Why don't you go and talk to your sister while I'm away for two weeks, and then when I come back, there will be plenty of time for me to go to see my relatives. Summer is two months, and I was planning to go and see Aunt Vera. I think this will work out for both of us."

Looking at me, she said, "Okay, but your report card had better be good."

I wasn't worried about my report card. I knew that I was a good student—people like me who have no place to go, sit home and read and listen to the radio, and I did like school. I had some friends, but not close enough to ask them to come to my place. I was ashamed about my living situation, and I didn't want them to make fun of me because my place was in somebody's garage, and maybe even smaller. So I never asked anybody to come in for that reason.

There was one girl I liked a lot. (Olga was her name.) She was quite well off, but her life was a disaster. Many, many times I noticed her neck was black and blue, or her hands were scratched all over. Nobody paid any attention to that, because no one cared, especially if you were a girl. But one day she came with a black eye and I said, "That's it. I have to find out what's going on."

I asked her very quietly, "Why the black eye?" She looked at me with tears in her eyes and said that her father had been so drunk last night that he'd beaten her mother, and when she tried to help her mom, he hit her as well. I knew her dad from people's talk about him. I don't think anyone on our block liked him. He was a very mean man.

She lived in a beautiful big house, had nice clothes to wear, lots of food, and most importantly she had a mother and father. If you think about it, I never had any of that, but looking into her eyes, I thought my life was not so bad. Having all these good things, but not being able enjoy them, what's the point of having all that? I felt sorry for her. Knowing there wasn't anything I could do, I decided to ask her to come to my place, even though my whole apartment was probably as big as her closet.

To my surprise, she almost jumped from happiness and said, "Yes, yes, I'd love to go to your house."

Right after the sound of the bell, Olga ran to me with a big smile, ready to go. Well, I couldn't say no, could I? Therefore, with a smile, we went. My place wasn't so far from school, and as we were approaching the door, my mother came out. I was surprised because she worked until five, and it was only 3:30.

The first thing that came to my mind was that something was wrong. I wondered if it had anything to do with Sasha. Mom looked at Olga and me and said she'd be back about six or seven. "It's nice you have a friend," she said, and then she left without any explanation.

For a minute or two, I didn't know what had just happened. Olga noticed that there was something wrong and as polite as she could be, she offered to come some other day. To make the situation better, I wouldn't hear of it, so I invited her in.

The place was beautiful and clean, but we had only one chair, so I told her to jump on the bed. I could tell she was a bit shocked. She'd known I had a small place, but this place was so small it was suffocating. I saw her face, and I offered her a game of chess and said that if she liked, I had some cookies.

In a very soft voice she asked me if I had always lived in poverty. I noticed she was sad, but I told her that I was okay with all this. Then, out of the blue, she jumped up with a great suggestion, though not a possible one. "Ramona, I have a big house, well not me, my parents, and I'm always home alone. My mother always goes to the neighbour's and cries, and my father is out at a bar drinking. I'm all alone and sad, so why don't you ask your mother if you can come and live with me as long we go to the same school?

My room is so big that we could put five beds in it, not just one, and we could pretend that we were sisters. Please, Ramona, what do you think of that?"

"Olga, do you hear what you're saying? We can't do that. I'm not a piece of rag that you'd like to have in your room to play with or to make sure that you're happy. Olga, I do thank you for your offer, but trust me, I don't mind living the way I do. My mother is an emotional person, but she's always home except when she's at work (that was a lie), and we are happy (another lie). No one yells at us, and we never get beaten by anyone. I'm telling you that it's okay with me not to have what you have. We can be friends, but not if you're ashamed of having a poor one like me. It's up to you, and now I think you should go home."

I could tell Olga was sad, but I didn't want her to know that was the best offer I'd had since I came to live with my mother. I just could not tell Olga that, but my secret was my secret and it had to stay that way for now. She was a beautiful person, and you never knew, perhaps one day I'd tell her everything, but not now.

As soon as Olga left, I went next door to Slavko's to see if he'd heard anything from my apartment. My bad luck, no one was home, so I decided to go and see the old woman, to find out if she'd seen anything out of the ordinary at my place. I knocked and knocked but there was no answer.

What was going on? Nobody was home this day, and I wondered if anything was wrong. Jumping to any conclusions was unnecessary, so I took a book and listened to the radio, and I guess that's how I fell asleep.

When I woke up, it was about six a.m., and I jumped up wondering where my mother was. Had I been home alone all night? This time, I got scared. Not knowing what else to do, I just sat and stared at the wall, and then I started to shake. What if something bad had happened?

I found myself talking to myself, and I knew doing that was just going to make it worse, so I went out to wash, and as I was going to make a tea, my mother walked in. She looked like she'd been through a tornado. I had never seen my mother so sad. I could tell she'd been crying, when she asked me to sit and listen.

This is not good, was my first thought.

"Ramona, there was an accident in the army where Sasha was. Two boys were fighting, and Sasha came to separate them. There was a struggle, and then one of the boys took a pistol and in a rage, shot Sasha. The hospital tried all night to save him but they couldn't. Ramona, Sasha is dead."

I think I actually had a pain in my heart. Emotionally I was going crazy. That couldn't be correct. I hadn't seen enough of him. I couldn't express my feelings except o say, "Oh please, God, help me! He was the only one who cared about me, even though we only knew each other one day. I don't know what I'm going to do now."

Crying, I put my arms around my mom, but she just pushed me away. I realized that he meant to her a lot, but I didn't. Quietly I said, "Mom I'm so sorry. I'm going to miss him as much as you do. If I can do anything to ease your pain let's do it together. Please Mom, sit down and talk to me. It will help us both, but more so you."

She stood up, and her eyes were like fire. For a moment I thought she was going to hit me, but instead she started to shout at me. "You! It's all your fault, you brought this tragedy, you're to blame for everything. I never wanted you before, and I still don't. I was happy before you were born, and then you came along to destroy Sasha's and my life. You—you're to blame for his drinking. Trying to find you made him crazy, and look what's happened now. Get out of my way and get out of my house and don't come back."

She was yelling so loudly that Slavko and his mom came knocking on the door, asking if everything was okay. Yelling and screaming, she opened the door and just pushed me out. I fell and I started to cry. She was going crazy for sure. Slavko's mom took me to her apartment and asked me what had happened. I thought for sure that they'd know about Sasha, but I guess not. While crying, I managed to say, "Sasha is dead."

They both were in total shock. "Ramona, what do you mean Sasha is dead? What happened and where? Moreover how?" Slavko was crying, and his mom just could believe what had happened.

"I'm not so sure about all details," I said, "but my mother said that there was a fight in the army, and one of the guys got mad and shot Sasha. She won't tell me anything else, and I don't know what to do now. She blames me for everything that happened, and I'm so scared now. Where am I going to go now?"

Slavko and his mother offered to let me to stay with them until my mom calmed down a little bit. All three of us just sat there without talking. I think we all had our minds on what had happened to Sasha, and what was going to happen to me. I was crying, trying not to make a scene, but I was hurting very badly. My mother was going to hate me more for sure now. Just when I thought that things were going little better—now this.

Any real feelings that she had for me were gone for sure, even though I had nothing to do with Sasha's death. I was struggling to calm down; my body was shaking and at one point I thought I was going to faint. Slavko noticed and jumped to my rescue. They put me on a bed to lie down for a while and let me rest. I was experiencing a nightmare in the middle of the day. My head was like a roller coaster and all I wanted was to die. Then a loud voice made me jump.

"Ramona, get out here right now! Don't make me wait; I have to go, and you're going with me."

I just stood there looking at Rosa, Slavko's mom, wondering what I should do. Should I go out, or just wait until she calmed down. With my eyes looking for an answer, I heard Rosa say, "Ramona, wait. Don't go, let me see if I can help you, she sounds outraged, just stay inside."

Rosa went out and the moment my mother saw her, she started to yell. "Get that girl out; I didn't ask for you. She's my child, and I'll do with her whatever I want."

"No Elsa, you can't do that. You're very upset now and there's no need to take it out on Ramona. She's all you've got now, why can't you be nicer to her?

That child needs you now more than ever, as well. She lost a brother that she met only once, and her hopes were to be with him when he finished his army duty. Please don't destroy what chance you have to be with your daughter."

"All right then, you think she's a sweet girl then you can have her. I'm going out and don't look for me. Rosa, you asked for this, and you got it. Ramona is all yours."

"Now look, Elsa. You can't just say she's all yours. We are talking about a child, not a dog or a cat. Elsa, you're under a lot of stress; get some quiet time and some comforting, and as you said, you have to go. I don't mind looking after Ramona for a while, but don't tell me I can have her. Be a mother to her. She just lost a brother too; how do you think she feels. You go now and do what you need to do, and come back when you're ready. In the meantime, school is going to be finished in about five days for this semester and after that, I'll be going on vacation and we'll bring Ramona with us. You don't have to worry about anything, just make sure when we come back that you have sorted out what you're feeling about Ramona and try to make a better life. She's all you've got left, so attempt to keep her before you destroy everything."

Elsa was struggling to find the proper words, but all she was able to come up with was, "I don't care. Do whatever you like, and thank you."

Right after that she left, and I was so upset that strangling her was crossing my mind. I walked in and saw a scared child, shaking like a tree; Slavko was in shock as well.

Rosa looked at us scared kids and seemed to decide to try to make it little more comfortable. So just out of the blue, she asked us to get ready to go to dinner, and said we could talk about anything we liked, and could plan our trip for next week.

"So who is going to follow me?" she asked, but there wasn't a sound. "Okay then, we can all sit here and stare at the wall, or maybe we can feel sorry for ourselves, or maybe we can just get up and like I said, let's go!"

"Mom, you're right," said Slavko. "Let's go."

Going out was an excellent idea, I didn't want them to worry too much about me, after all, we were just neighbours, and we all had some problems at home.

At dinner, Slavko and his mom tried so hard. I did a laugh a bit, but deep inside me, I was crying and screaming in pain. I didn't know why this was all happening to me; my mother should have thrown me off the train, I wouldn't have had all this pain. We talked about the trip and how it was going to be. The plans were to see Dubrovnik and Herzegovina, and then find a hotel in Kotor. It sounded magnificent, but I just couldn't bring myself to enjoy it.

Rosa was watching me, and I could tell that she understood my pain. When she took my hand in hers she made me felt better. After dinner, we talked about how we were going to work this out. Rosa suggested that Slavko sleep in my apartment at night since he was seventeen and not scared. Then in the daytime we could be together, or whatever we liked to do. "That doesn't mean that Slavko has to stay home all the time. Ramona, you're old enough to be by yourself in the daytime, and it's not as if you never were alone."

We all agreed to that, and I was glad to have them both as my friends. In a bit of a shy voice, I told them how much that meant to me, that I'd never forget them, and that maybe one day I could do something good for them.

When we got home, Slavko took his clothes and was ready to go next door to my place. We all said good night, and then Rosa showed me Slavko's bed. She had changed it and put on all clean sheets and a warm blanket. It was summer, but the warm blanket was fun.

I told her that I was going out to wash up, and she was okay with that. As I walked back in I saw Rosa waiting for me at the edge of the bed that had been prepared for me. I knew she wanted to talk, and I was amazed at how she knew that I wanted to talk as well. She saw me crying, and holding my hands she whispered to me, "Don't cry Ramona. Let's just talk for a while."

"Mrs. Rosa? Can I call you Mrs. Rosa instead of just Rosa, because to me calling you Rosa doesn't sound too good, you can't be my mother, so I'd like to call you Mrs. Rosa out of respect."

"Ramona, we are friends, and you can call me what ever suits you. It's okay with me. Ramona, can you tell me something? Do you have any other relatives that you know of, because then we can get in touch with them. Maybe you could live with them if it came to that point."

"Mrs. Rosa, I don't know. As I told you, I was in an orphan village all my life, and learning that the woman in the orphan village wasn't my mother was my first shock.

Then she and I found out that I had a mother and a brother, and some relatives on my mother's side, but I don't know where they are. I know the name of my aunt, but that's about it. My mother never talked about any of my cousins or relatives. Looking for her, we found out there were a lot more, but I never met any of them yet, and don't forget I've been with my mother only a year or so, and my relatives probably don't even know about me."

"Do you remember your aunt's name or where she lives?"

"The one and the only thing that I can remember from my mother telling me was an Aunt Jana and an uncle. They live in Branovbrdo, but that's the only information I can recall at all. We didn't even know where my mother lived until 1959."

"Well, then I guess we'll just have to wait and see what will happen when we come back from vacation. And now young lady, let's go to bed."

"Mrs. Rosa, thank you for everything. I don't know what would I do without your help."

The next day, Slavko and I went to school pretending nothing had happened, and I was thankful for that. Slavko was my best friend, and I knew he would not tell anybody about my mother or me. We had only three more days, and then school was over for this grade. I hoped my grades were good, but on the other hand, who cared? I didn't have anybody to share them with. It was so sad, so very sad, but I knew I'd survive, I always did. A week went by very fast; school let out for summer, and most kids were happy but not me.

School was the only place I loved going because I knew I would have a good breakfast and lunch, which was free every day for every child. Also, the school was my second home. I was safe there, and I had someone to talk to. At home, I was always alone unless Slavko wasn't too busy. Other than that I had no one to share my day with me or to ask, "How are you, Ramona?" Just no one, so you see school was the place for me, but for now I'd have to see what was going to happen in the next two months or so.

The next week I was going with Slavko and his mom for a two-week summer vacation, but what happened after that was what scared me. I didn't know where my mother was, and no one else knew. It was a very tragic and emotional time for me.

As I was packing, there was a knock on my door. It got me scared at first, I wondered if I should open it. If it were Slavko, he would be sad if I didn't answer the door, but no, this was someone new. Slowly I said, "Who is there?"

Then I heard a very soft voice. "Ramona, please open the door, I won't hurt you. I'm your Aunt Jana, and we have to talk."

I approach the door to open it, and then I heard Mrs. Rosa's voice. "Miss, can I help you?"

"Yes, you may give me a hand. I'm looking for a Ramona. I know she's inside, I have to talk to her."

"Let me introduce myself first. My name is Rosa, and right now, I'm looking after Ramona until her mother decides to come back, and that was okay with her before she left. Now we don't know where Elsa is, or when she's coming back. She just left this poor child; I don't understand that woman."

"Thank you, Rosa, my name is Jana. I'm Ramona's aunt, I don't know if she ever heard of me or not, but I never knew that Elsa had a daughter till two days ago. It's a sad story but let me explain. I got a telegram from the hospital that I had to come because it was a very urgent matter about Elsa. I knew she had some problems when her husband died, and then she was cruelly raped, and at that time she was suicidal, but that was all thirteen years ago. She also had a problem with her son, and now that he is dead I think Elsa is back in a dangerous state, and that's why she's in the hospital. She will be there for some time. In the hospital, she told me about Ramona. I was in shock; I never knew anything about her. She put that poor girl into strangers' hands, and she ended up in an orphan village for thirteen years.

"If Elsa wasn't so ill and a danger to herself, I don't know what I would do to her. I have looked after her son many times, and I can't believe she never told me about Ramona. You see I have two boys, and Ramona would be a blessing to me. I always wanted a girl, and if I had known about Ramona, she would have been with me, not like this. I'm sorry that Elsa has put you through this, but Ramona will be staying with me. I do have signed papers from Elsa that Ramona is going to live with us."

"Jana that is all so sad, and I feel so sorry for Ramona. My son and I, we just love her. She's a good girl, but I can tell you that she's also the saddest child that I ever saw.

I have a big favour to ask you before you take Ramona. We had made plans a long time before all this thing with Sasha happened, that we were going for a two-week vacation, and at that time Elsa had agreed. So now I'm not so sure. What do you think? This trip will do Ramona good, and if you don't mind, I'd like to do this for her."

"Well, I didn't know anything about that," said Jana. "I was planning to go home today with Ramona, but like you said this would do her good. I'll tell you what. She can go with you, but as soon as you get back let me know. I'll leave you my phone number where I work, that way you can reach me anytime, and meanwhile, I have to go and tell your property owner that she can rent this place, Ramona and Elsa will not be back."

"Jana, can you tell me where you work that you have a phone? To me, it's very strange, that these days phones are available to people outside the office or some government places!"

"Yes, you're right. I work for a military school for boys. My husband and I work there as superintendents. We take care of the grounds and cleaning; the phone is available in the hallway of the main entry, and we are there most of the time. We have a three-bedroom apartment; it's a charming place. Even though we like it there, I wouldn't put my boys in that school. The teachers are so tough on those kids, and I've seen a lot that maybe I shouldn't have, but it's a living, and we do all right. I know Ramona will have everything she needs."

"All that sounds superb, let's go and tell Ramona, I'm sure she's all ears by now."

I was standing by the door waiting for them to come in, and to see my Aunt Jana. I had first heard of her back in Bosnia from Branko, but I was shocked that she never knew that I existed. As soon as she walked in, she started kissing, hugging, and crying— you name it she did it. No one ever cared that much, or gave me hugs as much. She kept looking at me and crying, saying it was her fault for not seeing that Elsa needed help. She didn't make any sense, so I just looked at Mrs. Rosa for help. Finally, I took her in my arms to calm her down, and with Mrs. Rosa's soft-spoken words, she stopped crying.

Then again, she burst into tears. "Ramona, my dear, I'm so sorry about everything; I never knew you were alive. She told us that the baby she was carrying from that man... that baby died, and we never asked any more questions. I'm so sorry, my child, your mother, she lied to everybody. I didn't know that you were in the orphan village, my dear, I would have taken you to live with us. Please forgive us all. I'll make sure that you are taken care of from now on."

"Please, Aunt Jana, let's sit down and see what we can do now. I'm confident that you know I'm going on a vacation with Mrs. Rosa, when we come back I'll go and live with you, but can you tell me where my mother is?"

"Ramona, your mom is in the hospital and the doctor told me she's going to be in there for a long time. You see, your mother had nervous breakdown. She had one a long time ago when her husband died too. That's why I'm here. I didn't know anything about you until two days ago."

I smiled at her. "I'll eventually get used to living with you, perhaps that's not my choice, but I do know I don't have any other options. So let's go now and tell our property owner about the apartment, and I do believe you have a bus to catch. As soon as I come back from vacation, I'll call or I'll write to you. I'm sure that we have a lot to talk about, but for now, I'd like to take a moment and thank you and I'll see you soon."

Our property owner was sad to see me going, but that was my life; no one understood but me. Slavko and I walked my aunt to a bus station, and our goodbyes were sad, but she knew she'd see me soon, and she gave me some money for the trip. And in about an hour or so she left.

Slavko and I walked home, and we both had so much on our minds. I was thinking about my next home with my Aunt Jana, and Slavko was happy about us leaving tomorrow for a holiday.

CHAPTER 17

Going on a vacation with Slavko and his mom was an excellent opportunity for me to see our seaside country. I was looking forward to a little happiness. I knew as soon we got back I'd have to move again. My thoughts were so mixed up. But in trying to enjoy my vacation and attempting to forget what was coming after that, I just could not find time to enjoy anything. I think that Mrs. Rosa had the sense that I wasn't with them all the time.

"Ramona," she said comfortingly, "let everything go for now. You'll have plenty of time to worry when the time comes. For now, let's have some fun."

As I looked around, discovering many happy faces, I knew that if I let go of my emotions, I could be happy just like them. Yes, it was easily done, but my emotions were so deep, and it was hard to handle. But I did try.

The situation did improve, though, especially when Mrs. Rosa took us to a small house and with a big smile, asked us what we thought of the place. Slavko and I both looked at each other, wondering why she was showing us this house. I said the house was beautiful, and Slavko just said it was okay. I didn't know why she was interested in that house, but she never said anything. We didn't talk about it again, and our vacation went on and on.

We had a good time, but like all good times, they must come to an end. I struggled to hold back my tears, knowing I had to leave these two beautiful people; our true friendship was going to end in a day or so. We would each have new lives; I, moving to my Aunt Jana and Slavko going to trade school, and no one knew if we would ever see each other again.

When we got home, I was hoping that my mother would be there, even though I knew she was in the hospital. We didn't get along well, but I had been getting used to her and to managing all by myself. Now I had to start all over again.

Because I didn't have my apartment anymore, I was wondering where I was going to sleep until my Aunt Jana came to pick me up. Mrs. Rosa was quick to come to my rescue. She must have read my mind, or that's how a mother knows what a child is thinking. I guess I will never know; my mom never cared much about wondering what was on my mind.

Mrs. Rosa was just about to explain what we were going to do when there was a knock on the door. We all looked at each another, wondering who it could be. Slavko got to the door first, and to our surprise, the property owner, Miss Selka was standing there.

"Well, are you going to invite me in?" she asked. "I wanted to see how everybody was, and did you have fun on your vacation?"

I jumped up and gave her a friendly hug saying we'd had a great time, and we were happy to be home. The only problem we had now was me. "I don't know where to go until my Aunt Jana picks me up. I've taken up Mrs. Rosa's and Slavko's space for a long time, and I just don't know how to arrange to find my Aunt Jana today. I can go to the post office in the morning and give her a ring, saying that I'm back, or I can write her a note, I just don't know what to do."

"Ramona, this is why I came. Your Aunt Jana gave me some money to look after you until she gets here, so that you can stay with me. I've plenty of room and you and I will get along just fine. Slavko and his mom, they need some time alone, because you know he's going away soon, and I'm sure Rosa would like to spend as much time with her son as possible. So, pack up your bag and let's go to my house. I've made you some of that pita that you like, and the bed is all made up."

"Oh Miss Selka! Thank you so much but wait for just one moment, please." I threw my arms around Mrs. Rosa. "Mrs. Rosa, I can't express my feelings for you and cannot find enough words for thanking you for everything you have done for me. You made me part of your family, and as long as I'm living I will never forget you and Slavko."

My next hug was for Slavko. "Slavko, you were like a brother to me, the one I never had, and maybe one day we will cross paths and get together again, but for now, let's just say goodnight, and I should see you tomorrow or before I leave."

Later on, as I lay down and Miss Selka was just next to me, I asked her, "Miss Selka, are most mothers like mine, that don't like children? Or maybe it's because I'm a girl that she never wanted. Or are many mothers like Mrs. Rosa? Why am I so unlucky? You know sometimes I think about my situation, and

I'm surprised that I've not ended my life. I'm so tired of being pushed around and not having a family. What's the point of living if you're alone and sad? I cry almost every night, and in the daytime I pretend that I'm happy, but no one sees my tears...only me. I do struggle to tell people how I feel, that I'm so heartbroken that I struggle to get by."

"Oh my dear child, I don't have any answers for you, but you're so young and a free spirit. Time is on your side. I'm sure your happiness will come—just be patient.

Loneliness is very hard to live with; I know that just like you Ramona, but for a different reason. I'm very lonely and sad because I don't have anybody, but you, look you have your Aunt Jana who cares about you, and you have Slavko and his mom, and when you grow up I'm sure everything will be okay."

"I'm not so sure about that," I said, "but we'll see."

In the morning, the smell of fresh French toast made me jump out of bed. That elderly woman was something else. I did like her. Too bad she was hiding her true nature; she could have ended up with lots of friends, but I wouldn't tell her that, she'd get mad at me.

Over breakfast I asked, "Miss Selka is the post office open today? I'd like to mail a couple of letters, and can I write a letter to my aunt to pick me up on Friday? That is if she doesn't mind. That will give me some free time to say goodbye to my friends and be with Slavko and his mom."

"Ramona, you can stay as long as you like, I don't mind, and the post office is open. You'll need stamps and envelopes. I presume you don't have any, but I do. After breakfast, you can go to the sitting room—there is a desk you can use it for writing a letter or if you'd like quiet time to read. The room is very comfortable for studying and good for just relaxing."

I just didn't know why I had to let go of people that were so nice. Like Miss Selka. She was a beautiful woman, but if I asked Social Services to let me stay with her, the answer would be no. I just didn't know why. Going to live with my Aunt Jana was opening a new door. I was closing the door that I'd just opened and I wondered if I would keep opening and closing doors all my life. I prayed that this time would be different.

(However, my gut was telling me this would be not the end of me closing a door and opening a new one.)

After breakfast, I wrote a letter to my aunt and a letter to Mr. Nemic. The post office was not too far, so on my way back I stopped to say hello to my friend Karla on the south corner where she always was. Karla was very surprised to see me. Going to school, and then on vacation, I'd had little time to go anywhere else, and that's why I wanted to see Karla one more time before I went. She was my first friend and a good one—friends like that you don't just forget because you don't have time.

We sat on a large log, and I told her that I was moving again. I told her about my brother and his death. I had tears in my eyes when I talked about my brother but also a wave of anger in my heart when I told her about my mother.

Karla hugged me and told me not to feel sorry for myself and that crying wouldn't do me any good.

I just sat there without any words; I was so sad and depressed to move again…to leave the friends that I had made in this city. Before I went to the post office, I took some money that was left from Aunt Vera; I wanted to ensure that Karla had some. There had been a time that she had helped me, and now it was my time to give her my gift. Before Karla had a chance to say no, I took off, but not far enough. I wanted her to remember me as a friend, and you could never tell if we might meet again or not. She tried to give the money back, but I was in tears. I told her that she was my best friend, or my first friend after I got out of the orphan village, so finally she accepted it.

As I walked back to my place, I could hear Karla shouting. "Ramona, that is too much. I never had that much money. Wait, Ramona, I want to talk to you. Please hold on."

I pretended that I didn't hear her, walking faster and faster, and finally we were apart. I'm not sure; I think there were about 1200 dinars in my hand. Karla had been kind to me, and this was my turn to be nice to her. Deep inside me I was happy about it.

The next day I told Miss Selka that I'd like to go and see my friend Aunt Vera. She lived beside the river, and it wasn't that far. I liked walking—it was a way to forget all my trouble and sorrows. I hated to go and say goodbye. Like Karla, Aunt Vera had been helpful to me as well. Aunt Vera had taught me a lot, and I kept all her advice in my heart.

Walking through the city all by myself, I wondered how many other girls were like me. Why was my life so full of disappointment? I had been full of revenge before; now I was full of loneliness and struggling to understand the world. Why me? By walking and thinking, I didn't realize I was at my destination.

Aunt Vera was sitting on the porch, like she knew I was coming, and that was just so funny. We both laughed and gave each other a big hug and kiss. She sensed that something had happened; she could tell by looking at me. I always showed on my face when I was sad or happy. Now my face carried a worried look, and that's how she knew I was going to give her bad news.

"Mrs. Vera, I know you already see that I've got bad news, so I'm going to come right out and say it. My brother is dead, my mother is in the mental hospital, and I'm moving again; this time to my aunt who I never knew until last month, and I cannot take it any more."

"Ramona, slow down, please. Let's go in and have a nice cup of tea and you can tell me all about it. First, what do you mean your brother is dead? And why is your mother in the hospital?"

I told her everything that had happened during the course of the year, which had led up to me preparing to move in with my Aunt Jana. I ended with: "So, you can see now why I'm so sad and mad; there is no justice for a poor person like me."

"My dear Ramona, I'm so sorry about all this. Is there anything I can do for you?

Do you need any money for spending while living with your Aunt Jana?"

"No thank you, there is not enough money in the world that can heal my broken heart, but I do appreciate your offer. I just came to say goodbye and to say that I hope to see you sometime."

"Take care of yourself Ramona, and if you like, you can write me. I'll be here for the next year or so, and then I'm moving to Switzerland, but we'll talk about that later.

She gave me a big hug, and then she squeezed my hands. I didn't notice right away, but she put some money in my hand. I couldn't say no. I gave her a big hug and kiss, and then I thanked her again.

I rushed home because I was sure Miss Selka was wondering where I was all day. Rushing so much I didn't notice that I was crying at the same time. I saw a few looks that people were giving me, but was not sure why. As I was going home, I bumped into Slavko.

"Hey, Ramona what's wrong? Why are you rushing, and why are you crying? Slow down, talk to me. You know we're best friends; you can tell me anything."

"I'm sorry Slavko; nothing is wrong. If I'm crying, it's because I just said goodbye to a lady that was so good to me when I first came to this city, and on top of that, I was rushing home because I left this morning and Miss Selka will be going crazy wondering where I am. So, let's go back, my friend."

As I thought, Miss Selka was very upset. I explained to her where I had been, and then she calmed down, and with a worried look and a bit of smile she said supper was ready. I thanked her and gave her little kiss, and I could tell that she was happy again.

For the next two days I didn't go anywhere. I stayed in thinking about all the people that I'd met. Spending time with Slavko and his mom was not easy, I was sad most of the time, because I knew that the next day I had to go.

My final night in Novisad was sorrowful; Miss Selka was crying, but I didn't say anything. We all had our thoughts, and crying wasn't going to help me, that's what I said to myself, but I'm sure I fell asleep crying.

Morning came so fast, and jumping out of bed got me thinking about running away. I was not ready to go and live with another stranger again. Nevertheless, if I ran, run to where? With my thoughts so far away I heard a knock on the door.

"Ramona, are you up? Guess what! Your Aunt Jana is here already. Come on honey; I've got your favourite pita for breakfast, and some for you to take on your trip."

I got up, but I was taking my time. Going to live with Aunt Jana was scaring me. I just didn't want to go, but truly I had no choice. So I slowly came to the kitchen, and gave my aunt a hug. Then I kissed Miss Selka, and I whispered in her ear, "I don't want to go. Please, I want to stay with you. Tell her that."

She looked at me and started to cry. "Ramona, you're not allowed to stay with me for good. I've asked around and talked to the social worker. Ramona, you see your mom signed a legal document. Before she went to the hospital, she made it clear that you have to go and stay with your Aunt Jana, and questioning her record won't do us any good because the social worker agrees with it. So you don't have any frustrating thoughts, just let it go. Changes can be made only in the case of your aunt getting ill so she can't take care of you. Only then, can I apply for you to stay with me. I'm so sorry, my dear. I'd like you to stay with me, I care about you more than you know. Please stop crying and be a good girl. I'm sure one day you'll come and see me. Nothing is forever, and you staying with your aunt won't be forever. Please, my dear, keep your head up and stay strong."

Who on this earth could help me? No one, so I pretended that everything was okay, and with a fake smile I told my aunt that I was ready to leave.

I could see she knew I was sad. To calm me down she said we had two hours before the bus left, so if I wanted to say good-bye to Slavko and his mom, there was plenty of time.

"No Aunt Jana, I said all my goodbyes yesterday and to see them again will hurt me more. Why don't we just go—I can explore more of downtown."

"As you wish, Ramona. Let's just go then."

I turned around and saw Miss Selka was crying in her bedroom. I approached her very slowly, so she wouldn't be startled, took her in my arms, and told her that I'd never forget her. It came to me that I'd used the same words too many times to too many people, but it was true. All the ones I'd met; they all helped me. I'd never had that many people who cared about me before. But only one I really wanted to love me and care for me was my mother, and she was the only one who didn't care. That made me sadder, and my tears were coming down like a fast and furious river. I knew in my heart that I had to let go. I would always keep my good memories of Novisad locked up in my heart.

Just before I closed the gates, I saw Slavko running towards me. He hugged me for a long moment. "Take care of yourself, Ramona."

My eyes filled with tears and I nodded, unable to speak. That was the last time I saw Slavko.

CHAPTER 18

THE BUS RIDE to my aunt's house took about four hours. I was getting bored and didn't know what to talk to her about, so I pretended I was sleep. As we got closer, she woke me up and asked me to get ready. I wondered if anybody was going to be waiting for us, and as if she knew what I was thinking, she said that my uncle and my cousins would be there. I just looked at her blankly, like *So what, I don't care.*

On the other hand, my aunt was excited, she was smiling like a child. But I just could not feel any better than I had when I was going home with my mother for the first time. There were no feelings. I had no choice—I was going to live with them because the law said so, not because I wanted to. That is how I felt.

As I got off the bus, I saw all three of them standing there and smiling, and then they start walking towards us. My uncle took me in his arms and welcomed me to their family, and the boys just stood there. I froze. It was like we were a bunch of strangers, which we were, and I didn't know what to say. So, two boys and me, ha that should be fun. I hoped they didn't think that because they were boys that I'd do everything they wanted. I'd give them a chance and would see.

Finally, the one I believe was about my age, came and gave me a hug. He said,

"I'm Nenad, and that one over there is Andy. He's a bit shy, but he'll come around. I'm glad to see you. I knew your brother Sasha, and we met your mom couple of times. We never knew anything about you until last week, and having a girl as a cousin is nice. You and I are the same age, so we should get along good. In September, I'll be going to grade seven, and I think you will too if I'm not mistaken. We can probably go to the same classes but we'll talk about that later. Let me have your suitcase and let's all go home."

Well, it looked like one was shy and one was a talker—not bad, but my uncle was weird. Something about him struck me as odd. He kept staring at me as if I was somehow different from any other girl he'd seen, but maybe it was my imagination because all older men freak me out. I guess this was all because of Mr. Tekish, but I liked my aunt's

house. It was very nice and neat, I guessed my aunt took good care of it. She showed me my room and I was surprised. I thought that I'd have a little bed somewhere in a kitchen, but no, I had my own room. It was the first time I'd had a room all to myself. I may have shed a tear or two, which my aunt noticed.

With a hug, she whispered, "Ramona, you are going to be all right here, I'll take care of you, we all will. Please don't cry anymore. If you need anything just let me know."

"Thank you, I promise to keep my room neat and clean every day. Thank you, Auntie, you will never know how much this means to me; a room just for me, my room." I kept repeating the same thing, I was so happy.

By now, it was getting late, and my aunt said that the next day she'd show me everything that they do and the job that they have every day.

When I woke up it was almost nine am. I couldn't remember when I'd had such a good sleep. Everybody was in the kitchen when I walked in. With my eyes down I said, "I'm sorry for sleeping that long, you should have woken me up; it won't happen again. I always like to get up early. I was so tired and lost track of time, but either way, it won't happen again. I'm not here to be special; I'd like to help you any way I can, so boys, don't forget, seven o'clock, up we all get. Right?"

They all laughed, and breakfast was delicious. "Now that breakfast is done," I said, "what are we going to do now?"

My uncle got up first, and he explained the daily schedule. "Ramona, you are going with your aunt, and the boys will be with me. We stop for lunch and finish daily work at four p.m. After that, you kids can do whatever you like, and your aunt and I will proceed with our regular stuff. Ramona, you can go with Nenad and explore the town, and maybe go and see your new school. It's all up to you—there's plenty of time for everything, so everybody can enjoy themselves."

As superintendents, they had a lot to do. Uncle and the boys were cleaning the indoor/outdoor training center. Aunt was in charge of making sure the hallways were clean and picking up all the garbage from the bedrooms and classrooms. The boys always helped, and that was a plus for them. The military building was not so big; they had about sixty students if you can call them that. I would call them young soldiers. There was a lot of work, but I enjoyed it. I had done a lot of cleaning in the orphan village, so it was nothing that I couldn't handle. My aunt was pleased with my work, and she said that I was a big help to her. I gave her a big smile and told her that I would help her anytime.

....

I wrote a letter:

Dear Mr. Nemic,

I'm sure by now that you thought I forgot you, but guess what, I have not. So many things have happened, and I was just waiting for the right time to write to you. By the time you read this letter, I'll be living with my Aunt Jana, my uncle, and two cousins (boys) that I never knew I had—the place is actually not far from you. It is a lovely town called Branovbrdo.

My mother and I still are not getting along. First, she lied to you about our lovely place. What you saw was the place she was looking after. If you had seen what I came to there was no way you would have let her keep me. The apartment was so small, we had one bed, one small table, one chair, and a stove. One person could sit, and the other had to use the bed. That didn't bother me as much as the fact that there was no water. I had to go outside to wash and the same thing for the toilet, but I was slowly getting used it. When we left the orphan village that day, it took us about three hours to get to Novisad. When we got to the apartment, she just left. She gave me ten dinars and said to go to the store to get myself some milk and bread, and then she just left. I was so scared Mr. Nemic I started to cry, "Why me? What have I done so bad, that my mother hates me so much?"

She was back very late that night and told me that she worked nights. For me to stay home alone all night was not a good idea, so she took me to her friend that had a cargo boat. Your might have heard of her. She's the only woman in East Europe that is the captain of a cargo ship—her name is Vera Babic, and I spent two months with her. She was a very nice lady, and she taught me a lot. My mother never even came to see me until it was time for me to go to school. So far, my mom and I could barely stand each other.

The school was all right, I kept all my grades excellent, hoping she would be happy to see my report card. I had almost all A's and three B's, but she never even cared.

Then one day my brother showed up. I had never seen him before. We spent a day together, and he promised me that as soon as he finished the army, he'd come for me and find me a good place to live. My mother and my brother never got along either, she just had no heart for us. Then, my brother got shot dead in the army by accident (although I don't believe them), so my mother got crazy over that. Now she is in the mental hospital and the military is paying for everything, and I'm with my aunt and uncle. The army is paying them to keep me until Mother gets better, if she ever gets better. To tell you the truth I don't care. Now you can see why I never wanted to go with my mother. All this time, I was always alone. Thank God that my neighbours were friendly. Otherwise, I would be crazy. Many times, I packed my bag and wanted to run away, but where to? Now I'm starting all over, with a new family.

Mr. Nemic I'll write you a new letter and let you know how I'm doing here. Meanwhile, because we are not so far you can drop by, the address is on the bottom.

One more thing before I go. What is happening in the orphan village? Is it closed? Also, that monster Mr. Tekish, I hope he is dead by now!

All the best.

Ramona

....

Living with my Aunt Jana turned out to be okay for me. The boys were always friendly, though my uncle was a bit strange. But maybe it was just that I couldn't trust men because of Mr. Tekish. I hoped that would change.

Summer was coming to an end, and it was time to get ready for school. I asked my aunt if I could go to town to buy some school supplies and maybe a new dress. She didn't mind, and she offered me some money.

"Aunt Jana, thank you, but I don't need any money. You see I have a lot of cash, in total about 10,000 dinars. Before you get shocked, thinking I've stolen it or something worse, don't. Remember the lady I told you that I spent last summer with? Well, she is very wealthy. She has one child that is on her deathbed, and no one else. We became very close friends. Last November she sold her business and right now, she has a lot of money. Last week I went to say goodbye to her and we had an excellent talk. Once her daughter passes away, she is moving to Switzerland. To make a long story short, she gave me that money to use for important things. She knows that my mother doesn't care about me, but she does care about me. So I'm well off, for a long time."

"Ramona, why haven't you told me about that money? That is too much cash for you to keep around just like that."

"Aunty yes, I know, but no one knows about it, only me, and I'd like it to stay like that. Also, if you ever need any money for anything, please let me know, I do trust only you, and please don't break that trust, please."

Ok Ramona, but how are you going to explain your new stuff?"

"I don't plant to overspend Aunty; I'm excellent at keeping my spending under control. I had a good teacher, a gypsy girl who showed me the value of money, so don't worry. I would like to talk to you about something else, but will do that when I come back from town."

As I was getting ready to go, Nenad came and asked me if I'd like him to go with me. Actually I didn't, and told him maybe next time. When buying things for myself, I liked to be alone, and I didn't want him to see that I had money.

I just strolled by myself to town. There were a couple of stores to choose from and a bookstore as well. I managed to get everything I wanted and made sure nothing was too expensive. When I got back I was pleased with myself. My aunt was in the kitchen, and I asked her if we could talk. She nodded.

"Aunt Jana, there have been so many secrets in my life, and most of them I know about now, but I have a question for you. Do I have any other relatives that I don't know about? I would like you to be honest. In my fourteen years, all I've heard were lies and I'd like one person to be frank with me."

"Yes, Ramona, you do have some relatives, I was going tell you that later on. I was waiting for you to be settled down here and happy."

"Aunty, I'm never going to be happy. You have no idea how long I was abused. You don't know what I have gone through. For me to be happy is a long way away, and happy is not even a word that I use. For God's sake, my mother doesn't want me, what does that tell you? Be happy now, we like you? It is going to be a long road for me to feel happy; never mind saying it."

"I'm so sorry Ramona; I had no idea that you had been abused; your mother never tells us anything."

"My mother, my mother doesn't even know my birthday, and she never asked me anything about my life in the orphan village. She doesn't care. Yes, I was sexually abused and at some point raped—that was my happy life, Aunty Jana. So now you know why I'm not happy or if I'm ever going to be."

"Come here you poor child, come. I'll take care of you. Please trust me, I'll never let you down."

"No Aunty, don't say never. I have heard those words before, and they were lies. I'm okay, don't worry. So who are my other relatives that I don't know?"

"Well, I'm only counting one from our side of the family. You have one more aunt. Your aunt is in Canada; that is in North America. She is married and they don't have any children. Your mother never told you about her because they never cared for each other. Your aunt in Canada is younger than your mom or me. Her name is Vesna, and your uncle's name is Janos."

"It sounds like he is Hungarian!" I said.

"Yes, and no. Yes, your uncle was born in Germany, moved to Czechoslovakia, and then moved to Hungary. If he had other names we don't know them. Your mother, and honestly me too, we never liked him. There was something about him that was scary and your mom, she called him a fascist. So you see, maybe that's why she never told you about them."

"Maybe, but if so why did she never say anything about me to you? Did you two ever talk at all? If you did, then why did no one know about me until now? It looks to me like everybody gave up on her. It's possible that all of you abandoned her when she needed help, and now you, I, and everyone are blaming her for everything, and on top of that she blames me most of all. What a mixed-up family. So, are you in touch with your sister in Canada?"

"Yes Ramona, we write each other maybe once a month or so. She's been there since 1957, and now they are the Canadian citizens, so it's easier for them to get jobs and the medical care that the government offers. I think she's happy, even though she doesn't have any children. My sister Vesna lost two sons in the massacre, if you know what that means, so now she just works and takes care of herself and Janos.

"Not having any children must be a dreary life for her then. Why did she never adopt any?"

"I don't know; we never talk about that. If you like, you can write to your aunt, and see what she says. You never know, she might adopt you. Why don't you give it a try?

"Well, it won't hurt to try. I know where the post office is. Tomorrow I'll get some airmail envelopes, and I can give it a shot. Aunt Jana, can this stay between us? I don't like to get my hopes too high for nothing."

School was starting in about a week, and I was excited to meet new friends and see what they had to offer students in grade seven. As school was approaching so was my birthday. I didn't think my aunt knew, and I wouldn't tell her. My birthday didn't mean anything to me because I had no one who loved me to give me a hug and big kiss, or wish me another happy year. I was used to that, so no big deal. I wondered if I should write a letter to my aunt in Canada now, but I decided to wait for a while. After all, I'd just gotten here, and so far, I did like it. My Aunt Jana and Uncle Stefan were excellent people, and the boys were like boys, but not so bad. Also, I did like living with them, for now.

My school was a truly excellent one. This one was like new, the classrooms were so clean, and we had breakfast and lunch every day. There was a new gym and a new stadium, and I just loved it. The teachers were not bad either. I really liked one of them, she was teaching us history and geography, which were my favourite subjects. She noticed this and told me that I was her best student in history. I told her that I loved to learn all about the past and the future, but the past was my favourite. Geography was fascinating to me too. I'm almost sure that I knew every capital of every country in Europe; east and west.

We hadn't learned much about America, so one day I asked my teacher if she had any books on America, especially Canada. She asked me why and I told her that I had an aunt there and that maybe one day I would like to go and see Canada. She said that she had some and would bring them, but she also asked me if I was new in this town. I told her that I had come from Novisad.

She also noticed I was sad most of the time, and after she gave me the book on Canada, I was always reading it, so one day after classes she asked me to stay. I got scared, thinking I'd done something wrong, but no, all she wanted was to find out more about me.

I wondered why, so I just came out and asked her. "Miss Sofia, why are you so interested in me? Have I done anything wrong? I thought asking you lots of questions was okay with you. After all, you are the teacher. I'm very very sorry if I bothered you. I didn't mean to—it won't happen again."

"Oh no Ramona, you're no bother at all. I was just wondering why you want to know so much about Canada. Are you hoping to go there one day, or are you going there soon and why? Your mother must be sad knowing your plans."

"My mom doesn't care if I go or not, she doesn't care if I live or die. My mom is in a mental hospital, and I live with my aunt and uncle for now. If you like, I can tell you my life story but why should I waste your time? I'm not so sure if you are interested in the story of the loneliest girl that no one cares about at all."

"Ramona, you are wrong about that. I was a girl like you once, a long time ago, and I didn't give up when no one cared. I cared about myself and look at me today. I'm proud of myself, but once I was a girl that no one wanted or cared about, Ramona. I grew up in an orphan village until I was eighteen, and then I worked hard and went to school, and now I'm a teacher, who hopes to help all children rich or poor. If you have a secret that no one knows in here, it's fine with me, but if you'd like to talk to me I'm always open to everybody. There's no need for you to go into the corners of the classroom or outside to try to hide your pain and sorrow. Speak up. I'm here to listen and together we can find a solution to your sadness. You see, at least you have a mother. I never knew my parents at all and never had relatives that were able to take care of me. So you see, you are not as bad off as you think.

"Miss Sofia, you can have my mother anytime you want to have any parents at all. You don't know my side of the story, and to tell me I should be happy to have at least a mother is very wrong. I thank you for all the books, and I'd like to be left alone."

I was very upset with Miss Sofia, but I knew she meant no harm. When I got home, I asked my aunt for the address of my Canadian aunt; it was time to see if she would take me, so I could get out of this place and put all this behind me.

I thought writing a letter to my aunt in Canada might bring me some hope. I wrote her a very long letter, and when I got to the post office, I asked the man at the counter to mail it by airmail. I knew it would cost, but I had money and didn't care. He told me that my aunt would get my mail in about five to eight days. Going home to my Aunt Jana's house, something told me that I was making a terrible mistake. But I don't know why... I just felt that way. I knew that if I went to Canada, I'd never see my friends like Slavko and his mom, my gypsy friend Karla, my old landlord, and most of all Aunt Vera and all the rest of the really nice people that I'd met. However, I was determined to go, no matter what my feeling was telling me. Anyway, you never knew, they might not want to take me to live with them. So I'd have to wait and see.

CHAPTER 19

Living with my Aunt Jana turned out to be good. I had no problem with anyone in the family. I always kept my eyes on my uncle but discovered he was a just simple older man. One Saturday he was going fishing with the boys, not knowing that I love fishing, and he said they would be back very late. So, I just went right out and told him I love to go fishing as well. He was surprised at first and laughed, but I said I could catch a fish probably better than any of them.

"So where did you ever fish? I can't see you going fishing living in the orphan village! How can I take you fishing if you've never been fishing, and what do mean you can catch fish better than any of us?"

"Well my dear uncle, yes you are right, I never went fishing while I was in the orphan village, but you also don't know that last year I spent two months on the water, and I had an excellent teacher. I was with mother's so-called friend, she is the only woman in eastern Europe that can take care of a cargo ship, and she had two of her own ships as well. So, I was with her, and she taught me all the tricks about fishing and how to steer a big boat. So can you do all that, eh? I'll bet not. Do you have any more questions? If not then just get me one of your new fishing rods and let's go, and don't bother telling Aunty, she knows. Just look at her through the window, she is laughing at you.

"Very well, then let's go. Our boat is not big, but it will hold all of us, and once we get there we're going to fish offshore—that's safer than having all of us in a small boat. Ramona, you'll have to show us what you can do."

The day turned out to be one of the best. My uncle was lots of fun; he made us bacon and sausages on an open fire, and he let me have a little, I mean a little bit of red wine. I was competing with the boys about bigger fish, and as I told them I knew all the tricks, and guess what! I did catch two big ones and three medium. My uncle was funny and said, "Not bad for a girl."

It was a lot of fun, and I felt for the first time that I was part of a family. When no one was looking at me, a couple of tears rolled down my face because I was happy. My favourite days with my aunt and uncle were the weekends; we were all home, and it was like a real family. They were not rich people, but the love they had for their kids no amount of money could buy. The boys were just as kind; willing to help and do extras if their parents needed them. The place was excellent. The military kids never interfered with the family.

I met some of the older kids who were there, and most of them were very nice guys. I did talk to some of them whenever I saw them. Some of them told me that when they grew up, got married, and had a family they would not send their boys there. The military school was one of the most brutal schools in the country. The kids couldn't go into the service until they finished all sorts of programs that took about ten years. Some of them were about twenty-five or six when they completed all the programs. That's a lot of private military school if you ask me. In other words, they did further hidden service for their country. The school was strict, but if you liked that kind of life I guess it was okay.

There was one boy I did like, but we both knew that our paths would never meet, so before we went any further we became good friends and that was okay with me. Anyway, I was hoping to go to Canada one day if my aunt ever answered my letter.

....

Dear Aunt Vesna,

You probably haven't, or I'm almost sure that you have never heard of me, so let me tell you a little about me. I'm your niece, your sister Elsa's daughter. Yes, Elsa did have a girl that she never told anybody about, and that is me. My name is Ramona; I'm fourteen years old now, and for the time being I'm living with your other sister Jana and her husband. Most of my life I lived in the orphan village where your sister left me at the age of three months. Elsa is in the hospital now, and no one knows when she will come out, so I'm staying with Aunt Jana. There is so much to be said. I just wanted to write to you first and see if you can help me. Since you don't have children, Aunt Jana suggested that I ask you if you would like to adopt me. I know your might like to adopt a little one, but I don't have a home, and I promise to be good. I have learned that you and Elsa did not get along good, but please don't take that on me. I'm not her, and I'd just like to find myself somewhere and maybe Canada is it.

I would be jubilant to hear from you, and Aunt Jana said hello from all of them. Thank you, Aunty Vesna and Uncle Janos.
From Ramona

....

It was a cold November day. Leaves were flying everywhere, and you could feel that winter was coming soon. I was wondering if my aunt in Canada would ever write to me, and my answer was right there. When I got home, my cousin Nenad told me there was a surprise in the kitchen for me. I never had time to say thank you; I ran so fast. Something was telling me the letter from Canada had arrived, and I was right.

"Aunty Jana, Aunty Jana, Nenad said there's a letter for me! Please let's sit down before my knees give out. Oh!...Look, it says it's for Ramona. Aunty, they did write back. Let's hope the news is good; I don't think I can bear any more bad news."

With trembling hands, I opened the letter.

Ramona my dear,
Ask my sister Jana to help you with everything she can. Your uncle and I will get a lawyer and will see what we have to do. Meanwhile, stay well and we'll talk soon.
Your Aunt Vesna.

"Aunty look, they got my letter, and they both would like to adopt me, even though I'm fourteen years old. Yes! I'm going to Canada! It looks like there's a lot of work ahead of us now. The first thing we have to do is go to my mother and ask her to give us a letter stating that she's okay with this, and then I need a birth certificate showing where I was born. Getting my birth certified is going to be one of the hardest things to do. My mother never registered me in Bosnia, and the orphan village made a fake one, so this is going to be a big problem. But I think we can talk to Mr. Nemic about that, I'm sure he'll tell me what to do. If we have to, we can go to Bosnia. There's a police officer named Branko, and I think Aunt Jana that you might remember him. He was Peter's best friend, and he did tell me if I ever needed anything just to let him know. "You see Aunty, that money I have will come very handy for all our trips. Oh Aunt Jana, I'm so excited. I can't tell you how happy I am right now. But many times, I've thought about all this. Is it that I want to go, or do I just want to disappear and start all over? But for now, I'm going through this and whatever happens will happen."

My aunt was struggling not to show her tears, but I just pretended to look the other way. I knew she was hurting, and would be sad if I went, but this was my chance and I chose to go. I would always be grateful to them, but I had to find my home if not to-day, the some day. So maybe Canada was my home?

"Ramona it looks like we are going to need lots of time for traveling, and yes you are right, your money will come in very handy. The first thing we will do is go to Novisad to the hospital to see your mother and explain to her very politely with no fighting or screaming. We just have to be very careful with her. Once we see what she says then we can look into your birth certificate. One thing at a time is the best way. Now that we know your aunt in Canada does wish to adopt you, there is lots of time to think about everything and I mean everything. Please, Ramona, do ask yourself if you really want to go, or if you're just using this as revenge against your mother. I just don't want you to have any regrets later on. Please think very carefully, and remember we also love you—you're not alone anymore. I want you to know I love you just as if you were my daughter. Please Ramona, tragedy can sometimes make people make bad choices."

"Aunty Jana, I see what you're saying, and you are correct in many things, but I have thought about it, and I do want to go. I'd just like to see if my destiny is there! I can always come back. So let's not think about that for now. I'm not leaving just yet."

The first thing my aunt and I did was to go see my mother in the hospital. When we got there she was asleep, so we waited for a while, and then after an hour or so she got up. You'd think she would be happy that we came to see her, but not my mother. All she said was, "What do you two want now?"

I looked at my Aunt Jana with a question, but I remembered that we had agreed to be patient with her…otherwise it could be goodbye to everything. I didn't say anything, but Aunty spoke to her in a charming and calm voice. I could see she was getting better.

"So Ramona, you'd like to go to live with your aunt in Canada? What is wrong here, that you want to leave us? If you are looking for a better life, go ahead, you have my full support. I will give you a letter, but one day, trust me, you'll be sorry that you left us all in a search for a better place. You have everything here now. Your Aunt Jana is the best person you could ever find, but going to live with that fascist... go ahead, but cry on my shoulder later on."

"Mother, I'm looking for a better life, yes you're right. You never cared for me; you gave me away when I was three months old. Aunty Jana has her family to take care of, and you, you, look at you. You're not well—how do you expect me to live with you after you come out? I know you will go away and leave me with some other relatives that you find, so yes, I'm looking for a better life. I'm well aware that you don't like Uncle Janos, but your sister Vesna needs to have someone, and so do I. Maybe my life in Canada will turn to be worse, but then I won't have to blame you for that. Thank you for the letter and you know there is no turning back now. Maybe one day you'll be sad for giving me this message—you might just think about that as well. Thank you one more time, and goodbye for now, I'll come to see you before I go, that is if everything goes well."

Once we got to the bus station to go back, I told my aunt that I actually couldn't believe my mother had given her that letter; that it showed me how much my mother didn't care about me at all. So I did let go a few tears, but not for long.

Next was to get my birth certificate, which was going to be very hard because I didn't have one, except the fake one. The next day I needed to write to Mr. Nemic to ask him for advice.

As I was occupied getting all my papers in order, I ignored my schoolwork and that's why my homeroom teacher came to see me after school.

I was not surprised, and I told her right out. "Mrs. Obranovich, I know that my schoolwork is getting behind, but I'd like you to know that I'm getting ready to go to Canada, and getting all the papers in order takes time. I promise I will catch up with my work, but in the long run, it won't matter."

"Ramona, you can't talk like that. School does matter, even if you go or not. Let's just ask what will happen if you don't get your passport, or whatever you need to go. What then? Look, young lady, take my advice and get back to those books because in about three weeks a new semester is starting and you don't want to be left behind just because you claim you have a lot to do with getting your information in order."

"But Mrs. Obranovich, my school is not necessary anymore, I'm more than sure that by this time next year I won't be standing in front of you. There's no need to be so mad at me—I'll do my homework, you'll see. I'm very sorry if I upset you, but going to Canada is a big deal to me, more than you know."

"All I want is for you to be careful, Ramona. Lots of disappointments can happen, and I hope you can meet all the challenges."

"As for me, Mrs. Obranovich, if I go I'll be happy, and if I stay I will try to find my life one way or another. Doesn't matter to me."

Determined to prove to Mrs. Obranovich that I could do it all, I studied hard and at the end of the semester, I passed with flying colors. Mrs. Obranovich saw me in the hallway and gave me a smile. I wanted to say *I told you so*, but I just said hello instead.

The school was closed for the winter holiday, and I had fifteen days to do whatever. I was thinking of asking my aunt if we could go to see Mr. Nemic, and at the same time, I could show her the place where I had spent thirteen years of my life. The military school was closed as well, and I knew she would be free.

My aunt jumped at my offer—I think she needed a break. Going with me would be just what she needed. Approaching the boys and my uncle to tell them where we were going was a bit hard because they would be home by themselves and have to do everything, but to my surprise everyone agreed it was a good idea, and off we went.

Vrnjac was not too far from us, about hour or so on the bus. I didn't tell Mr. Nemic that I was coming. I wanted it to be a surprise, and then we could talk about my birth certificate. I knew that there was a small hotel there run by two sisters, and they were happy to give us a room for as long as we needed. I told them that I had been living in the orphan village for thirteen years, and they were so happy to hear that. Because it was Saturday, I knew Mr. Nemic wouldn't be in his office. So I suggested that we should take a walk around town. It was hard for me to come back so soon, but Mr. Nemic had answered my letter and told me that Mr. Tekish had died. Knowing that monster was dead made it bit easier.

I took my aunt to the orphan village or whatever was left of it. To my surprise, there was not much change except that the gate was open and in my time, that had not been allowed. The building was still there but looked sad. They were making offices for the government in it, and there was a big sign that said: "An Orphan Village for Girls was here from 1943-1963." I could not help but cry. My aunt hugged me and said everything was going to be okay.

We went through to the courtyard, and my heart started to give me pain. Mr. Tekish's quarters were still there, but you could tell they were being taken down—there were no windows or doors. I turned around and said to my aunt, "That was the place where I lost my youth."

She looked at me very sadly as I continued.

"You see that house over there? That is the place where many other girls and I were sexually abused for years. That's the main reason this place closed. The man who did that to us is dead, and so is the teacher who knew what was going on, but never told anybody. That is my sad life that not many people know, not even my mother. She never asked me about my life in here, so I never told her. I do carry a significant pain in my heart, and that's why I'm so afraid of most man, and can't trust them."

Oh my dear child, I'm truly so sorry Ramona. I'm here for you, and nothing like that will ever happen to you again. Oh my dear child, come here. I'm so, so sorry."

"Thank you, Aunty, maybe one day we can talk more about it, but right now let's go back to the hotel. I'm getting tired, and I just feel like I'm going to explode from how much I hurt."

As we walked back, I noticed some changes, and I showed her my school, which was the same. I'd had a good time there. I told her that I'd had a big crush on a boy who sat right beside me in class. He used to bring me little things; the kid was rich, but he never cared if I was rich or whatever. I remember one time I told him I lived in the orphan village, and he wanted to know all about that. He knew that after the war, there were lots of girls left alone and having an orphan village was a good idea, so we wouldn't be on streets. He was one of the nicest boys I ever met. Saying goodbye to him was very hard, but we all have our paths to run.

I would always have my disappointment about how the law never cared much about the problems in the orphan villages; not only in the one that I was in, but in so many. The abuse of one monster was still in my heart. I knew that I would never forget this place and the man who made our lives so horrible. I would carefully try to heal my wounds, and in time, I hoped I could forgive myself for not being robust enough to speak up or to say no. Being scared was wrong—I knew that now, but I wished that I could tell the world that taking advantage of innocent girls was wrong. One day I hoped that we would all be equal, but for now, I was approaching my days vigorously and trying to do my best.

We spent some more time sightseeing because Vrnjac is a small city but beautiful. Monday came pretty fast and my aunt and I were at Mr. Nemic's doors right at eight a.m. The shock on his face almost made me laugh—he was so surprised but happy to see me.

He approached us very carefully, not knowing why I was at his door. But before he got too confused I told him we were here to talk to him about my birth certificate, which I need very badly if I wanted to go to Canada. The situation changed very fast; he was actually happy to see me.

"Well, hello Ramona. I'm so glad to see you."

"Thank you, Mr. Nemic. I'd like you to meet my Aunt Jana, she is one of my aunts that I never knew, and guess what…one more aunt is living in Canada. That's why I'm here to talk to you. I came here to ask you if you know how to get my real birth certificate. I know that the one I had in the orphan village is a fake one. I just wonder if you can tell me how to get proper documents. I know I was born in Bosnia in a small village not too far from Sarajevo, but my mother never registered me there. I just don't know what to do, and that's why I'm here, I need your help."

"Ramona this is going to be a very complicated procedure. You see, Mr. Tekish's sister burned a lot of documents before we arrested her, so we have not a clue about a lot of girls including you. We can't prove anything. Only one person can help you with that. You must go to the village where you were born, and I'm sure that there must be someone in that office who can help you. I can give you a letter that will explain your situation to them, and that might work. I'm so sorry Ramona that I couldn't help you, but look at it this way…it's fun to see you again. Now tell me, what is this about you going to Canada?"

So I told him about my plan to go live with my relatives in Canada and he wished me luck and then gave me a letter for Officer Branko, requesting birth documents for me. He suggested to my aunt that perhaps it might be too stressful for me to go there and that she do it alone, and then he said, "Ramona, let's have a big hug and make sure you take care of yourself." Then he shook my aunt's hand and thanked her for taking such good care of me.

"Thank you, Mr., Nemic," she said. "I will continue to look after Ramona, and I'm so glad that she has a friend like you. Ramona it's time to say goodbye to Mr. Nemic. We have a bus to catch."

CHAPTER 20

IT WAS PARTY time at the military school and Jovan, a boy I liked, invited me; I was happy to go. Sitting home every day and dreaming of my trip was getting to me, so to go and have a good time was perfect. My aunt wasn't happy about it, but my cousin Nenad was going with us, so she finally agreed that I could go. I had never been to a New Year's party, so this was all so new to me. I had a lovely dress and the party was next door so I didn't need a heavy coat.

Jovan came and picked me up at nine p.m., and I told him that Nenad had to go with us, or I couldn't go.

"That's perfect," he said, "because one of the commander's daughters came and no one wants to take a chance with her, so Nenad you have saved our day. Her name is Maya, and don't worry, she is very kind, you'll see. So, let's go."

When we got there the place was almost full and everybody there including us had fun dancing and singing. Some older boys were drinking and smoking, but I guess it was allowed, after all it was a New Year's Party. As I was dancing with Jovan, I noticed that one of the officers was always looking at me. I tried not to look at him but with all the noise, music, and drinking no one else noticed what was going on. My eyes were open all the time, and I saw danger. I knew how some guys liked to control girls. I had been there, not once but twice, and I had promised myself that no boy or man was going to touch me unless I agreed.

Then I felt a hand on my shoulder and he was getting between Jovan and me. I heard him saying, "Get lost kid."

If I said get lost to him, that means get lost. Jovan just stood there, scared, and not knowing what to do at that moment, and the officer said again, "If I said get lost, that means get lost."

"Jovan, it's okay," I said. "One dance won't kill us. But I had the feeling this man didn't want a dance; he was drunk and I wasn't. He grabbed my arm and pulled me to the door. No one paid any attention, so I knew I had to be ready to protect myself. Outside, like every drunk man, he grabbed me from behind and tried to pull down my underwear. For a second Mr. Tekish's picture was looking at me, and that gave me the energy to kick him right between his legs. I never heard a man scream like him. Standing over him I spat on him and told him if he ever tried this again that the next time I would kill him.

Looking for Jovan, I saw Nenad looking white as a ghost. When he saw me, with a warning in his eyes, he asked me to go home. I had no idea what he was talking about, so I said I was staying, and that I was looking for Jovan.

"Ramona, let's go home."

"Nenad! What is wrong with you? Why do we have to go back?"

"Ramona, don't you know what you did"

"What I did?"

"That man who is in pain outside is the top commander, and you hurt him very badly. The whole academy is making fun of him, and I guess he's going to do something dreadful to us. We work for him, so what the hell did you do?"

"Nenad, don't worry. He'll be lucky if I don't report him to the police. And if you must know, it was him or me. Just go home and don't worry."

Just as I suspected, no one said anything, but I did tell my aunt what had happened that night. She wanted to sue him, but I told her it was not a big deal, he was a pig, and he always would be.

"But Ramona, if we don't report him he can try again with someone else. Think about that."

"If I report him, then you and my uncle might lose your jobs and I don't want that. He didn't hurt me, it was the other way around. I think he won't be touching anybody for a long, long time. I've learned to protect myself from people like him, unfortunately too late, but I'm okay, don't worry."

A week or so passed by and there was no talk about the New Year's scandal. As I thought, the army always took care of its own, but I did learn that the commander of Jovan's unit was still not feeling good, and that made me feel good. Busted wouldn't forget me for a long time.

It was the middle of January 1963, and I was starting to worry about whether I was going to Canada or not. My aunt had written a letter to Branko about my birth certificate and so far, no news. Because it was winter and there was not much to do, I was bored most of the time. I wrote a letter to Slavko, but he hadn't replied just as yet. Maybe he and his mom had gone to Kotor. I knew he had been excited when his mother told him that she might buy a house there, but either way, I did miss him.

....

Though I didn't know it yet, the news from Canada was good and my aunt and uncle only had a few more papers to file. In the meantime, I was getting a bit worried that I might not be going to Canada, so I started to do my homework, which I had ignored for a long time. Winter break was over and I was back in school. If I went to Canada, this would be my last year in school, and in grade eight I would hopefully be taking English.

It was the first week of February when I finally got a letter from Branko and it was a happy one. There was a Ramona Birth Certificate! One for me to keep and one to send to my aunt in Canada. In the letter Branko sent, there were two little notes; one from Aunt Sofia and one from himself. They were both so sorry that I preferred to go to Canada instead coming to live with them. Aunt Sofia said she missed me so much, but that if I wasn't happy in Canada she hoped I knew I'd be welcome back with her. Reading that made me cry. I knew that my life in Bosnia would be plain and straightforward, and that later on there would be too many memories of a father that I never knew. Branko's note was just as sad, full of apologies and sorrow, but I knew that he had been young then and couldn't help my mother. I still respected him for saying his doors were always open for my mom and me.

Now that I had my birth certificate, I knew that I would be going somewhere; I wouldn't be staying in the spot all the time. If for some reason or another I didn't go to Canada with my other aunt, I was going to explore the world as soon as I turned eighteen. I had to thank Branko for his work. So, for now, all I was waiting for was a letter from Canada.

Sometimes I thought people didn't understand why I wanted to leave this place so badly. It's not that I wanted to go so badly, but that I had to find myself in the world. I was so empty inside of me; I didn't have many feelings for anything, and I didn't know what the real meaning of love was. Yes, I was young and had time to find all that out, but as a fourteen-year-old girl I just didn't care about anything, and that was sad. All the people I'd met in these past two years had been kind to me, and I liked all of them, but did I love any of them? No. And it was true. I'd been hurting all my life so badly; I just couldn't forgive the whole world. I knew that was wrong, but that is how I felt, and looking for love was going to be the most challenging for me, because I didn't know what love was.

To me the days felt longer and longer. I was getting bored with everything I did—all I wanted was to go, go somewhere. I had no desire to stay with my mother. My aunt noticed that I was silent and sad. With a soft voice, she asked me to come into the kitchen for one moment; she had news for me. I wondered, what news? I'd seen the mail carrier and there was no mail. It crossed my mind that Aunt Jana might be afraid to let me go and had tried to delay the process of getting all the documents in order. No, not my Aunt Jana, she was one of the best people in this world—she wouldn't hurt a fly, so why would she hurt me?

Something must have happened; I was not going to Canada. No, no that couldn't be, but the whole family looked so sad, and my aunt was crying. Oh dear God, what was happening?

"Ramona, why don't you come and sit beside me, I do have news for you. The news is good for you but sad for us. The letter came by special delivery, so that's why you didn't see it. It's from Canada. Come sit down and read it—it's good news for you."

My hand was shaking, thinking if that if it was good news that meant I was going to Canada. Reading the words aloud, I was so deeply touched at how all four of them started to cry. I'd never thought that they cared for me that much—I guess I was wrong. Carefully folding the pages, I began to cry as well. I was going now, no turning back. All I had to do now was to go to the Canadian Embassy in Belgrade, to get the rest of the documents. My aunt from Canada was sending adoption papers to the embassy by special courier, and I had to make an appointment to see them. With nervousness and sadness in me, I had tried to prepare myself for this but wasn't sure if I could take it. I'd always said I couldn't wait to go, and now I was so scared... scared that I was going to regret going so far away. There was a little voice in my head telling me to wait now, to just calm down and that what would be would be, as they say, for better or worse.

I hugged my aunt and the others and with a smile, I shouted, "Hey you all! I'm not gone yet. Let's just have some fun. Uncle Stefan, let's get that bacon, and the boys can start a fire and let's have some fun. Maybe my going will be good for all of us. Perhaps one day you can join me in Canada, I will see to that. So Aunty, make some of that pita and let's's put on some music. I'd like this to be a fun day. We still have a long way till I go, and for all we know something could go wrong, and I won't be going. Let's put all our feelings aside and have fun."

There was no movement at all; they just set there with long faces and did nothing.

"Okay, if you want to cry like babies, go ahead. I am going to my room, and if you decide to have a little fun, you know where you can find me." I was struggling not show them how sad I was, so I went to my room and cried myself to sleep.

When I woke up, to my surprise I was still in my clothes, I hadn't changed. I guess that crying most of the night had put me into a deep sleep. As I was just getting up, there was a soft knock on my door.

Before I even opened the door, I knew that it was my aunt. She always cried over every little thing. I know, me going was not a little thing, but she and the rest of them had known this was going to come one day, and that day hadn't come yet, so why upset yourself ahead of time? There would be lots of days to prepare for goodbye besides today.

"Ramona, we're all so sorry for acting like a bunch of children last night. We love you so much and every time I see a letter for you I panic. I love you so much, and I don't want you to go."

"But, Aunty Jana, why did you give me the address of your sister in Canada if you didn't expect me to go?"

"I don't have an answer for that, and I know you've made up your mind to go. To tell you the truth I will never forgive myself for telling you about your aunt in Canada. I have to live with that the rest of my life. I won't stop you going, though, maybe you will find some closure and happiness in Canada."

"Aunt Jana, I don't know what I'm looking for. I never had a home, it was always somebody else's house or the orphan village. But I want you to know that I am very grateful for what you have done so far for me. Now that we're almost sure that I'm going I'd like to ask you one more thing. I'd like to stay till school is over for this year—that means nearly two months. After that, you and I can go to Belgrade and the Canadian Embassy will tell us what we need to get a passport or any other documents. So let's just forget that I will go one day, because that one day is not today. Now come here and give me a big hug. I do love you Aunty Jana."

Because I wanted to finish my grade seven with a good report I studied even more. My teacher noticed my improvement and one day in the hallway, she asked me if she could talk to me. "Ramona, I'd like to ask you a simple little question. Are you going to Canada?"

"Yes, I am. What is your interest in that?"

"Nothing Ramona, I just noticed that your work is excellent and I thought maybe you care about your homework because you're staying, but if you're going why are you studying so hard? Your grades won't matter over there."

"Well, my grades won't matter to them, but they will matter to me. I want to finish my last year as one of the best. That's my reason."

"Very well then, good for you, and thank you for being so honest with me." By now the days were just flying by. I studied so hard and in the end it paid off. My report card was all A's, and I was so happy. My teacher gave me a present; a Yugoslavia and English Dictionary, which I had been planning to buy when I got to Belgrade. I gave her a hug and promised her I would try to be good for the rest of my schooling in Canada.

I was so happy that I was singing and jumping around and then I saw Jovan standing by the end of the yard. Seeing him made me even more comfortable. "Hey you!" he yelled. "What's your rush?"

I noticed he was holding a bouquet of flowers. Smiling I came running and gave him a friendly kiss, hoping the flowers were for me. They were so beautiful and no one had ever given me flowers. I didn't know it was the last time I would see Jovan.

"Jovan, are those flowers for me, for my good grades? Well thank you, but hey we're friends, no need to buy me flowers. Don't do this anymore."

He took my hand and pulled me onto a bench beneath a tree. "Ramona, can you just shut up for a second. The flowers are for you, but not for your good grades; it's me saying I'm leaving on Saturday. I don't like it here, you know that, and there's no point in me staying—I'll never be a soldier. So before you say anything, don't let me see any tears; tears are for kids. I'd like to remember you as my best friend, but do give me a big hug and yes kiss me if you like, because I'd like you to do so."

That was my first real kiss with a boy, and I don't think I'll ever forget it.

"So Jovan what are you going to do now?"

"First of all, I'm going to take a long vacation. I'd like to think about my future, so going away from everything will help me. But I do have one thing on my mind, and that is to study human behavior. I think it's sociology, or I'd like to be a scientist. I'd like to know, why we're all so different. What I'd like to do will probably take me a long time. To get to know people you have to see the world. I have a cousin in New York, that's in the USA, not too far from Toronto, so we'll see, maybe one day I'll just come by and say hello. What are your dreams, Ramona?"

"I'd like to travel first, just like you, but that's not going to happen. I'm going to live with strangers, so for the time being I have to do what they say, but as long I can find some happiness I'm going to be okay."

"Happiness, what is that for you? I've known you for almost a year now, and I don't remember you ever being happy. Yes, you smile, but behind that smile is a lot of sadness."

"Jovan, let's just try to remember each other as we are now, and a big hug will keep me happy."

We embraced for a long time, and I let him go. I didn't want Jovan to see me crying. As I walked home, I heard him saying, "Ramona, please don't cry."

Now that school was over it was time to make arrangements for me to go Belgrade and get myself ready for my long trip. My aunt was getting supper ready, and my uncle was reading the newspaper. I walked in with a big smile and with a happy face I asked my aunt, "Guess who's the best student in grade seven, and who got all A's?"

(I know she was just joking but she said it was Nenad.)

"Aunty, are you kidding? I hope so. Guess what? It's me. I'm so happy that I finished as the best my last year school."

My saying that made them both sad again, so I just went to my room, and wondered if it was too late to change my mind or not. Lying down I thought of my life then and now. Since everything was good here, why I should go Canada? I had a real life now; they were my aunt and uncle just like the ones in Canada, and I was getting comfortable here, so why was I going? I was going to talk to them after supper. For once in my life I had to make a decision, and it wouldn't be easy.

Supper was somehow silent, and I wondered what was going on. Then my uncle spoke. "Ramona, you know we all love you, and we don't want you to go, but all the adoption papers are ready, and it's time, to be honest with each other. We know that you have to go, so the military school is closed for twenty-one days, and your aunt has some free time. She can go with you to Belgrade to finish the rest of the documents, like getting your passport and visa at the Canadian Embassy. Your uncle in Canada called yesterday and told us that everything is ready on their side, and they have sent money for your ticket. You'll get that in Belgrade as well, not all on the same day, so you ladies can stay there as long as you need to."

I watched my uncle talk, and at the same time I looked at the rest of them. My aunt was crying, and the boys were so sad neither one wanted to look at me. My uncle's hands were shaking and his voice was full of nerves. Watching them, I asked myself why I had done this. I should have canceled everything before it was too late. All I could do now was enjoy my time with them for little longer, or perhaps it would be better if I went soon.

My uncle went on, "Ramona, this has to be done as soon as possible; the more you put it off, the worse it is for all of us, and I can't imagine what you think. We have saved some money for all your expenses and..."

"Uncle Stefan, please stop. I have to tell you something. (I looked at my aunt hoping that she wouldn't say anything.) I have lots of money, and I'll cover all my own expenses." And then I told him about Aunt Vera and how I had more than 25,000 dinars because she had given it to me.

"Ramona, I don't know what to say to that. Where do you keep all that money?"

"It's in my room; I have put it in my traveling bag."

There was silence for minute or two. My uncle was so shocked and my two cousins were just staring at me. I could see they were unclear on what I'd just said. We all hugged and my uncle whispered to me, "Thank you, Ramona."

After we had a good talk, my aunt and I made arrangements for our trip to Belgrade on Monday morning. We went and made train reservations for both ways. Packing for my trip was not sad as yet, because I knew we were coming back at the end of the week.

Monday came pretty fast. I liked going to Belgrade; it was a big city and beautiful, but I could tell my aunt wasn't as excited. I tried not to show my excitement, but it wasn't easy. The train was on time, and the trip was about three hours. We took a slow train so that I could see more of the countryside. We didn't talk much,—we both were deep in our thoughts. She was sad, but we managed in a nice, calm way to enjoy the trip.

As we arrived in Belgrade, the first thing we did was find a hotel for us, and that wasn't hard. Once we unpacked, we agreed that for the first day we would pretend we were tourists, so we could enjoy some time together. Our day went so fast. My aunt wanted me to buy some stuff that I might need for my trip, but I decided to wait until I knew the date of my departure. Deep inside me, I was hoping not to go until late fall. I wanted to go to Novisad, my first home after the orphan village, to see if Mrs. Vera was gone, and I wanted to see my first friend Karla, and the old lady in my first apartment, but the time of departure was not up to me. I had to see what the Canadian Embassy had ready for me.

Next day after breakfast we took a taxi and went to the Canadian Embassy. Boy, that building was so beautiful. As we walked in, there was a soldier standing there with a funny hat. Well, it was funny to me, but that was the Canadian army uniform. And then, a young man approached us and asked us if he could help us. *What a beautiful people,* I thought. I told him we had come to see somebody about my papers, and that I was going to Canada, but I needed some information, and I wasn't sure what I needed to do at the embassy. I handed all my papers to him. As he looked at them, he asked me if I was Ramona Miklush! Boy, that was so funny. I laughed and said, "I am Ramona, but not Miklush; my last name is…" and then I stood there like an idiot. I honestly didn't know what my last name was. Was it the name from the orphan village or the one that my mother had, or my father's name?

The young man saw that I was confused. He looked at the paper and said in a very kind voice, "Ramona, can you please come with me?"

I thought I was in trouble, but he took us into a very nice room and told us to wait there and with a light smile he said someone would be with us shortly. I smiled and said thank you.

It was about half an hour before she walked in. And then the door opened, and a young lady came in and said, "My name is Miss Sandy Clark, and I am in charge of your documents. We have received everything we need from Canada, but there are few things we still need. So I presume you are Ramona, and you are her temporary guardian. Am I right?"

"Yes Miss Clark. I am Ramona and this is my Aunt Jana. I'm very pleased to meet you."

"Thank you, what a polite young girl you are. Okay, I need a letter from your mother stating that she is no longer able to take care of you, and that is why she is letting her sister Vesna give you a new home, and their family name. I also need, if you have it, a letter from the orphan village, saying how long you lived there, and then we can start. But before we go any further Ramona, can I ask why you want to go to Canada? And another thing comes to my mind. Ramona, how come you don't want to stay with your Aunt Jana till your mother gets better? Perhaps then you could go back and live with her. Am I missing something?"

I told her my mother's story and that I liked living with my Aunt Jana, but that she had a family to take care of and my aunt in Canada did not. "And by the way, why not Canada?" I asked. "It's a big country and most beautiful as well, and I'm truly looking forward to going there as soon as possible. All this is not easy for me, but I have chosen to do it, and I realize that me going is hurting lots of people, but I have made up my mind."

"Ramona, you have answered all my questions, and this is all we have to do now. All your documents are ready, so now you have to go to the passport office and get a passport. You'll need four photos of yourself. Once you get the passport, which will probably take about three days; then you can bring that passport back to me, and I will issue a visa so that you can land in Canada with no problem."

"Thank you, Miss Clark. I sure hope to see you very soon."

She was right; the man at the passport office told us to come back in three days, and everything would be ready. Now we had three days to spend and do whatever we liked. I was very excited, but my aunt wasn't. I wanted her to be happy for me, but she just could not let go. I didn't know how she was going to handle my last day with them. To make her little happy I asked her if she had ever been to a zoo, or I suggested we could take long rides on the Dunav river and see a lot of different places, or we could do whatever she liked.

"Ramona, if you don't mind, all I want is to go back to the hotel for the rest of the day. Perhaps we can go to the zoo tomorrow, since I've never seen any animals except ours and I would like that."

I approached her carefully and gave her big hugs. "No problem Aunty, I can use some rest myself as well, and tomorrow is another day.

I didn't know how to handle the emotional situation, and I felt so lousy. Three days went pretty fast, and my aunt enjoyed herself for the time we had left together. Like we planned, we went to the zoo, and then took a ride on the river. We had done some shopping for my trip, but I didn't want to spend too much money. I had a big surprise for my uncle, and it had cost me a lot of money. I kept it as my secret.

Friday came pretty fast. We went to pick up my passport and then we rushed to Canadian Embassy to see Miss Clark. She was glad to see us. She was a lovely lady. Once we got there, she smiled at me and said, "Ramona, give me your passport for a minute, and I'll be right back."

In five minutes she came back with my passport, and I saw her holding a book and a large envelope. She handed me my passport and the book, and with a warm hug and a smile, she said, "I have one more surprise for you. In this envelope is your ticket for the airplane. Your aunt and uncle have paid for all this, and all you have to do now is go to the airport. And now my dear, everything is in order, and you are ready to go. Welcme to Canada, Ramona. Your passport has a visa for you to enter Canada anytime you're ready. Hope you enjoy your trip, and I sure hope you like your new country. Good luck and all the best."

I took the passport, envelope and book in my hands, and I just dropped them. My hands were shaking so badly, that if I had been holding a bomb, we would have all died. Miss Clark noticed my pain and emotional situation. She picked up what I'd dropped and with a cautioning look she said, "Ramona what's wrong? Are you all right? Come here, you know what we say in Canada? Cheer up and don't worry."

I started to cry. "I'm sorry. I just got so nervous holding my ticket and passport and my mind went crazy, telling me that it's all over; goodbye, go, run, so that's what you wanted, smile and be happy. I didn't expect it to be that fast, and I wasn't prepared for leaving as yet, but according to my ticket, I have only two weeks to get ready. Miss Clark, I'd like to thank you for all you have done for me, and maybe one day we will meet again. If you go home to Toronto and you can find me, I would like that."

"I will Ramona. Good luck and see you. Take care of yourself, my child."

When we came back to the hotel to pack, my aunt burst into tears. There was no way I could stop her, so I just let her cry and get everything out. And as she cried, I cried with her. We both knew that the crying must stop, but neither of us had the heart to do so. I took her in my arms, and held her for quite some time. Standing like that we wanted that moment to last forever, but we knew it couldn't. She finally let go and went to clean up. Our train was leaving in about two hours, so we had a few hours to be together with our thoughts. I had a bad headache and felt so lousy. All I wanted was to get home and take care of other things before I went. My ticket said July 10, 1963. I honestly couldn't believe that I was going. I was so scared and sad, but I knew I must not show that to them. I must put my emotions to the side and pretend that I didn't care; pretend that I always wanted to leave. But deep inside me, I was the only one who knew that I was lying to myself.

As we got on the train and found our seats, we were both silent. That was what I needed for now because I knew what was coming later. I kept telling myself to be strong, that everything was going to be all right, but all I could think was that I might have made a big mistake. (Little did I know then, that I had made a mistake.)

After the long train ride, we got home okay. The boys and my uncle were so happy to see us, but looking at them I knew how sad I was about them. My aunt went to her room, holding her tears, and so my uncle knew that something was wrong. He looked at me with sorrowful eyes and his voice sounded sad. "Ramona, you're leaving very soon, am I right?"

Yes, I'm living on July 10th, which gives me only two weeks to get ready, and Uncle Stefan, I'm not ready for that. How am I going to say goodbye to you all? How am I going to leave my aunt, the person I love so much? Please uncle, you're going to have to be strong for me and all of you."

"My child, you're not leaving us, you are just going a little bit far away, and hey, you never know, maybe you'll come back one day. But we will all carry each other in our hearts, and that's more important. So now let's go and see how your aunt is.

....

Meanwhile, in Canada, Janos and Vesna got a letter.

Dear Mr. and Mrs. Miklush,

I am happy to inform you that Ramona's documents are all in order, and she has picked up her passport and her ticket. According to the airline, she will be leaving on July 10, and by the time you get this letter you probably will see her in a few days.

We thank you.

Miss Clark

Canadian Embassy Director

....

I knew two weeks would come fast, faster than I wanted, and I had so many things to do. The next day I went to see if my surprise for my uncle was ready, after that, I had to write a couple of letters and many other little things. Before I went to the shop for my uncle's surprise, I dropped by the military school hoping that Jovan was still there, or maybe had left his forwarding address. The school was so strange when no one was there; so quiet and spooky. The office stayed open, though, and the principal was there. He knew me; we were not strangers. With a light smile, he asked me what I was doing in school.

I told him what I'd come for and he answered, "No Ramona, all the students left last week, and yes we do have a forwarding address for any students that are not coming back. But Ramona, those are confidential documents, and we are not allowed to give them out."

"But please sir, you know that Jovan and I were friends. I'm leaving for Canada in few days, and I'd like to send Jovan my new address, that's all I need. No one has to know, please."

"Ramona, this is against the law, but please keep it to yourself. Give me one minute, and I'll be right back."

He came back in about five minutes with Jovan's address. I thanked him and left before he changed his mind. I knew it was against the law, but hey who was I going to tell? I never even looked at the address, I just put in my pocket and left. Next thing was the shop. My surprise for my uncle was ready; it was just beautiful and he was going to love it. I told the store manager I would be back in two days with my payment in full, and with my uncle. I wasn't sure what to give the boys for a going-away present, so I decided to give each 1000 dinars, which was a good amount, and they could buy whatever they wished. As for my aunt, I had purchased in Belgrade, a charming handbag and two scarves like the ones she always wore on her head, and I would leave her the rest of my money, once I saw how much money was left.

Now that I had done most of my planning it was time for me to go to the hospital and say goodbye to my mother. I hated to bother my aunt for everything, but she wouldn't let me go by myself, so I had to ask her.

Every time I asked her for anything, the answer was always okay, and always with tears in her eyes. This was going to be the last thing I was going to ask her, except for taking me to the airport on July 10th, which would be the hardest one. I had to make sure she would be okay on that day, because she never told me but I knew she had a weak heart, so I had no idea how this was going to work out. To tell her to stay home would be worse. I had only a few days to talk to my uncle about that.

Aunt Jana and I took a bus to Novisad and in an about hour we were there. As we approached the hospital, I was emotionally getting sick. I couldn't believe that this time I was saying goodbye to my mother; a mother who for the second time had given me away, so why was I so upset? My mother was a heartless person; she never wanted me in her life. Taking a deep breath, I handled my emotional chaos pretty good. She was in her room looking like a zombie, with not a care in her face. I came very close to her and told her I was there to say goodbye. As I was saying those words, my eyes were full of tears— after all, she was my mother. I bent low to kiss her, and at the same time, I whispered in her ear, "Mother I forgive you for everything."

She never even looked at me, so I ran outside and waited for my aunt. As I was sitting on a bench crying, I asked myself why I was crying. Was it because I was leaving her or because I was so mad at myself for coming to say good-by to her? There was no answer to that. I expected at least a hug and a kind word, but a cruel person like her is just unbelievable.

Sitting on the bus later, all I could think of was my mother. With going so far away, all I wanted was a hug and maybe a little kiss goodbye. How could a mother be so cruel? What happened to her was that she was blaming me for all the abuse that my father did to her, so there was no way she wanted anything to do with me.

As soon as we got home, I went to my room. What I wanted was to be alone for a little while.

Like before, I slept without knowing that it was the next day. I jumped up so fast and ran to the kitchen. They were all sitting there. "Look Aunty, Uncle Stefan, and you two," I said. "You have no idea how I feel. Every night I cry in my room, and in the daytime, I hide my tears because I don't want you to see me so sad. So please don't be sad. I'm not dying. Me going away is not so bad. I'd like you all to be happy for me, and please we have only three days left, and I don't want to spend them crying. Now after breakfast I have a big surprise for you all. Mostly it's for you Uncle, but I'm sure that you'll all be happy. We're going to a shop cross the river, and you will get your surprise."

As we approached the store, my uncle was getting restless. He started to walk so slowly that I thought he was going to faint, but no, he must have seen a little boat sitting at the dock. The boat was blue and the most beautiful little thing on the water. Once we got closer, I said, "Uncle Stefan this is Ramona, and she is all yours."

I was sure he was going to pass out. He hugged me so hard that I that I lost my breath. Crying and laughing he said, "Thank you, my child. No one ever thought that you would do this. I am going to show Ramona to the world!" We all hugged and had fun. I don't remember ever seeing anybody so happy, and I was so glad that I'd left something for them to remember me.

The next two days were hard on me. My going was getting closer. So I took my cousins to the movies and on our way back I gave them each an envelope with 1000 dinars in it. At first, they both refused to take it, but with a little nagging, everything was okay. I told them to spend it on anything they liked, and like always we hugged and laughed. On my last afternoon, my uncle took us all out in the boat, and we had lots of fun. He knew everybody was looking at him kind of jealously, but I was so happy that he could enjoy himself and the rest of the family. On the way back my aunt said she was making my favourite food, and my favourite cake. I knew it was hard on her that it was my last supper with them, and I thanked her.

Supper was equally excellent. We all felt happy; there were no sad faces or tears, which made my day. After helping my aunt to clean up, I went to my room for the last time. I had some more packing to do and wanted everything ready for first thing in the morning. Our bus was living at eight a.m., because it took about three hours to get to Belgrade, and my airplane was living at three p.m. We had some time left to be together, and that was the reason I wanted a bus, not a train. We all got up around six a.m., and we had a good breakfast, which we needed because I wouldn't have an appetite to eat at the airport. Once we cleaned up, we took a taxi to the bus terminal and when got there I paid everything for them and me.

Four tickets were for return, but mine was one-way. It struck me very hard; a one-way ticket for me. I turned around with eyes full of tears. I didn't want them to see me crying, but my aunt noticed and grabbed my hand. In a tiny voice she whispered, "My child everything is going to be all right. Please be strong for me." We were all calm and quiet while the bus was running fast… if you ask me it was too fast, I wanted to tell the bus driver to slow down, but looking at the family I knew we shared the same thoughts. When we arrived at Belgrade airport, it was 1:30. I had to check in at least an hour before I boarded the plane.

As I went to check in my bags, a flight attendant from Air Canada came and wanted to talk to me. "Are you Ramona Miklush?"

That last name always confused me. "Yes I am."

Okay then, my name is Rhonda Simon, and I will look after you while you are traveling to Canada. Because you are under sixteen, we have to have someone take care of you. I do speak Yugoslavian, so there will be no problem. If you need anything, I'm right here. You have about a half hour, and then you must come aboard. We are leaving in thirty-five minutes. Take your time and don't worry."

As the four of us realized this was it, we kind of all started to cry, nearly at the same time. I couldn't believe that I was going—there was no returning. My heart was totally screaming out loud. I struggled to talk. My aunt was sitting, she had no energy to stand up, and I knew I had to be little stronger, or she would be very ill. I came and sat beside her and gave her the handbag that I'd been hiding all this time, which was her present from me. Inside that handbag, there was quite a bit more money left, and I told her to take care of herself, that she was the most important person to me. I asked her one last favour, which was that I never wanted her to write me anything about my mother. "I'd like to start free and don't need to know anything about her at all. I know I'm asking you a lot, but please promise me."

She just nodded her head, and I knew it was time for me to go. I hugged my uncle and my two cousins one more time, and I was ready to go. Before I took the last step, I heard my aunt saying, "Ramona, please don't cry. Don't look back, there is nothing that's important. Always face front. Leave your past here, and start a new, fresh life. Take care of yourself, my dear child."

And that was that. I went on the plane and never looked back.

CHAPTER 21
Ramona arrives in Canada, July 11th. 1963

I DON'T REMEMBER CRYING so much in my life, and crying must have put me to sleep. When I woke up and looked out at the window, all I could see was water…water, nothing but water. The flight attendant, Rhonda came and asked me if I was okay. With a confused look, I just said yes, but that was a lie. I was so afraid and sick, and I felt sick to my stomach and my head. I asked her if I could have some water, and maybe an aspirin for my headache. My head was spinning, and at some point, I felt dizzy and sick. Rhonda sat beside me, holding my hand, and it made me feel little better.

"Ramona, don't worry, your headache will soon go away. It's just a change of pressure. We're going to be in Toronto about two hours. You slept most of the time, and that's good. Now just relax and in about ten minutes you will see some land, and that is eastern Canada. I'll bring you something to drink. Did you ever have a drink called Coca-Cola?"

"No Rhonda."

"Then Coca-Cola it is. I'll be right back."

She came back with a chocolate bar and Coca-Cola. I took one zip and almost gagged. There was so much of a chemical taste or something. I didn't like it.

She noticed my funny expression on my first drink and laughed. "Ramona, when you drink Coca-Cola, you have to take it very slowly. Now try again."

"I don't think so, I just don't like it. If you bring me a glass of water I'll be more than happy." It took me a while but I started to feel better, and when I looked outside the window, I saw land. We were still high up in the air, but you could see we were flying over Canada, my new home. At first, I wasn't sure if I was happy or sad, all my sad memories and good memories were mixing me up.

An announcement over the speakers startled me, because up I didn't know where that voice was coming from. He said that we would be in Toronto in an about two and a half hours. So we could relax for the time being. We were still high up, and all you could see was water and some land, but not much of anything else. Looking out the window my thoughts were far away—away back home. I wondered what my aunty was doing now and if Uncle took his boat out for fishing, and if I was ever going to see Jovan or Slavko or my friend Karina? I almost fell asleep, but Rhonda came and said it wouldn't be long now.

She pointed out the window. "You see that big city there! That is Montreal, one of our beautiful cities in Canada. Most people in Montreal speak French, but don't worry, in Toronto it's all English and maybe about fifty different languages, so you'll be okay. You can go to the toilet if you need to wash up because in about an hour and fifteen minutes we'll be in Toronto."

Hearing that I was so quiet. I had no idea what was waiting for me there. Starting all over again was not easy, no matter where you went, but I had gone so far away now, and if I didn't like my new parents I'd have no choice but to stay, and that was the scary thing for me. I wouldn't have anybody to turn to when I was sad. I wouldn't have a friend. I wouldn't even understand anybody, except my aunt and uncle.

Oh dear God please help me!

I wanted a better life but I was so mixed-up emotionally, and wondering if this country was going to give me what I was looking for. I felt so lousy and scared. Then I looked out the window, and there was a big city again. Rhonda came and said, "Ramona, there is your new home. That is Toronto, and you see there is a big lake, so if you like swimming, fishing, and all the outdoor activities, this is the place for you. When the plane stops, I'll be here with you to take you out to an immigration station where your parents are waiting for you. So set tight, and I'll be back for you. Don't go anywhere till I come. Do we have a deal?"

"Yes Rhonda, I won't move. I'm too nervous to go anywhere, but Rhonda if I didn't say it before, I'd like you to know that I'm grateful for all your help. Thank you very much."

It had struck me funny when she called them my parents. I guess she didn't know that they were my aunt and uncle, but for someone to say my "parents," it was a strange word for me. I'd never had parents, and now I had to remember to tell people this was my mother and father. It was so weird and confusing, but I had to stop thinking of the past. And then I realized that the airplane had stopped, and so had my heart. This was it—my new home. Most of the passengers were ready to get off, and I sat there waiting for Rhonda. When I saw her I thought I was going to pass out. I got dizzy and sick. I needed to sit down and relax.

"Ramona, are you okay? What's wrong? Don't be afraid; you'll love Toronto, and your parents can't wait to see you. So my dear, let's go, just follow me."

My legs were frozen, I just could not move... something was holding me back. "Rhonda, I don't want to go. I want to go back home. Those are not my parents. I want to go home, this is a mistake, please." I started to cry, and I was talking a lot of nonsense.

"Ramona, tell you what. Let's talk. Would you like a glass of water or maybe a chocolate bar like before? Why don't you want to go to your parents? What's wrong? Please Ramona, you can tell me. This can be just between you and me. We can talk as long you need to; just take your time, there's no rush. Or we can just sit and wait until you feel better."

"Rhonda, can I tell you something? Those people that are waiting for me are not my parents. They've adopted me, they are strangers to me, and that's why I'm so scared. I wish I could go back home to my aunt and uncle. Do think you can help me and take me back to my country? I'll find somehow to pay you for everything, please."

"Oh my dear. You're just scared. I know that the people that are waiting for you are your aunt and uncle, just like the ones you have back home. They expect to see you, and I'm sure you will love them. Don't be scared. I'll be with you and we can meet them together. Your aunt is such a sweetheart. I met them before I came to take you downstairs."

"Rhonda, promise me you'll be with me for a while, please. I can't do this on my own."

"Don't worry. I'll stay with you as long as you need me. So now it's time for you to meet your new family."

As we walked towards a tunnel, my heart was going bang-bang so loud, I thought that Rhonda might hear it. She was holding my hand and smiling, and then they were standing there. Two people that looked so strange to me. I just stood there and didn't know what to do next. I heard Rhonda whispering, "Go Ramona, don't be afraid."

Yes okay, go, but what do I say to them? Oh dear God, I want to go back home, please tell me what to do!

And then she started coming, almost running, (I mean my aunt). With a big smile on her face and open arms, she just grabbed me so hard, I thought I was going to burst.

"Welcome to your new home Ramona," she said. "I'm your Aunt Vesna, and this is your Uncle Janos. We are so glad that you came, and now we can all start a new life, with our new daughter."

"But I'm not your…"

I was going to say daughter, but Rhonda pulled me to the side and told me not to be so hard on them. "You can talk about your relationship after, now just say yes and get on with it. Can't you see how happy they are? Please Ramona, just give them a chance, and later on you'll see how things are, and then you can make up your mind. Right now go there and hug them or kiss them or whatever, but be gentle, please, okay?"

"Rhonda, thank you. Can you promise me one thing? If I ask you to look me up from time to time would you do it? I don't know anybody here, and if I need any help, I would like it to be you that I can talk to."

"Ramona, I'll come and see you, but remember that I'm a flight attendant, and I'm not home that much. I'll tell you what. Let me give you my telephone number, and you can call me anytime. I'd be happy to talk to you."

"Wow! You have your own telephone!. Do I have to pay to call you?"

"No Ramona, most likely your parents have a phone as well. In Canada a telephone is not a big deal. It was maybe ten or fifteen years ago, but now everybody has one, so you can call me anytime. But now Ramona I have to go, and I see your father wants to talk to me. Be good and take your time to get to know each other and everything will be okay. So bye for now, and be good."

My uncle went to talk to Rhonda, and I could see him giving her something. It must have been some money for her good job looking after me. Rhonda turned and gave me a kiss. It sounded like Canadian people were very friendly, and I was glad because I'd need lots of help.

And now I had another friend that I probably wouldn't see. Every time I met someone and I liked them they went away, and I always had to make new friends or in this situation, a new home. I sure hoped this would work out. I was so tired of moving from one place to another.

Aunt and Uncle looked okay to me, so I was ready to go home and find out. I noticed that we were quite far from the city and wondered how we were going; by bus or taxi, but it looked like my uncle read my mind and he pointed to a couple that was standing beside a nice, big, black car.

"Ramona, this is Mark and Jonna, they're our friends, and Mark has a car. Therefore, he will take us home. Mark has helped us many times in getting proper letters to immigration, and Jonna was helping us in getting your room ready for you. Please be polite to them."

Why would he ask me to be polite? Did he think I was uneducated or something? I didn't like that. When we got to the car, I walked towards them very carefully and told them that I was very pleased to hear about the help they'd given my parents. I had trouble saying "parents," but I had to find that out. Mark and Jonna were an attractive couple and since my English was zero, we couldn't talk.

The trip to the city or my new home was so weird to me. No one talked much at all, and my aunt told me not to worry, that everything was going to be all right. She was a lovely, sweet little lady, and she looked like her sister Jana and my mother, but my uncle...I was having second thoughts about him. We didn't connect right away, and something about him bothered me, but for now I just wanted to get home or my new home.

The trip was only twenty-five minutes, and then Mark stopped in front of a lovely building, which had about seven floors. I noticed that the neighborhood was beautiful and clean. As we got out of the car the only words I knew were thank you, so I told Mark and Jonna thank you for everything. They were so surprised by my words and I guess I just wanted to show off. It was just a little fun I had, they were friendly people.

I saw quite a lot of people looking through their window curtains, they must have been interested in me, it was fun for me. Our apartment was on the fourth floor, and there was an elevator so it was easy to get up. As we walked in, the first thing I noticed was a TV, a great radio, and a big sign that said, "Welcome to your new home." It was all so strange to me; I didn't know what to do. They just stood there and looked at each other. There was no love there or happy feeling that I felt, but this was nothing like I had expected. To make it easy on all of us because of my disappointing situation, I asked my aunt if she could show me my room, because I would like to go and have a rest since the trip was long, and I was all drained out.

The room looked very nicely done, mostly in pink. It made me feel like an eight- year-old, but I just said, "Thank you and we'll see you later on." It was about eleven a.m. when I lay down to rest, but rest was not what I needed. I just put my head on the pillow and cried...cried so much. I don't know what came over me, all I wanted to do was cry. I was so sad and felt so lousy. I knew that we were all going to need time to get to know each other, but there was nothing there. Communication between them and me was hard, and there was some struggle to look at each other. And I'd noticed something about my uncle that made me think about Mr. Tekish. His eyes were so blue but cold as an iceberg; there was not a trace of love in them. It made me wonder about my aunt; why she married him, but I'd let that go for now.

Maybe I was too tired, and being tired can make you judge people wrong, so I lay down and slept till about three p.m. when I heard a door open. I looked up, and there was my uncle standing beside my bed. Boy did I jump, and I asked him, "What are you doing in my room?" I was so upset and told him that from now on he was never to come into my room unless he knocked first. "And you have to wait for my answer. I don't want you to do this. I'm not a baby; you don't need to come to check on me. Please, can you leave now, and let me be? I'll come out when I'm ready. Please go out right now."

He was shocked at the way I talked to him, and I could tell he was mad. I had seen that look before, and I knew the danger. I'd promised myself a long time ago, no more Mr. Tekish ever, and my uncle had better be careful. He left without a word, and I knew from that moment that my aunt Jana had been right about him. He sure looked like a mean man.

I stayed in my room for a long time. It made me wonder how come my Aunt, Vesna never came to see if I was okay or not. So I changed my clothes and put on a clean dress and went out. Both of them were sitting and watching TV. Slowly I walked towards them and said hello.

My aunt was so happy to see me. "My dear, did you have a good rest? I went out to buy you some tiny things that you'll need till we go shopping together."

"Thank you, Aunty. I was not aware that you left, but please can you tell me when you go out next time? I would like to go with you. I'm not comfortable staying home alone with a stranger and him coming into my room. Aunty, I grew up in the orphan village where there were no men, except for a monster, but that's another story. I don't know my uncle well enough that he can just walk into my room without knocking. I'm almost fifteen and I do need privacy, he can't do that anymore."

"Ramona, I'm so sorry. I didn't realize he did that. I'll have a good talk with him, and trust me that won't happened again. He was just probably worried about you; I'm sure of that."

"Well then okay, but please tell him not to do that anymore. Aunty Vesna, when can I watch TV? I have nothing to do now. I have put away all my clothes and the room is all clean. Maybe I can help you make supper. Whatever you need me to do to help you just ask me. In the orphan village, they taught us almost everything to do and then some! So please just let me know."

"Oh my dear. You don't have to ask me to watch TV; I'll show you how to turn it on and you can watch it anytime you like for as long as you like. And thank you for offering me your help. Right now I'll be home for ten days so that I can show you the city, and we can spend time together and try to get to know each other. I know you were in the orphan village for a long time and after that, Elsa didn't care for you very well, and I understand that you are not too comfortable with a man. But don't worry, Uncle Janos is a great man, and he cares for you. So try to get along, it would really please me. You see Uncle Janos is home most of the time for now because he's waiting to get a job at the hospital and it is very hard. But one of his friends is working on it, and I work every day from seven a.m. to three p.m., except Saturday and Sunday. For now, I'm going to start supper, and you just relax and watch TV. Uncle Janos went out to grab some fresh watermelon and he'll be back in a minute."

There were some new things to see on TV; I was so amazed by it. I had seen a television once, back home in the military school where my aunt and uncle worked, and that was all, but this is just great. I could learn English quickly by watching them talk, and it was something for me to do till school started in September.

I was far away in my thoughts and never heard my uncle come in, so it startled me when he sat beside me. I gave him a slight smile, and I saw his beaming face looking at me. If didn't know better I could have sworn that it was Mr. Tekish staring at me. I jumped up and ran to my room. I was having a flashback from my old days with Mr. Tekish's lap. My uncle reminded me so much of him. He had similar cold eyes and I could smell on him that he'd been drinking.

Then I heard a knock on my door. I was hoping that it was not him and thank God it was my aunt. "Ramona, what's wrong? Your uncle said you just looked at him, and you ran to your room. Did he say something? Tell me honey, what's wrong?"

"I'm sorry Aunty, nothing is wrong. I just had a flashback of an evil memory from the orphan village. One day I'll tell you everything that happened to me while I was there and maybe then you will understand me. For now, if I go off like this, crying or going to my room, please don't worry that it has anything to do with you. I'm very sorry if I gave you a reason to be scared. Aunty can I ask you one question, and please be honest with me. Does Uncle Janos drink?"

"Oh my dear, why are you asking me that? Did he do or say something to you?"

"No, no, no Aunty. I just thought that because I smelled whisky on him, that's all."

"Okay then, let's go and have our supper, and after that we can go for a walk. You might like to see your neighborhood. There are lots of stores, and you'll be amazed how many different nationalities are in this city. After that, we can watch some more TV, and you can go to bed whenever you like, but try not to stay asleep too long. So let's go."

Toronto was a big city, and I liked it. There was so much to do and see. I found a night school where I could take English classes, and I discovered real record store because I loved to listen to music and a new group from England called the Beatles. I just had to ask my aunt for some money, since I didn't know anybody.

One day, as I was walking down to the store, I noticed that some young kids, girls and boys, were looking at me and laughing. I wondered why, but then I realized that I didn't have the same clothes as they did. To them, I looked like some nerdy kid, so I needed to change. I asked my aunt if she'd like to take me shopping like she'd promised before. She was wondering why now, I explained to her about the difference in fashion between my clothes and what they were wearing here. I needed to change. All I wanted was a pair of blue jeans, some t-shirts, and running shoes. After that day, I knew I that there would be no difference between me and other kids, except my English, but I was working hard on that.

Summer was almost at an end, and I was glad to go to school, mostly to learn English and to get out of the house because my feelings about my Uncle

Janos were still in limbo. There was something about him. Most of the time he was drunk, and that bothered me. Why was he drinking every day? Was he in some pain or trying to forget his past or worse? Mind you, even when he was drunk he didn't bother me or anybody; he just lay on the couch and fell asleep. What kind of life was that? One day when I caught him sober, I'd talk to him, but for now, I'd just stay away from my uncle.

The day before school I met a girl that lived in the next building. She was from Denmark, and her English was just as bad as mine was, so we became friends. The way we talked English, a lot of people were wondering how on earth we understood each other, but that's called street English, and we were okay with that. Her name was Megen, and she was my age. We were registered in the same class; grade 9. The school was within walking distance and it was always nice to meet new people. Megen was a little bit shy, and I wasn't much of a talker myself, so sometimes we would walk without a word, but we enjoyed our friendship. Because our English was not quite right as yet, most of the teachers gave us a little more time to submit our work. I always carried my dictionary for help. I had to keep myself busy. All I wanted was to learn English fast, so I could go and get a job. I was fifteen by now and to work you had to be sixteen years of age.

Time just flew so fast, and before I knew it winter came; my first winter in Canada. And winter was something else. By December, there was so much snow I often laughed saying we lived at the north pole. With the winter came the holiday for Christmas. I had never even heard of Christmas, so it was fun for me. Back home we always celebrate new year Eve, but Christmas was a new to me. I asked my aunt to explain to me why people celebrated Christmas. It was hard for me to understand, because I was born in a communist country, and we never learned or talked about religion. I wasn't asking too many questions though, just enjoying my free days. The school was closed for the holidays until January 6th.

For Christmas, my uncle got us a lovely tree, so we put all party decorations on it, and my aunt and uncle put lots of presents under the tree for me. Since I was too young to work, I had no money, but my aunt gave me twenty dollars to spend any way I liked. I asked Megan to go downtown shopping with me, and she was happy to do so.

The holidays went fast and just as fast was the new year. As my first Christmas was a good one, so was the new 1964, and we were all happy to be together. Back to school was approaching fast and I was looking toward to seeing the rest of my school friends. My English was getting better and better every day, and most teachers were happy for me. Grade nine was going to have a good finish for me if I continued to study like that and I did. Except for studying, I loved to listen to music. The Beatles and most British groups were my favourite and with music and school, my time just flew by so fast.

Winter was very harsh; there was lots of snow and it was so cold. I didn't like it at all, but that's how winter in Canada was, so they told me.

By now spring was approaching by the calendar, but I'd never seen snow in April before. My aunt said that was nothing new, that snow sometimes could fall even in May. Well I guessed there was nothing I could do about that. Everything was still new to me. Like there was another holiday called Easter. Again I asked my aunt what kind of holiday it was. She told me that like Chrismas, Easter was a Bible holiday, and everybody celebrated it. I was wondering how many holidays they had here in Canada, but I'd learn one thing a time.

By now I had survived summer, fall, winter, and now spring. Weather in Canada was very strange. If you went by the calendar weather was early, either winter or early summer. Spring and fall didn't last too long, but I noticed that winter lasted the most.

School finished for this semester, and I thought I did pretty well, for a person that had been only one year in Canada. Report cards were due June 15, and after that I'd be free for the summer.

Megen was wondering what was I doing for summer vacation, but I had no plans so far. There was no one that we knew in Canada so we'd usually stay in the city, go to Center Island, or the EX, or just bum around. She was going to Montreal; she had an aunt there, and was planning to stay there for three weeks. After that she and I could just have a good old time in the city.

Finally, report cards came, and as I guessed, I had passed. Only my English grade was little off, but that was understandable. I was planning to take more night classes in summer so that I could be more ready for grade ten in September.

CHAPTER 22

I COULDN'T BELIEVE THAT it was one year since I'd come. Time just passed too fast. I was still homesick, and my uncle hadn't changed. I did feel sorry for my aunt; she was the most caring person I ever met. What she was doing with my uncle I could not figure out. Once she told me that my uncle had saved her from an abusive man, so I guess that was why she was so good to him. So I didn't bother him about his drinking, but I tried very hard to stay out of his way as much as possible, because those eyes were telling me how dangerous he was.

Summer was scorching, and the good thing was that there was a public pool not too far from me. Otherwise, the heat might have killed me. We had no air conditioning in our apartment, and nights were so hot. Sometimes I would take a towel and put in the freezer, and then I'd wrap that cold towel around my head to keep me cool. It was okay with me though, because I knew winter would come soon, and I just didn't like cold weather.

Then one day just before I was returning to school, my uncle's frustration at not getting a job at the hospital came to an end. Finally, they called him for a position as a CSR; that meant something to do with an operating instrument, and how he got that job was a puzzle to me. That post required a person with skills in that field, and he never said anything about working in hospitals before or anything close to that.

Before he went to work that day for his first day, he wasn't drunk. so I thought it was my chance to talk to him like a reasonable person. So right out I asked him how he got the job without ever having worked in a hospital before? His answer shocked me.

"Ramona, you're just a kid and there is so much that you don't know about me and you never will, but I can tell you one thing about this job. When I was in the army, I worked with doctors, and that is how I learned. I did go to university, but war destroyed all my dreams and Ramona this is all, and please don't ask me this anymore, because you won't get any answers. I know you hate me for drinking so much, but I'm not as dangerous as you think, so next time you see me drunk, please mind your business and just let me be. I do love your aunt, and you are here because of her, not me. Your mother and all of your relatives hated me; they called me names. Your Aunt Vesna was the only one who understood me. So now you know that my drinking is not your thing to worry about."

"But Uncle Janos, drinking is hurting you, and all of us. I can't bring any friends over to our place because I'm scared of what you'll say to them, and what about Aunt Vesna? I know it isn't my business, but I'd like to help you. I don't like to see you like this every day. I'm sorry, but I do care, and if you feel that way I won't bother you anymore. It's your life, and if you'd like to kill yourself, it's up to you."

After that talk with my uncle, I just gave up. I never bothered him again, and when he was drunk, I just turned my head. I did ask my aunt again how she could live like this and this time she told me. "Ramona, I was married to a man that was well off, and had a good job, but that man never had a heart. He beat me almost every day, many times I slept in the barn with the animals. He never drank, but he was a monster. So one day I left him, and while I was hiding, I met your Uncle Janos. He was always so sweet to me, so I told him about my husband, and I also said I was in hiding. Uncle Janos helped me to get free, and from that day on, he protected me, until the day we got married and ran away to Yugoslavia. Yes, he is German, but what happened before I don't care. I saw lot of things that occurred in wartime—no one was perfect. Soldiers had to do what a soldier does, kill or be killed, and if you were German, a partisan, English, or Russian, they were all the same. War is war, and we have to forget it, or we will never have peace. I know he drinks a lot, and I'm the one that brings him a bottle almost every other day. His drinking doesn't bother me that much, so please let it go. If you don't like our way of living you are free to go as soon as you turn eighteen, but in the meanwhile leave him alone. He is my problem, not yours. And Ramona, it's because of me that you're here, so please if you can help me, don't make it worse. I've lived with him now almost nine years, and we do get along well, believe it or not. We both love you, and we are here for you, and you have to do that for us. I know that he looks scary to you, but believe me he is not that bad. Let's all just try to be nice to each other for now.

"Tomorrow we'll go shopping for school again. I know you need more clothes and some notebooks, so tomorrow is our day. We can have a beautiful day out, just you and me."

"Thank you Aunty, and I'm sorry, but all I wanted was to help him. If that hurts you emotionally I will never bother Uncle anymore. I'll stand by you."

With my English improving because of my extra night classes all summer, my going back to grade ten was much easier for me. Now that I understood more, there was more homework to be done, but it was okay with me. I wanted to finish grade twelve and get out of school. I wasn't struggling in any class, but all I wanted was to get a job and start having something of my own. I always wanted to be a teacher, but that was back home. Now that I was in Canada everything had changed. English writing, reading, and all that spelling were so hard, and I didn't think that I was going to be able to learn it properly, so going to work was my choice. There was nothing wrong with that, it wasn't so bad. When thinking about these things I suddenly realized that the next week I was going to be sixteen years old, and that meant I could go to the employment office and apply for my S.I.N. Then I could start working at least part-time. That was my dream.

My aunt asked me if I'd like to have a sixteenth birthday party. She said she would like to do that for me. Since I was a kind of a loner I never had many friends; it was always just Megen and me. Nether one of us had a boyfriend. I knew what boys were like, so I wasn't interested in them. I told my aunt that throwing me a party was unnecessary. I just wanted to go to the movies and maybe order pizza for dinner and have my favourite cake. I asked Megen if she'd like to come to my house on my birthday, and then the two of could go to the movies and we'd see after that. She was surprised that I didn't want a party. Most girls like to have a big sweet-sixteen party. I didn't see why it was a big deal, but she agreed to go to the movies with me. So my sweet sixteen was sweet because I had a good cake, and I was happy.

After my birthday, I waited for a couple of months, and then I went to apply for my S.I.N. I thought quite often about my Uncle Janos, and wondered what was so bad that he did, that made him drink every day. I never asked him any more questions, but just watching him killing himself slowly was sad, and my aunt just pretended nothing was wrong. It was a sad life, so I wanted to get out of that unpleasant living situation. They never bothered me; it was the opposite. I had everything but a happy home. My reason for coming to live them was for a happy home, but look what I entered into—pretty sad.

My disappointment made me struggle more with my future. I was lonely, and I wanted to scream so loudly that I wanted to go back home. Even back home I would be more happy, with the friends and the relatives that I had, and maybe my mother would change, but anything would be better than this. Now I knew, it was much better if you didn't have anything, then having everything but no happiness.

Feeling lousy, lonely, frustrated, and full of revenge I was so determined to find love and happiness. I wanted happiness, and I was scared. I hated my life, and I knew I had to do something about that. Happy home, happy thoughts; those were not there. My life was like a roller coaster, and I had to do something. Struggling to find my way, I decided to run away. I wanted to see the world on my own. At sixteen, I knew this was a mistake, but I was so unhappy. I had no money, absolutely nothing, but I took a train from Toronto to Windsor Ontario, hiding in the washroom, from one car to another. Once I got off the train, and I looked around, I got so scared I knew I couldn't do this. Right away I was sorry I ran away. So not to make a terrible mistake a problem, I took the same train right back. Funny thing, my aunt and uncle never even knew I was gone. It was about nine p.m. and my aunt thought I was with Megen, but she did notice something was wrong.

"Ramona, are you all right? You look like a ghost. What's the matter, did something happen in school, or did someone say something to you?"

"No, Aunty, nothing is wrong. I just did something stupid, but I'm all right now. Sorry for coming home late."

Okay then, your supper is in the oven. I'm going to bed, and I shall see you tomorrow. Good night dear."

I was so hungry, I hadn't eaten all day. A trip to Windsor one way was three hours, so I'd had six hours of my life wasted on the train. How stupid was I? As I was eating I thought a lot. Since I'd gotten my S.I.N., the next week, I was going to look for a job. Christmas was just around the corner, and the job would be just great to let me have my money, but at sixteen I knew it was going to be hard. Still, just sitting home and feeling sorry for myself wouldn't do me any good. The next day I told my aunt about looking for a job and wondered if she could ask at the hospital if there was any opening in any department. I was willing to do just about anything. She told me that at sixteen it was going to be a bit hard, but she knew people in the office, and she promised to ask.

I went to some restaurants, theaters, and lots of stores, but when I told them I was sixteen most of the people asked me to come back in two years. I was so very disappointed. There was nothing I could do. So now all I had left was going to school and watching TV and spending time with friends. Life was so boring for me at that point. Sometimes all I did was play my records and like many girls my age fantasize about the Beatles and other pop groups. So Christmas came, and New Year's. Winter was frigid again this year, and like always I hated it.

My New Year's was no different than any other day; I had nothing to do, and that made me depressed. I would lie down and think about my friends back home; wondering about Slavko, Karina, and Jovan, wondering about my aunt and uncle and the boys, and yes often I thought about my mother. Thinking of her, even now I couldn't believe that she hated me so much. She'd loved Sasha, but not me. If I ever was going to have children I wouldn't let anyone ever harm them. I would love them forever, that is what every mother should do and does, but not my mom. Sometimes I cried and always tried to understand, but there was no answer. Crying was my escape falling into sleep.

CHAPTER 23

THE NEXT TWO years went pretty slowly or I thought so anyway. I guess I was just impatient to get out of school and start something different. I had finished grade twelve, and that was all the schooling I was going to take. My friend Megen was going to college; she wanted to be a photographer for a big fashion magazine. Me I wanted nothing except to get a job and be my own person. I didn't mind living with my aunt and uncle, but to be dependent on them all the time was getting to me. So, for now, I didn't continue school. Megen and I graduated our grade twelve, and she went back to Montreal to study photography. It looked like to me as if she liked Montreal. She asked me to go with her, but I was determined to find a job. My plan was to hit the pavement and look everywhere. I was almost eighteen by now, and no one could tell me to come back in two years unless there were no openings.

Searching and searching for weeks with no luck I was getting emotionally disappointed and thinking that I would never find a job, and finally after seven weeks of running to companies, hospitals, and many small businesses I got a call from a fashion designer, Patrisha Geyer. She was the organizer for most pageant shows and some C.N.E shows every year. I had heard of her but not in a million years did I ever think she'd call me. I was so excited and the next day at 8 a.m. I was in her office. To my surprise she didn't have her own offices, she ran the shows from companies like fashion magazines or pattern designers, but I didn't care, all I wanted was that job. I wasn't sure how to dress, so I took a chance and put on my best jeans and my long t-shirt, but I knew I looked decent, thinking she was into fashion and she wouldn't like it if I dressed up like a business person, and I was right. The interview was at McCall's, a pattern and magazine company that was located on Front Street, maybe fifteen minutes from my house, and that was another plus for me.

I won't deny I was very nervous. First of all, my English was totally broken, and I was not quite eighteen. So I was scared that she might be looking for an experienced person. Although she never said on the phone what the job was about, so I took my chances. Seeing her personally was my pleasure just as well. I wanted that job so badly that I was so excited and nervous that I forgot to lace my running shoes, and when I walked in I'm sure she saw my runners, but she gave me a warm smile. From that moment I don't know how I know I got the job. She told me to sit down and relax, and she was kinda joking saying, "I don't bite, just relax." In my head, I was asking her to be in my shoes, and I just smiled.

"All right, Ramona tell me a little bit about you. By your name and your English, I guess you are new in this country."

"Yes, Mrs. Geyer, you are right. I'm from Eastern Europe, and I have been in Canada for about three years. I have finished grade twelve, and now I'd like to find a job. I'm very familiar with your work. Last year I watched a show at the C.N.E. I'm not eighteen as yet, but in October I will be, so I hope you don't hold that against me. I'm willing to work very hard, I'm available to start anytime you need me, and to start from the bottom is something I'm not afraid of. I promise you I will work hard, and you won't be sorry for giving me a chance. Right now I live with my aunt and uncle, but by law, they are my parents. They adopted me, so that is how I came to Canada. I'm not sure what else to tell you, but if you have any questions, I will be more than glad to answer them. Oh, one more thing Mrs. Geyer, I have never worked before, so please don't hold that against me either."

"Ramona, I'm interested in you. As for the job, I'm sure that you do qualify. I don't need people with a lot of experience. No, I need a fresh, new look. You are young, and I can see your fashion is almost like mine. I'd like to explain to you about the job. Right now I'm getting ready for the C.N.E. in late August, and I need someone that can be my right and left hand all the time. There will be times that you won't have a chance to go pee, and you will spend some of your time in a warehouse helping with magazine and pattern orders. There will always be something to do, and there is room to grow in the business with me. If you think you can be free for me almost eighteen hours a day, then we can talk about it. As for your wages, you will be getting student's pay, but as soon as you turn eighteen, you will have a full salary and benefits after three months. The job is not easy, so Ramona I'll give you a couple of days to think about it, and I will call you. As for your English, don't worry, in time you'll be okay.

One more thing. Ramona, why are you so sad? Your eyes are telling me you are somber and lonely."

"Mrs. Geyer, I have been sad and lonely as long as I can remember. There will be a time when I will tell you about my life, and then you'll know why I'm so sad, but I'm actually happy now. Meeting you was my pleasure, whether I get the job with you or not."

"Okay. Ramona, thank you for coming, and you'll hear from me in two days. I do have a couple more people to interview."

A "couple more" struck me so hard. What if the others were better than me? I was driving myself crazy. It was Friday evening, and I just went to my room and closed my eyes and pictured Mrs. Geyer working on the show with me. A knock on the door made me jump. It was my aunt.

"Hi Ramona, I just wondered if you're coming to have supper with us? I haven't seen you since I came from work, and your uncle said you were out all day. Do you feel all right? Is anything wrong? If you're upset about not finding a job yet don't be silly. Now that you finished grade twelve you have lots of time to look for a job. Don't rush into that, you have the whole world in your hands and just as much time. You'll find one, so let's go and have supper."

"Okay Aunty, no problem and thank you." I felt so bad not telling her that I'd had I thought I'd keep quiet about it..

Two days were like two years to me. All weekend I stayed home just in case Mrs. Geyer called me before, but for a busy woman like her it was not likely, so I had to wait until Monday. Both my aunt and uncle left for work, and as soon as they left, I jumped out of bed, washed up, and sat beside the telephone, hoping it would ring soon.

It was nearly noon time and no phone calls. I was slowly losing hope of getting a call from Mrs. Geyer, and then at about 2:30, the phone rang. I must have jumped five feet in the air, but to my disappointment, it was not Mrs.Geyer.

"Ramona, are you doing anything?" It was my aunt calling from work, which surprised me, she had never called me from work before. "I have been to our office and the woman in charge of hiring would like to see you tomorrow. Should I tell her you will come, or do you have other plans?"

"Aunty, I do have something in mind for tomorrow, but tell her I will come Wednesday morning with you, if that's okay with her, and thank you, Aunty." I wanted to get off the phone so badly, and finally, she hung up. Just as we hung up, the phone rang. My hands were shaking. It had to be Mrs. Geyer, please…

and yes it was her, and yes it was her! With a trembling voice I said hello, and I knew she can tell I was nervous.

"Ramona this is Mrs. Geyer, I'd like to give you the good news. I have carefully studied all of the applications, and I'd like to give you the chance. I'd like you to come tomorrow, and you can start working. I'm very busy as you know, the Ex show is in August, so you are going to be a very busy person too. I hope you can put all your plans on hold till the show is over. If you don't have any problem with all this, then my dear I'll see you tomorrow morning at eight a.m."

"Thank you, Mrs. Geyer. I promise you won't regret your decision, I'll see you in the morning, and one more time thank you." I was so excited and happy. And if I could, I would have jumped over the moon. I laughed because she'd said, "my plans." If she only knew that, Ramona never had plans.

I called Megen and told her my news. She said I was very lucky to be working with the most talented woman in Canadian fashion. "Maybe one day I can help you, Megen," I said. "Maybe I could set up a meeting for you, some photo shoots on the show, that is when you finish college." We both laughed and said goodbye because she was living in Montreal and wouldn't be back until the end of September.

I decided to make supper for us to surprise my aunt and uncle. I knew they would be happy for me, even though my aunt wanted me to continue school. But she knew that getting a job was imperative for me.

It was about 4:30 when they both came home, and supper was on the table waiting for them. If I'd only had a camera to take a picture of their faces when they saw the table ready for dinner.

"Ramona, what is this?" asked my uncle. "You never made dinner before! You're not leaving us, are you? I can't take this surprise any longer, tell us what's happening."

I saw my uncle getting a drink, and he poured a glass of wine for my aunt. Maybe he was hoping that I was leaving, I don't know for sure. I told him to pour a half a glass of wine for me. They looked shocked that I was asking for a drink and I wasn't even eighteen yet.

So I went on straight out. "Uncle and Aunty, I'm celebrating this moment with you, so raise your glass to my first job. I'm starting to work as a full-time helper to one the most famous fashion coordinators in Canda. She's the host of the Canada pageant shows, and she is putting on fashion shows every August at the Ex. I'll be helping her all the time in every way she needs. Once the show is over, I'll be in the warehouse helping with the orders for magazines and patterns. When I turn eighteen I will have full pay and benefits, so I hope that you're proud of me. Why she picked me over the other applicants, I don't know, but I'm glad that she did. As of tomorrow, I'm a full-time employee. It took me a long time to get a job, but I finally have one. And today we are celebrating my being employed."

My uncle was smiling. "Now I know what you were doing in all your free time. I use to think you were just running around with those hippies and war protesters. With your ripped jeans and long t-shirts you always looked like one of them. Your aunt and I were worried about you a lot of the time, but I guess I owe you an apology—you were looking for a job. Well done Ramona. I'm proud of you and congratulations."

"Uncle, to tell you the truth, she liked the way I dress. She said that the other people she interviewed in fancy clothes were just full of themselves. She needed young blood; someone just like me. She will train me in everything I need to know, and you guys might not see me home for supper all the time, or I will be home late. She told me that the job requires me to be available 24/7, and that's when I'm available… anytime. She loves that. Now let's have supper, and I'm going to bed early because I want to show up for my first day right on time. One more thing, Aunty. Please tell your office thank you for me."

CHAPTER 24

THE PHONE RANG early on Saturday morning, I thought it was Mrs. Geyer, because she had the habit of calling me on the weekend for some help. Sound asleep, I answered,

"Hallo."

"Happy twenty-first birthday, girl. Get up, and this time, you're not going to tell me you don't care. It's your twenty-first! I have a friend that gave me their cottage for the weekend, and that's where we're going. Get ready and I'll pick you up in about an hour. Happy Birthday, Ramona—love you."

"Oh Megen, I'm going to strangle you. Do you know what time it is? It's my day off, and you know I don't care about birthdays. Birthdays are for happy people, not like me. I need some sleep. I was working until ten p.m. last night, so let me go back to bed, but I'll see you later."

"Not this time, I'm picking you up, whether you like it or not. I made this plan a long time ago, so you better be ready, or I'm carrying you off in my car. You can sleep in the car if you want because the trip is about two and a half hours, so there."

"I hope you're not setting me up with somebody, you know how I feel about that, but if I can nap in the car, okay then, I'll see you in about hour. This is just to let you know I'm doing this to get you off my back. I thought maybe you and I could go to one of the new bars in Yorkville and have some fun, but if you'd like to drive, go for it. Just tell me where are we going that it takes two and a half hours to drive?"

"Okay, I wasn't going to say anything before, but because you love fishing, then I might as well tell you now. We're going to Midland; there is a lake right beside the cottage, so you can fish all day and maybe catch a fish for supper. I have the cabin for three days, and I know you'll enjoy it. There will be only you and me. So, now you're satisfied?"

"Well okay then. That sounds good. I'm getting up as we speak, and you know why I agreed? It's because of the fishing, not because of my birthday. So, see you in about fifteen minutes, I'll be ready. And Megen, thanks."

As I was getting ready, I wondered where three years had gone, just yesterday I was eighteen, and now I was twenty-one. I'd been working almost every day, and I hadn't seen anybody seriously. All I wanted was to save some money, and I did. This year I'd I kept enough to buy myself a new TV, and the next week I was going to make a down payment on a car. I wanted it all, and I made it all possible, but deep inside me, there was still a sad person in there. I had tried to go on with my life, but every time I met someone, after a week or so I broke it off. The face and hands of Mr. Tekish were always there. It felt like he was looking and laughing, and touching me all over again, and I just could not seem to have a healthy life. The best thing for me was just working. Working those long hours didn't leave me any time to think about the past. I hoped that this trip with Megen would give me some peace of mind.

Before Megen come rushing through the door, I thought I'd better go and tell my aunt that I was going on a short trip with Megen, and that at the same time I'd try to catch some fish.

My aunt thought this was an excellent idea, but at the idea of bringing fish home, she just laughed. "By the way Ramona, happy birthday, my dear girl. Have fun and take this and get yourself some food; you look like a toothpick. Some folks think we don't feed you enough. Have a safe trip and we'll see you in a couple of days."

"Thank you, Aunty, and do me a favor. If Mrs. Geyer calls, just tell her that I'm taking three days off because it's my birthday. Tell her I'll be back Tuesday night."

I was getting my fishing equipment from the storage locker in the basement when I heard the horn. She didn't seem to believe that I was coming, but I did love her, she was my best friend. I'm sure some tenants were telling her where to go with the noise, but knowing Megen she probably laughed.

I ran outside. "Hey, hold your horses! Help me put this in the trunk, and let's get going before we get some tomatoes thrown at us."

"No problem, but first let me give you a big kiss. Happy birthday, my friend and I want you to know that I love you."

"Slow down girl. I love you too, but let's just enjoy this trip and have some fun. Did you bring some good stuff, just for a little more relaxing?"

"Yes, I did, and this time, you're going to have fun. It will be only you and me and your fishing, ha, ha. It's going to be a long trip, so we can stop and have a good breakfast, or you can go to sleep."

"Megen, you sound like my broken record player, which is on my list to buy a new one. You keep assuring me that there will be only you and me, but I'd like you to tell me the truth. Let me be prepared for a surprise, even if I don't like it, but this time and only this time I'll forgive you. So let it out. Who all is coming and when?"

"Ramona, you're impossible. The surprise is a surprise or it's not surprising is it? I promised I won't say and I won't. Be patient and act like you're surprised, and anyway, you don't know who is going to be there. If you ask me, I'd prefer to be just you and me, but what I discovered was that you have more friends that care about you than you think. I was surprised myself, and glad and happy. There are a lot of folks that just like you and some, like me, love you."

"What's with those words you love me? Are you a lesbian or something like that? I get shivers when you talk like that. I love you Megen, but as a friend. I hope you know that, and stop with that love talk. Some people might think that we're a couple, or whatever they call them."

"I'm sorry if I offended you, Ramona. No I'm not a lesbian, but I do care about you a lot. I have odd feelings when it comes to men and women. Like you, I don't have a boyfriend. And deep inside me I'm not interested, but I get along very well with females. I always thought or hoped that you were like me, but I can see I was wrong. So I'm sorry for that and let's forget that we ever talked about this. My feeling will stay with me from now on, so let's not spoil this party. This is all about you, not me. We can always talk about this later on if you wish."

I pointed out the window. "Look there's a restaurant. Let's stop and have breakfast. Since I can't sleep now, let's eat. I'll pretend that we didn't have that kind of conversation, so let's just have fun, and yes Megen I love you too, but in my way."

We ate very quietly with Megen trying to avoid eye contact. I was thinking, maybe she and I were the same. If you thought about it, I didn't have a boyfriend and I had no feeling at all for the ones I went out with. *Ah! Megen, you're confusing me now, but let's just try to enjoy this trip.*

"Good food," I said. "Maybe they can tell us if we're close to our cabin, and if there's anyplace I can buy a can of worms for fishing."

"Ramona, are you kidding me? After all our talk, or my talk you're still interested in the fishing. Aren't you excited about the party? What's wrong with you? Maybe you don't like to admit it, but you're like me at least a bit."

"I'm not too excited about the party, but having friendly faces around on your birthday is not a bad idea. If no one shows up that will be okay with me as well. I can fish all day, and you can get lots of photos of nature here, and we can have fun just the two of us. So to answer your question, I'm not too excited. Now let's go, I can't wait to get there. It's almost eleven, and we've been on the road for two and half hours, and I'm getting tired."

Soon we were in the car and approaching the end of the drive. "According to the map, you should turn left on the next road, and then go straight to the lake," I advised Megen.

She slowed down. "Look and listen," she said. "It's so peaceful here—not a sound, and there's the lake. Look how beautiful it is here."

"Wow! Look at that cabin; you could probably fit a hundred people in it, it's so big. You sure must have planned this for a long time, and I wouldn't be surprised if Mrs. Geyer had anything to do with it. This place is more like her style, but it's free, so let's go in. All I want right now is to lie down and listen to the birds and the sound of the lake. It looks like no one is here because there are no cars. I guess we're the first ones."

There was no response.

"Hey Megen, you're very quiet. What's wrong? Are you okay?"

"Yes, yes, I'm all right. Just grab your stuff and let's go in. I'm tired as well."

"SURPRISE! HAPPY TWENTY-FIRST BIRTHDAY, RAMONA!"

"Wow! How did you guys pull this off? There aren't any cars outside, and how did you all get here?"

Someone explained that the cabin next door was empty, and that they had all parked there. Otherwise, the surprise wouldn't have been surprising.

"Thank you very much, this is a surprise. Honestly, I thought that maybe in the afternoon, some people might show up, but this...this is amazing. Thank you from the bottom of my heart. Megen has been so quiet about all this, and she tried to make up some stories about how she and I are going to have a good time, but nothing like this. Mrs. Geyer, I'm sure you had a lot to do with this, so thank you and your husband.

It's not quite noon yet, but who cares! Let's all have a drink, and Megen brought some good records, so let the party start!"

I thought that Mr. Geyer and Mrs. Geyer would probably do a barbecue and I couldn't imagine who had prepared all the rest of the food. I was so nervous about it all, I needed something to calm me down, and Megen promised to bring a joint for us.

She must have read my mind and she took me by the hand, and we ran outside toward the lake and lit up our collective joint. Boy, after that I fell great, I even kissed Megen, and she laughed. No one noticed that we were gone. Except for Megen and two other girls, it was all older people, and all they talked about was business and a lot of other nonsense. I was very high, and I felt great. Later on, Megen told me I was a great hostess. Everybody had fun and it was close to midnight before most of them started to head back to Toronto.

Mrs. Geyer came over, gave me hug, and whispered in my ear, "It's about time that you loosened up. Good for you, my dear. I'll see you at work on Wednesday. Stay here and have a good rest."

After the last guests had left, I was ready to go to bed. Not only was I high, I was drunk as well, and the room was starting to turn and turn. I told Megen I was going to bed, and I was out.

I had no idea what time it was, but the sun was in my eyes whe I slowly opened them, and there was Megen beside me. She was sleeping like a baby. I looked at her and wondered what we had done last night. Whatever we did I didn't remember it, so I doubted she would. I got up and went to the kitchen, made some coffee and sat there, wondering if I'd made an ass of myself last night. But it was my birthday after all, so I didn't care. I scrambled some eggs and toast and waited for Megen to get up.

I guess the smell of fresh coffee woke her up. She was smiling coming down, and she looked good. "Hey, party girl," she said. "You were wild last night. I never thought you could be so much fun; everybody just loved you. That guy, what's his name... Peter, who works with you in the warehouse, the man was all over you, but you just kept dancing with everybody. I think you're just one hell of a party girl. I'll have to keep that in mind."

"You keep nothing in your head, my friend; it was my twenty-first birthday, and trust me, that won't happen again. And by the way, how come you were in bed with me? What's up with that?"

"Ramona, if you don't remember, then I don't remember either, so let's leave it that way. We've been friends for five years, and I don't want to break that friendship up over sleeping together. Whatever happened, happened and that's that."

"Well then, I'm going down to the lake to see if I can catch some fish, and if I do that will be our supper. You can come with me, or you can take your camera and start taking some photos. This place is beautiful."

It was a very nice October day. I sat on the deck throwing my line in the water. I was bending down trying to see if the water was cold, when I heard a boat coming. When I looked up, there he was, with a big smile on his face. I was still lying down and looking at him. I could not open my mouth. I was like a kid at a zoo—I was just staring at him. All I could hear was an echo in my ears.

"Are you all right, miss? Can you hear me? Talk to me."

"Yes, yes, I'm okay, I was just looking at the bottom of the water. You see, I dropped one of my lures, and I can't see it where it is. I'm quite good, thank you. Who are you? I thought we were alone. I don't recall seeing you yesterday."

"Well, I'm telling you, that party sounded good. That song, "I Can't Get No Satisfaction" was played maybe about fifty times; what was that all about? Looks like somebody needed some joy."

"What are you talking about?"

"I'm sorry, let's start over.. I'm staying right over there. You see that small cabin? Well that's me. My name is Keven; I'm pleased to meet you, miss."

Yes hi. My name is Ramona. I'm very sorry if the party kept you awake, but you should have come and enjoyed it with us. I would not have said no. I was celebrating my birthday, and now I'm trying to enjoy fishing for the next day or so. To get over a big headache, the best thing is fresh air and quiet time. So Keven are you staying here for long or just relaxing for few days?"

I've rented that cabin for a week, and Saturday morning I'm going back."

"Mmmm...Back to where?"

From the cabin we heard, "Hey Ramona!"

"Look, you've got company!" Keven said.

"No, that's my friend. Megen and I are the ones that are staying in this cottage for a few days. We're going home Tuesday night."

Megan came down the the dock grinning wickedly. "Ramona, I turn my back for a second, and you get a new boyfriend right away. What is this now? Are you making me jealous?"

"Megen, I'm going to kill you one of these days. Sorry Keven. Megen this is Keven, our neighbor. We were just talking, that's all. Don't be funny because it's not funny at all. He might think we're together."

Pleased to meet you, Megen," he said. "I'd just like to ask you girls, if you'd like to go for a ride in my boat. The lake is beautiful this time of a year, and later on we can go to dinner in town. There's an excellent Italian restaurant, and we can continue celebrating your birthday, Megen."

"Ha, is that what Ramona told you? She hates to tell anybody about her birthday, so she even lied to you."

"Actually Ramona didn't say anything, I just said that. Okay then, Happy birthday, Ramona. Now that we know whose birthday it is, would you like to come in my boat so that I can show you the rest of this beautiful lake?"

Not for me, thanks," said Megen. "I don't like water like lakes and river and so on, but if Ramona wants she can go. I don't mind."

"Megen, yes I'd love to see the rest of the lake, but leaving you by yourself is out of the question. Sorry Keven, not this time, but thank you just the same."

Okay ladies, it's your loss, so maybe we'll see you later or tomorrow. Ramona let me give you my phone number, in case you ladies change your minds."

Keven that won't be necessary because there's is no phone in the cottage, but you can drop by later on if you like."

Megen headed back up the dock. "Ramona, I'm going in. This fresh air is making me sick, but you promised me fish for supper, so we'll see you later."

"Goodby Megan," said Keven. "Hope to see you later!"

"Not if I can help it."

Keven looked perplexed. "Ramona, are you sure she's your friend? Maybe she doesn't like me or something, but I don't know why. Is she always moody like that, or is it just me?"

"Don't pay any attention to Megen; she's just drained from last night. She's usually a good sport about everything, so maybe come back later on, and then we'll see.

"The way I see it, Ramona, Megen won't change her mind about me. Let me give you my phone number; you can reach me anytime you like, and I sure hope to hear from you. But if you don't think you're going to call me, then it was very nice meeting you, Ramona."

All right Keven, thank you. "Talk to you later."

CHAPTER 25

Keven, 1968:
"Hi Chuck, how are you? I need your help with something."

"Don't tell me you're leaving earlier than usual."

"No, nothing like that. I have a question for you about cottage number three. There are some girls who had a party there on Saturday, and I met them the next day, and I like one of them. But the problem is I don't know how to get in touch with her. I gave her my work phone number but she didn't give me her number. I like that girl, so I need your help. You know everything that goes on at this lake. Did those two girls rent the cabin, or did someone rent it for them? Please Chuck, help me with this one."

"Man, I can't help you much. The person who rented that cottage was Mrs. Patrisha Geyer. She's the most famous woman in Canadian fashion, and fashion shows as well. All I know is her work phone number and address. That's all man. She must have done that party for a girl that works for her. Rosa, the catering woman in town, might know more because she made all the food for her, so try there and good luck. So is that girl a real looker, or is she hot? I don't remember you ever fell for any girl so fast. Well good luck, and let me know if you find her."

"Thanks Chuck. Will do. Okay, now let me see. Rosa's Catering, Midland.

Hallo, is this Rosa?"

"Yes, sir, can I help you?"

"My name is Keven and I'm staying in cottage number five over on Wolf's Road. There was a big party here on Saturday in cabin number three, and I'd like to find out something about a girl that was there. Chuck told me that you did all the food for them, so I was wondering if you had the phone number of the person who organized that party? Maybe this is too much for you to give, but please, I've just got to find that girl. There is something about her that I can't forget. She has my phone number, but like a little puppy looking at her, I never asked her for her phone number or the address. Please help me."

"Keven, yes I know her address, but that's a woman, not a girl. She organizes most of the TV shows about fashion in Canada. Is that the person you're interested in?"

"No Rosa, I'm not interested in her personally, but she threw that surprise party for a girl that was there. Her name is Ramona, that's all I know. Maybe she works for that fashion organizer, so I'll take that address, and I can start with that. And thank you, Rosa, if I ever find her, I'll marry her one day, and you'll be my catering person. That's a promise."

"I sure hope you find her, Keven. Good luck, kid."

I decided to go home early, just in case Ramona called me. If I didn't hear from her by Monday I'd try to call that famous Mrs. Geyer. Maybe she'd help me, or maybe not!

I thought I'd call Chuck to tell him that I was leaving the next, and then I'd start packing. "Hey Chuck, listen buddy, I'm leaving tomorrow and don't worry about a refund, I'll call you in a few days. Thanks for everything. You'll find the key in the mailbox."

Driving home was so slow, or I thought so anyway. Finally, when I got home, I called my boss to tell him that I was back and to see if anyone had called, hoping that Ramona had. But my hopes were too high. No one had called.

Well it's only Thursday, I thought, *so then I'll wait until Friday, and if she doesn't call me by then, I'll try a different way. I'll call the number I got from Rosa and Chuck and take my chances asking Mrs. Geyer about her.*

By now, it was Friday noon and there were no calls from Ramona, so I picked up the phone and called Mrs. Geyer. I was very nervous and scared, but all wanted was to see Ramona and just to have a friendly talk.

"Hello, this is Mrs. Geyer, can I help you?"

I froze—words would not come out. I could hear her asking if anyone was there, but I just could not talk. I felt like a kid telling his mother he'd done something wrong, but her voice was getting a bit mad, and just before she hung up I spoke.

"Mrs. Geyer, my name is Keven, and I wonder if I can come and talk to you?"

"Let me ask you this. How do you know me and why are you calling me? If you're looking for a job, then you've got the wrong extension, I don't do hiring or firing."

"No, no no, I'm not looking for a job. I just need to talk to you, and I don't like talking over the telephone about this. Please, Mrs. Geyer. All I need is five minutes with you. I'm not too far from your place, I can be there in fifteen minutes. Please."

All right, Keven, you've got five minutes, and you better be here soon. You're lucky that I'm in a good mood. Otherwise, the answer would be no, and now I'm very curious about.who the hell you are."

"Thank you, Mrs. Geyer, I'll be there." As soon as she hung up, I ran to my car and took a short cut to Front Street. As I was getting closer, I was getting more nervous and scared. How should I start asking her about Ramona? Maybe Ramona was her daughter; I never asked her that. *I'd better calm down, I'm almost there.*

The place was quite a large, one floor, but decorated very tastefully; I guess Mrs. Geyer must have decorated it herself. As I walked in, the receptionist approached me and asked me if I was Keven. Being so nervous I just nodded my head, and she said, "Follow me, please."

I knocked on the door, and a very firm, loud voice said, "Come in." I was amazed at the way she looked. She was tall, with short, blondish-gray hair, and she was wearing designer jeans, and a John Lennon t-shirt. At first, I thought I'd walked into the wrong office.

She noticed my confusion and came to my rescue fast. "Okay Keven, you've got five minutes, so start talking, I do have a meeting in about a half hour, so let's get it over with. Why are you so desperate to talk to me?"

"First of all, thank you for letting me see you. You don't know me, and I don't know you, but I ..." There was a knock on the door.

"Not now, I'm busy, come back in five minutes."

But the knock was even louder a second time. Mrs. Geyer got a bit mad and said, "Come in."

"Mrs. Geyer, I'm sorry, but I ..."

Then our eyes met.

"You, what are you doing here? Why are you here?"

"You never called me, and I was so disappointed, and I wanted to see you very badly, but I guess you didn't care about me as much as I did about you. Why didn't you call me? I was so sure you liked me, but maybe your friend Megen is more important than me."

"She is important to me, but the reason I haven't called you is I lost the phone number, and since you never told me your last name, I had no idea how to get in contact with you."

"Okay you two—this is my office, and I'm standing right here, can anyone tell me what is going on?"

I was still staring at Ramona. "You could have done just like me. I went to town to find out who rented your cabin, I mean the name, and that's how I got here, and voila surprise. Mrs. Geyer, I came here looking for your daughter and look who popped up. She's right here, Ramona."

"Slow down, Keven. Ramona is not my daughter, she works here, and she is my right hand and best worker."

Ramona's face lit up. "I'm all that to you? You never said that before. Thank you, Mrs. Geyer, I love working with you."

"Boy, this is too much for me. Mrs. Geyer I'm so sorry to act like a lost kid, but this my happiest day. I found Ramona., thanks to you and your name. Now I'll ask you if Ramona can take a fifteen minute break. I'd like to talk to her more privately, no offense to you Mrs. Geyer."

"None taken. Go now, and Ramona I'll speak to you later."

"Mrs. Geyer, it was my pleasure to meet you and I sure hope to see you again shortly."

"Keven, I was in the middle of something at work when I came to see Mrs. Geyer, and I do have to go back, but I'll tell you what. Write down my number and my address, and we can go out tonight and talk without anyone looking at us. I think that's best. Now that you know my phone number, you can call me anytime. I do live with my parents, though, so please don't call late. I really have to go, talk to you tonight."

"Ramona, are you sure that you'd like to see me? I don't want to force you to do anything, but I want you to know, I've been thinking about you all this time and to lose you now would be a disaster for me. So please be honest with me."

Keven, if I wasn't being frank with you, I wouldn't have given you my home number and let me tell you this; you're the first man that has my phone number, so that should tell you something. Don't worry, I have been thinking of you as well. I've got to go."

Driving home, I had lots of time to think about Ramona. I had fallen in love with that girl, although if I told her that, she might laugh. It sounds so corny, but it's true. At twenty-six years old, this had never happened to me before—to fall in love with someone at first sight. There was something about her that drew me close to her, and I had to find out what it was. Now at least I knew where she worked, and soon I'd know where she lived. It was going to be our first date, so I had no idea of what to bring her or where I should take her. I didn't know anything about her, so I was entirely in a hole. Maybe we could go to a small restaurant and that way we could have dinner and try to get to know each other. I know that first dates are the worst, but I knew Ramona was a sweet person, and she wouldn't care where we went. Just in case I'd call her about six o'clock, she was probably home by then.

....

Ramona:

I was excited about Keven; I liked him the first day we met and was upset that I'd lost his phone number, but not anymore. I was miles away in my thoughts when a pager announced my name; Mrs. Geyer needed me right away. I wondered if Mrs.Geyer was mad at me because of Keven—but I was wrong.

She gave a light knock on the door and walked right in. Mrs. Geyer was standing and looking out through the window. With a soft tone, she told me to sit. "Okay Ramona, start talking. Who is Keven and what do you know about him? To me, he looks like a bee that lost his best flower; he is so confused when he's looking at you. What in the world did you do that he's so crazy about you? He probably would have turned Toronto upside down till he found you. Maybe you're lucky to have someone like him or maybe not, so start talking."

"Mrs. Geyer there isn't much to tell. On Sunday morning I got up, and I went down to the lake to see if I could catch some fish…Yes, I love fishing, and don't laugh. And then I heard a boat coming towards me and there he was, standing like a saint. We looked at each other, and that's how it all started. He wanted to take us to dinner in town, or for a boat ride, but Megen brushed him off. I could tell he didn't like her, but I wasn't going to leave her there all by herself, so I told him maybe some other time. He gave me his phone number to call him as soon as I got home, but I lost it. To tell you the truth, I did like him right away. He was so sweet, not a pushy guy at all, and he didn't want to come between Megen and me."

"Speaking of Megen, what's with you and her?" asked Mrs. Geyer. "Many times I have seen the looks that you give each other! Is Megen your friend or is she your girlfriend? Which is it? I've never seen you going out with guys, so you have some explaining to do. Are you and Megen a pair, or are you interested in Keven? Which is it? Ramona, you can't play with people's hearts and minds. If you and Megen are so close then be honest with Keven and tell him. If not, then take my advice and go for it. Keven looks like a very decent young man. I'm not your mother, but I do care for you Ramona and either way I wouldn't like to see you hurt."

"I don't understand why people that think something is going on between Megan and me. We're just beautiful friends, and I mean superb. We know everything about each other, and we tell each other everything. Maybe she is more protective of me than others, but there's a reason for that. Yes, we love each other but in our own ways. Mrs. Geyer, Megen knows what happened to me a long time ago. I've only told some people, and I believe that it's about time that I tell you. Maybe this will shock you, but don't interrupt me, just listen and then you can see why Megen is so close to me, and me to her."

And then I told her my whole sad history, finishing by saying, "The memory will always be with me, but the images are getting a little bit better, thanks to Megen. Every time I'm sad or about to cry, she always reminds me that was before, and I'm safe now."

"Ramona, how come you told all that to Megen but never thought of saying it to me. I always knew that there was something sorrowful holding you; your eyes are always ready to cry. So now I know, and I'm so sorry that all that happened to you. If there is anything I can do anytime, please Ramona, just come to me. I care about you a lot.

So then are you going to see Keven? I think you should; he sounds very sweet young man, and I can tell that he cares about you. That kind of love is hard to find. Just take your time to get to know each other and then time will take care of the rest. Try not to think too much about the past, otherwise you'll end up alone, and that's not a whole lot of fun. You see Ramona, I'm married, but we don't have any children, and that is one thing that I'll always regret. I have everything, but my heart is empty. And do you want to know something else? Many-many-many times I've often wished that you were my daughter. There's something about you that draws people to you, but you don't see it. Take a chance with Keven, and I'm sorry if I said something wrong about

Megen. I think she's a one of a kind to help you like that. Now, it's Friday so go home early, and I'll see you on Monday, hopefully with a big smile."

"Thank you, Mrs. Geyer, and I wish you were my mother too, sometimes."

As soon as I get home I have to tell my aunt about Keven. There's not much to say, but I'd just like her to know that I've met someone that I like. She knows that most of my male friends never last a week, but I'm so sure that this time is different.

....

"Aunt Vesna, I'm home. Do you have a minute? I'd like to talk to you about something."

"Okay Ramona, is that something Keven?"

"What are you talking about? How do you know Keven? Please don't tell me he came looking for me."

"Don't worry, nothing like that, but he did call you, and he will call you back about six, that's what he said. So, now will you tell me who Keven is? It was so funny when he called. My, my, I said three times, 'Who is there?' and I almost hung up. He was so nervous, he sounded ridiculous. Are you going out with him, or is he just a friend from work?"

"He's not from work. I met Keven right after my birthday party on that Sunday. I lost his phone number, and in the meantime he was waiting for me to call, so when I didn't, he found out where I worked and so now we're going out. Maybe I can tell you more about Keven when I know more."

And right on time at six p.m. the phone rang. I wanted to play it cool, so I told my aunt to pick it up, and yes it was Keven.

After that phone call, Keven and I were like one person. Deep down in my heart I knew I'd found happiness. Keven picked me up right at seven p.m. as we agreed. Neither one of us had a car, so we met on Yonge Street, where there was a small cafe. We sat there and it must have been about at least twenty minutes before one of us started to talk. We didn't need to speak, looking at each other was good enough, but I spoke first.

"So, does Keven has a last name and what does Keven do for a living?"

He laughed, and with a sparkle in his eyes he said. "For you Ramona, I'll answer all you need to know, but I'm so dying to find out more about you. For starters yes, my name is Keven Show, and I just turned twenty-six on July 15th.

Right now, I'm finishing my pilot training with Air Canada, and later down the road I'd like to fly big planes for them. I'm stationed at the airport where the training is, and I live there and train every day. And if everything goes well, I should be a full-time pilot on May 1st of 1969. I come from a small town not too far from North Bay; that's way up north. My father owns a little four-engine airplane; that's what started me liking to fly. I was fourteen years old when I flew my first plane with my dad. Right now, my father is taking care of everything, and my plan is way – way- long in the future to go home and take over my father's business. I'd like to buy one more plane that can carry about six people because business in summer is magnificent. All that is my plan, but we all know plans can change, and maybe mine will change as well. I'm telling you all this, so you know where you stand. I might go home sooner, or I might not go at all; time will take care of that, and all I have to do is wait and see. Flying with Air Canada will give me a chance to save some money and more experience in flying bigger planes.

"As for personal goals, I'll be honest with you. I haven't meet a girl that I could settle down with…well not yet. I love to go to movies and listen to folk music, someone like Bob Dylan, Donovan, Cat Stevens, some rock groups—that's just about it. I don't have a brother or sister; it's just me, Mom and my dad. So I hope that I've given you some information about me, and if I missed something just ask. Ramona I have nothing to hide, and sure hope that you like what you heard. Now I'm dying to find out what country you came from. My first impression was that you're from Quebec, but then your name is most unusual, I have never heard it before, and the way you talk is so interesting. I know my mother will love you."

"Hold on Keven, your mom? You don't know me at all, and right now you said your mom would like me. How did that come about? You, yourself don't know me, so take your time with your parents. My life is not as simple as yours, as a matter of fact, my life has been complicated since I was born, but I won't go into all the details now. That will come later. Right now all you need to know is that I came from Eastern Europe, a small country in the Balkans, which is called Yugoslavia. I have been in Canada since 1963. I don't have a brother or sister either, I'm on my own and it has been like that as long as I can remember. I finished high school in Toronto, but my goal was always to get a job. Not having much of anything, all I wanted was to work. So at seventeen I got a job working with Mrs. Geyer, and have never looked for another job because Mrs.

Geyer took me in like I was her daughter. Why I don't know, and I don't care. I love my job, and one day I'll be manager of the warehouse, because I like to organize things. I love working hard, and I'm not afraid to try a new challenge. I don't have a boyfriend, and I never went on more than a simple date; nothing serious. Like you, I also never met anyone that I liked before, but then I'm only twenty-one, and I think I have lots of time. I love rock music. My favourites are the Beatles, DC5, the Animals, Jefferson Airplane, and like you, I like Donovan and some more. And most important, I love fishing, and I love to play tennis. Right now I'm playing tennis at the Centennial Club, and I know I'm excellent at it, but I sometimes find it tedious there, because of all those rich people. The only reason they accepted me in their club was because of Mrs.Geyer, and they play like big, spoiled kids. But I can fish all day, and that's not annoying for me as it is for some of my friends, who won't even go with me. But we all have something strange, right?"

"Keven, look what time it is. I think they'd like to close the café. Let's go for a walk, but I have to get up a bit early. I'm going to buy a car tomorrow."

"Wow, you must be rich! Or you're not telling me everything about yourself… like you haven't said anything about your parents. You told me you've been on your own all your life. What do you mean by that?"

"I told you my life is very complicated, not as simple as yours. I'll tell you everything but not in one day. Let's get to know each other before I go too deeply inside of my life. And as for my parents, well I don't have any. The ones I live with are my aunt and uncle, and as I said, it's a long story that I'll tell you later. And by the way, I'm not rich, I just work hard to get what I want. For my twenty-first birthday, my aunt and uncle gave me $2,000, and Mrs.Geyer gave me $500, so that's how I can buy a car. I need a car to go places, and for fishing, because I'm tired of asking people to take us, even though my aunt and uncle love fishing as well. Me having a car will work out just fine. So now you know some things, and being rich is not my goal. There are things I'd like to have, but in good time. I have lots of patience. If I have the money, I get what I like, if not I'll wait."

"Ramona, I'm glad that you're so amazingly organized, but what happened to your parents? If you don't like to talk about it then I understand. Maybe one day you'll tell me."

"Keven, to discuss my parents is a long and painful story. I'd prefer to speak about that some other time. I'm not saying I won't tell you, but not just now. Hope you understand."

"Okay then, let's change the subject. What kind of car are you buying, and would you like me to come and help you with the decision? I know a lot about cars, and maybe I can be of some help."

"Well, thanks, but I'm going with my uncle and aunt, and one of my uncle's friends is driving us, so it's not necessary, but thank you. I'm buying a Pontiac Laurentian, a nice big car, dark blue. I can't wait till tomorrow; I'm so excited about it."

"It looks like that's bad news for me. Are you probably going to go fishing all the time with your folks?"

"Yes I probably will, but that doesn't mean you can't come, and no I'll be home sometimes. Look at it this way; summer is very short, and we all have to enjoy it as much as we can, and you and I will go places, just the two of us. That is if everything works out okay."

"That sounds good to me, and now, let me take you home."

"Thanks Keven, I had a good time and was my pleasure to get to know you at least a little bit. As far as I know, getting to know someone takes time, and our relationship is starting on the right foot…not sure if this how you say that in English."

"I love your English. I love the way you pronounce the words, and if you need to know anything that you're not sure of just ask me. English-speaking people don't know how hard it is for you; you know how to speak more than one language, so don't be ashamed about saying it wrong. I'm Canadian, and trust me I need help in my spelling all the time. I do understand, and I do love you."

"What did you just say?"

"Are you questioning me about my choice of words? I did say I love you, and that is true. I loved you, Ramona, from the first day I saw you."

"Keven please. We don't know each other that well, and for you to say I love you, those are special words, and I have never used them unless I meant it."

"But Ramona, I do mean it."

"Keven, I like you a lot, but to love you I need time to know you better, so let's give us a chance and we'll see what happens in the coming days, but for now, I've got to get home."

"All right then, let's go. One more thing…can you call me tomorrow? I'd love to hear about your car and perhaps we can meet later on, and go to a movie or what ever you like."

"That sounds fine. Let's go this way, our apartment is right there and you see that building over there? That's where my best friend Megen lives."

"Oh yes, Megen. How is she these days? Have you told her about me?"

"No, not yet, but I will. She's going to flip."

"Why would she flip? Ramona, there's nothing going on between you and Megen is there? Anything I have to worry about?"

"Keven, don't be silly, we're just best friends, that's all. Nothing for you to worry about. I like you, and you can be sure it's only you, and now here we are. I'll call you as soon as I can tomorrow. Keven, I had a real good time."

"Good night and see you later."

And with that, I almost ran inside. I didn't want Keven to kiss me or anything like that on our first date. I could tell he was almost ready to say something or even to give me a hug. I sure hoped he wouldn't be mad at me for running in so fast, but one day I'd tell Keven everything about me…one day!

CHAPTER 26

KEVEN AND I became just like best friends. We had been going out almost two months, and I told him it was time that he met my aunt and uncle. My aunt had suspected that I had someone, but never asked me any questions, She was so careful about my personal life, and she always said, "You have one life, and you have to protect that life and cherish it as much as you can. Be true to yourself and others, and you will go a long way."

Keven was a bit nervous, but out of the blue I kissed him and told him that I loved him more than I could explain. He was almost in shock. That was the first time we kissed after two months' dating. He looked at me and gave me a big hug and this time I let him kiss me. That moment we were one, and both of us knew. He whispered in my ear, "I loved you the moment I saw you on the lake that day, and I'll never stop and will love you forever."

After meeting my folks, Keven was more often at my place for dinner and many times we went fishing, but it was getting cold, and I told him that the fishery was out for now. He was surprised, because he thought that I'd do ice fishing as well, but I said I liked to give the fish a break. I was joking, but ice fishing was not my cup of tea. By now it was almost Christmas, and Keven wanted me to go with him to meet his parents and stay there for the Christmas holidays and New Year.

Meeting his parents was too early for me. We had known each other only three months, and I needed more time to figure out what I wanted. I knew I loved Keven, but there was something deep inside me pulling me away, way back to my days in the orphan village. Mr. Tekish was constantly on my mind. Every time I kissed Keven and every time I tried to let him touch me, I froze. I knew I needed more time to find out if Keven was what I wanted or if it was all in my head. But at the same time, I didn't want to lose him. Keven was someone that I'd been waiting for all my life. He was so kind, decent, and understanding, but I didn't know for how long he would be like that, and that worried me sometimes.

I told Keven perhaps I could come in the spring, like for Mother's Day, because by then we would know each other over seven months, and I could be sure that I'd know if Keven was right for me or not. And you never knew...he could change, so I decided to wait until spring. He was heartbroken for a while, but like always he gave in.

Christmas was just around the corner, and Keven was getting ready to go home for the holidays. I was a bit sad, not having him with me at the holidays, but I told myself if Keven was right for me, we would spend many many holidays together, so I tried not to show him that I was sad. Keven didn't have a car, so I took him to the bus station, and to my surprise, I started to cry. I just wanted him to stay with me. I knew that was selfish but I loved him and I knew life without Keven was not meant to be for me. He asked me if I wanted him to stay, but if I said yes that would not be fair to him. He hadn't seen his parents for a long time, and he had asked me to go with him, so to be strong I just said, "No, just make sure you come back."

I heard the bus driver say, "Five minutes, all aboard please."

Before he jumped on the bus, Keven kissed me and gave me a small present, and I gave him my little box. As we were exchanging gifts, the bus driver yelled, "Let's go," and then he was gone.

I was standing there with tears in my eyes, wondering why I didn't go with him. Through the window, he saw me standing there, and our eyes met for a second. I saw a small tear fall out of his sad eyes, but as the bus was leaving, I just waved goodbye and ran to my car so that no one could see me crying. I held his little present in my hand and wondered what it was. In a split second, I was going to open it, but I stopped.

After the bus left, I went straight home. My aunt noticed that I was crying and gave me a shoulder to lean on saying, "He'll be back very soon, please don't cry, Ramona." I knew she liked him as well. I took his present and left it under the tree, and I went to my room.

Knowing that Keven wouldn't call me until late, I decided to see what Megan was up to and what her plans were for the holidays. I called her, but she wasn't home. Her mother said that she was spending Christmas and New Year's with her friend in Montreal. "But Megen is going to come and see you before she's gone," she told me. "I think she'll be home about eight p.m. I'll tell her you called, or maybe she'll come to see you before she comes home, because she's leaving very early, so I presume she'll come home to get some rest."

I thanked her and went to see if supper was ready. I always liked Megen's mom. She was one of a kind, and Megen loved her so dearly, which made me so sad that I couldn't have that with my mother. But I thought I might have it with Keven now.

Just before nine, Megen came rushing in. "Hey girl, what's up? I don't have much time—got to get up about three a.m. I'm going to Montreal with some friends and just came to see what your and Keven's plans are."

"I don't have any big plans. Keven is gone home for Christmas but will be back for New Year's Eve, so you and I could have some fun over Christmas, but I guess you have other plans, which I didn't know."

"How come you didn't go with Keven, is something wrong? Have you two had your first fight?"

"No, nothing like that. I'm just not ready to meet Keven's parents. I think it's too early, perhaps next year. Keven was sad but promised to come for New Year's Eve.

Tell you what. Why don't you come with us, and I'll make sure you get back for New Year's Eve!"

"Go to Montreal, I don't think so. You just go ahead and have fun, and listen I have a little something for you, nothing special. So go and have a good Christmas holiday and I'll see you... well, next year. Come here you silly girl, give me a kiss and go home and straight to bed."

Megen and I gave each other big hug. We both knew that we had grown up, so 'I love you' words were left behind. I'd always love Megen, but not in the way she wanted me to love her. Now that I was with Keven she had backed down, and I kind of missed it. After Megen left was almost midnight, so I thought Keven must have arrived. I didn't want him to call me too late, so I called him. At the first ring, Keven answered.

"Hi Ramona, I just got in about ten minutes ago, and I knew you were going to call, so I sat right beside the telephone, and my dad made fun of me, but I don't care. How are you? I miss you already. I have a lot to do here, my dad needs some help over Christmas, lots of people like to fly in a small plane. So I'll help him but will be back on the 28th of December so that we can be together. Are you getting together with Megen?"

"No, I'm staying home. Megen is going to Montreal. Mind you, she asked me to go with her, but no, I like to stay home, and at least I can talk to you at night or whenever you grab a minute."

"Thanks you made my day. If you went with Megen, I know I would go nuts, but you don't have to stay home because of me; I can trust you Ramona. I love you and that's good enough for me, but I do respect you for staying home, made me feel good."

"Listen, I have to you let you go now. It's very late. Have some rest and we'll talk soon. Just said hello to your folks for me. Love you Kev."

"Ramona, did you just call me Kev? You never said that before."

"That's my pet name for you; you're my Kev."

"So now I have to think a pet name for you, let me see, AAAA AAAA AAAA, how about my Cherrypie?"

"Cherrypie? Where did you get that?"

"Well your name is unyielding, and I can't see it for me as a pet name, but I love cherry pie, so just between us, you are now my cherry pie."

"You're crazy, make sure you call me that only when we're alone, and when you get back I'll give you a cherry pie. Listen it's getting very late, talk to you tomorrow or whenever you grab a minute. Stay safe. Love you."

"Love you too."

Christmas came and went. I wasn't too religious, and to me Christmas was just another day off, but because my aunt and uncle were Catholics, I respected Christmas, and we had a real good time. I gave my aunt a gorgeous new handbag, and to my uncle a very soft shawl. From them, I got a new Beatles record, which I was surprised about because my uncle called them four long-hair scorpions—why I don't know. In getting me a brand new album they must have asked Megen to get it for them, which I loved. And then I took my small box and went to my room. I wanted to be alone when I opened Keven's present.

My aunt saw me and followed me. "Ramona, can I see what you're hiding there? I saw you carrying a tiny box. Is it from Keven? You know that good things come in small boxes."

"Aunty, it isn't what you think it is. I know because we're not getting married until about two or three years from now, and I told him to save the money for later."

"So OKAY then, let's see."

I was nervous, like my aunt that it was a ring, but if it was, I would be disappointed. I wanted him to give me a ring personally, not in a box like this, so I was hoping it was something else. And to my relief, it was a chain with a half-heart. The small note said, "Please look for the other half. When you find it you have found your soulmate." My heart almost stopped. I turned pale as a ghost because I had given Keven the same present. Is that strange or what?

I heard my aunt asking me if I was all right. It took me a few seconds to get back. I just couldn't believe that we gave each other the same present. I couldn't wait for Keven to call me. This was very strange, or maybe it was meant to be. I still couldn't believe it. After all this excitement I went to my room.

A moment later the phone rang, and I knew it was Keven. Before he said anything, I rushed to say, "Kev, I love your present."

"Thank you, love, but I'm not Kev and who is Kev?"

Ah! Megan, you're nuts. Megen, listen to this. Kev is Keven, and don't tell me you didn't guess that. Anyway I gave Keven a chain with a half a heart for a present, and you know what? He gave me the same thing. How strange is that?"

"Yeah girl, that is something. Have you heard from Keven yet?"

"No, when you called I thought it was him, and by the way how come your calling me at this time? Are you all right Meg?"

"Yes, I'm okay I just missed you. Ramona. This girl that I came to Montreal with is very weird in some ways and looking at her made me wish that you were with me."

"Megen, please stop. I think you've had too much to drink. You know that you and I are always friends and only friends. Please Megen, calm down, and I'll talk to you tomorrow. Or call me later. Please Megan, don't do this to me. I love Keven, and you're my best friend, so find that girl and give her a big kiss and you'll be alright."

"Sorry Ramona, you're right, I did have too much to drink. I'll call you tomorrow."

As soon as I hung up, the phone rang, and I was hoping that this time it was Keven. My heart melted when I heard him saying, "Mery Christmas, Cherrypie, and I'm dying to ask you, did you follow me when I was buying you a present? Otherwise, how on earth did you give me the same necklace as the one I got you? That is a strange thing... and that note. Well, all we have to do now is connect those two hearts, and we're going to be one forever."

"Ah! You silly monkey, I was not following you, that is just plain old faith, and thank you, I just love it."

"So now I'm a monkey, OKAY. This is a war now, I have to think of the new name for you, but for now you're just my Ramona. We have lots of snow up here, and I'm going to be quite busy helping my dad, so if you don't hear from me in a day or so, don't worry, I'll call you as soon as I can. I tried to call you earlier but the phone was busy, I bet you were talking with Megen."

"Yes, good guess. Megen went to Montreal and it looks like it was a mistake, so she needed a friend to talk to and you know we're best friends. But now I'll let you go, and I'll speak to you later. Please take care of yourself up there."

"Don't worry Ramona, when I'm on a plane it's as if I'm in yours arms from now on. Bye for now, love you."

A few days passed by and nothing from Keven, and then finally on December 29th he called. He was very busy and would arrive back on the bus on December 30th at six p.m. I told him that I would pick him up, and he was happy. He said he couldn't wait to see me, and that he was very loony without me.

The weather was a little bit harsh, but I drove slowly. I had told my aunt that I would be staying at Keven's for a few days, and if she needed anything to call. I knew she wasn't too keen on that, but hey, I was twenty-one now, and it was time for me to make my own decisions.

As the passengers were coming out, it seemed like forever, and finally, there was my Kev. When I saw his face, I knew that I would never let him go, except when he got the job with Air Canada, but that was different. Looking at him standing there, tall and handsome, I knew I loved that man, and the way he looked at me I was sure we would be together all our lives. As soon we got to his bachelor apartment, we could not stop talking and kissing.

I told him that I was staying until next year, which meant about two or three days. He was happy to hear that, and at the same time, he looked like he was worrying abut something.

....

Keven:

I loved that Ramona was going to stay with me but I kept remembering Mrs. Geyer's words. "Be extra gentle because Ramona has a sad background." Ramona hasn't told me about it yet, and we haven't done anything except kiss, and now if she's willing to stay for a few days, I'm not sure how I should handle if it comes to love making. I love Ramona, and I'm going to be as gentle as possible and hope that she might open up to me about her past. The apartment is small but good enough for now. Once I get a full-time job with Air Canada, I'm moving to a one-bedroom, and then we can make a future for us, but for the next five months, this is it. Ramona always likes coming and cleaning up my mess, and we laugh that if we ever get married that I'll have to learn to be a little more decent or neat.

But that was a long way from today—now I had to figure out how I was going to handle these two days. Once I unpacked and she put some of her stuff in the bathroom, we began to relax. It was the first time that Ramona was staying at my place more than a couple of hours or so. Most of the time we would just go out or to her apartment, and then we'd go our separate ways, but this was different. I had some beer in the fridge and we both enjoyed each other's company. As I was going to turn on the TV, Ramona asked me to come and sit beside her. Then I got scared, maybe she was leaving me, but that couldn't be. Then I remembered Mrs. Geyer's words again. I did get nervous because I had no idea what was so wrong in her past that she was hiding it, from me at least. Playing cool I just laughed and said, "What's up cherry pie? You look so serious. You're not sick or anything, are you? What's wrong? Was that beer sour? Talk to me."

"No to all your questions, but please sit right beside me. I have to talk to you about something that has been long overdue. Kevin, the situation between you and me is very emotional for me. I love you more than I love anyone on this earth, but I have not been totally honest with you. I don't know if you've noticed or not, but so far all we've done is kiss, and that's as far I let you go, so now I would like to tell you the reason why."

"Ramona."

"Keven stop. I'm going to tell you this now, and only now and never again. So, please listen to me carefully and then you can tell me how you feel about me, but just listen to the whole story and please don't interrupt me, I don't know if I'll ever have the courage to tell you this again."

And then she told me the whole terrible story of her childhood.

"Keven, it's all up to you," she concluded. "I love you, and if you're not sure about me now, I won't be mad at you. We can stay friends and will take one day at a time."

"Ramona, that's a most sad and horrific story. I'm so sorry for what happened to you, but I'd like to let you know that as far as it goes for me, I love you, and what happened a long time ago we can work out together if you wish, or we can just close that chapter of your life, and we can start a new one. I'll help you all the way, and I promise you I'm going to be always available to you if you need to talk about it more. I love you Ramona, and give me a chance to prove it to you. Right now I'm not ready for us to get married, but that will come soon. I'd like you to wait for me, and you and I can make our life as happy as can be. Now get over here my cherry pie, and let's sit together for a while and just be together."

Looking at her I could tell she had relaxed a bit, and then I remembered Mrs. Geyer's words. "Be very gentle with her, and she'll open up to you. Ramona loves you, and now it's your turn to take care of her. If you're not serious about her, let her go now, or be patient with her and you will receive her love in return. Trust me on that. I've known Ramona since she was seventeen, and Keven, if you are ever going to hurt her, trust me, you will be answering to me."

Mrs. Geyer's words were so real. I'd show her that I wouldn't hurt Ramona, and in a year or two, we would be getting married.

After that, we went to bed. It was the first time she'd stayed over in my apartment and now it was our first time in my bed together. I felt like a kid that was hiding something from his parents. It felt good, but a bit scary for me because of her past. Ramona had never slept with anyone before, and I could feel her whole body shaking. She put her head on my chest and in about five or ten minutes she was asleep. I watched her for a while, and then I dozed off with Ramona beside me, my true love. And that's how the two of us became one.

I woke up very early and was making coffee when I saw Ramona getting up. I'm sure that she was confused about where she was. Once she saw me, everything went back to normal. We planned our first New Year's Eve together and hoped to have many many more.

The weather was getting bad, and Ramona hated driving in snow, so I went shopping on my own. When I came back, my place was so clean and neat I almost thought that I'd walked into the wrong apartment. She made supper, and after that, we went downtown for a walk, and about 11:30 we went home. I wanted to be with only her at midnight—only Ramona and me. I think she wanted the same thing, and as soon as we got home she got very comfortable, and we opened a bottle of wine, and just before twelve, we toasted to a Happy New 1970 Year to ourselves

CHAPTER 27

Ramona:
Keven and I were jubilant together; we had let time pass us by. New Year's Day we practically spent in bed. I think we were getting to know each other, and I felt healthy and safe in Keven's arms. From that day I often came and stayed at Keven's place, but I didn't want to move in, and he was okay with that.

As January began, so did reality. I went back to work, and Keven had only four more months of training left until he got his pilot license.

I called Mrs. Geyer, who always spent winter in Florida. Work was slow in the winter for her. She was happy to hear from me, and I told her about Keven and me. Before I had a chance to say anything else, she came right out and asked me if I'd slept with him. If only she could have seen my face through the telephone, she would have seen a smile on it. With a small voice, I said, "Yes, and it was nothing like I ever experienced." I knew she was happy for me, and I thanked her for her Christmas presents and said I hoped to see her soon. Mrs. Geyer was like the mother I never had. I felt so free to tell her everything; she understood me more than anyone I knew.

Mrs. Geyer also said that Keven had talked to her and wanted to know why I was so afraid of him if he touched me more than I wanted. She never told him why, only to be patient and that he would find out for himself, and that's how it happened. Keven never said anything about talking to Mrs. Geyer, so I never told him I knew. Some little secrets are okay, but I didn't want any more secrets at all. I loved him, and I'd never lied to him before and I never would in the future.

We both worked hard, and Keven studied very hard. His training was very challenging, but he wanted to finish so badly, because he wanted to start working full time and make money. That part I understood, so I never pushed him to go out, or for us to go somewhere. I wanted him to do well on his last writing test and flying test.

We spent winter nice and quietly, and not soon enough spring came. His last day of training was on April 18th and if he passed, he'd get his pilot license in May. I knew he'd do well.

We made plans that we would go to his parents' house on Mother's Day so that I could meet them, and by then Keven would have finished with his training, and that is how it happened. He was second in his class, and Air Canada offered him a full-time job, flying in Canada only for two years and after that, he'd be flying internationally. He was so happy; I'll never forget that day. Keven came to my place, and we went to a small cafe where he asked me to marry him. He didn't have the money to buy me a big ring, but he knew I never cared about the fancy jewellry. I said yes. That night we made love, and we were so happy. He was full of plans, but I told him to slow down. We'd known each other only eight months, and we needed to get to know each other more, but he said he knew all he needed to know and all he wanted was for us to be together. Little did he know that was all I wanted as well.

On May 18th, we went to his parents' house. It took us a five-hour to drive, which I liked. I had never seen that part of Canada and it was so beautiful—so many small lakes and trees everywhere, it was so new to me. Because it was Mother's Day, I had bought a beautiful scarf for his mother. I was very nervous, but Keven was always beside me, and that was a big help. His parents were very friendly folks, not like some I knew in the city; they were just plain country, friendly people and after a while, I felt comfortable. As we walked in, his father came first, and right away I could tell Keven looked like him. His mother was a real country lady, in an apron and a lovely blouse, pale blue like her eyes, which matched Keven's. I gave them both a hug and a kiss, and I think they were surprised at that, because in Canada you don't do that, but I did it out of respect. It was a bit quiet for a while until his father spoke, and from then on everything was just fine. Keven told his father and mother that we were engaged and planning to get married in about two years. He was starting to work for Air Canada on June first, and if everything went right, he would like to come home and help his father with the flying business. His father was so happy about that news, and his mother was crying, but they were happy tears.

After that they wanted to know a bit more about me and were surprised that my English was not that bad after being in Canada only five years. I promised that I'd take more English classes later on, and I just loved them. I'd never had a family like Keven's folks, and I thought I could live in this part of the country. Keven and his father went to look at a small airplane that they had, and it sounded like it needed some work. Keven asked me if I wouldn't mind staying for a couple more days, but that meant I'd have to call Mrs. Geyer and let her know. After all, I had a full-time job, and I didn't want to lose it. Even though Mrs. Geyer liked me, we had some higher bosses above us.

Mrs. Geyer was surprised that I liked that part of the country; she always looked at me as a city kid, but she said to just enjoy myself and that she'd see me later. I thanked her and went to help Keven's mom to prepare supper. I noticed that Keven's father looked tired after they came back from their short trip up north. I asked Keven to look into this, but he said his father was just fine, so I ignored my suspicions.

Spending lot of time with his mother made us a bit closer. I told her about my background and my life in the orphan village, but I didn't say anything about my harassment by the owner of the orphan village. I left that out because that was between Keven and me. She told me that Keven had a girlfriend a long time ago, but she never liked the place where Keven wanted to live, so they went their separate ways, and he never came out with any other girls until he met me.

I was glad she trusted me and told me all that, but she also wanted those words to stay between her and me, so I promised I wouldn't mention anything to Keven.

Four days passed by very quickly. I had to go back to work, and Keven was looking for a new place to stay.

As we said goodbyes to both of them, I noticed his father give Keven something in his hand, but Keven refused it. His mother stepped in, kissing him, and she said,

"Keven this is not much, but enough for now, just to help you get started. Find a new place to live and be happy my son. You're all we have, and we love you so much.

We are family and hope soon to be a big family with Ramona in our house."

I was very moved by that and finally Keven took the money and off we went.

I gave her a big kiss, and she whispered in my ear, "Ramona, look after my boy, we both love you. Don't forget to come back soon."

His father gave me a big smile, said aloud, "You are one of us," and gave me a fatherly kiss. I felt strange because no man before had done that unless he was after my body. This was so different, and I could tell I was blushing.

Keven tried to make me blush even more when he said, "Hey Dad, hands off, that's my girl," and we all laughed.

We had a long ride home, so we waved goodbye and off we went. It was still very early in the morning and the weather for May was excellent. All over the province you saw green grass coming up and the trees starting to bloom. It was like a picture postcard. As we drove, Keven was a bit quiet for a while and then out of the blue, he said.

"Ramona, I'm sorry for taking you to my house. I have a feeling you didn't like them. You were so quiet most of the time, but hey, as long as we're okay with each other, parents will come later. I love you and I don't want to lose you, not now or ever."

"Keven, how can you say that? I liked your mom and dad; I felt warm and happy there. It was a good home, full of honesty and love. Your mother is so sweet and full of love. She has the kind of a face you'd like to see on every mother, far from my mom, which I'll tell you about one of this days. As for your father, I'll need some more time to know him, and you know why, but other than that I love spending time with them, and I'm looking forward to living there in the future. So if I'm a bit quiet, you'll have to understand. I never had a family, or a mother and father that cared for me, so when I see thow they look at you, I'm so happy for you, and I love you and sure hope that one day we can raise our children with your mom and dad."

"Now you made my day, Ramona. No wonder why I love you. Yes, one more thing. You're right about my father. My mother told me that he wasn't feeling well last week, and he is too stubborn to go to a doctor, so I think I'll be going home at least twice a month, and if you like, you can come as well. I'm little worried about him, but Mom will call me if anything goes bad. So I'm sorry for telling you not to worry before, but you were right.

"So let's go back for now and we'll see what we can do to find me a beautiful apartment. That's the agenda for tomorrow. I know you have to go back to work, so I'll hunt for a good place on my own and surprise you. Are you okay with that?"

"Sounds good to me."

I must have dozed off when I heard Keven is calling me. "Hey, sleepy head, do you want something? There's a gas station, and we need some gas, and I need a coffee."

"No, Keven, I'm okay, but you can get me a bottle of water, thanks."

We were almost home, and I told Keven he could keep the car for the rest of the week because looking for an apartment taking buses is not easy, and my work was not far from my place.

"You're the best; I'll try to find something soon."

For the rest of the way we drove pretty quietly, I think both of us had something on our minds, and in no time we arrived at about two p.m. I was tired and so was Keven. He came in for a coffee and went back to his place because I needed to rest to go to work the next day.

The month of May just flew away so fast and on June first, Keven got his first job flying to Montreal. He was so excited and I was too. I was so happy for him. Now he had a good job, a beautiful apartment, and that was all he wanted and for me to move in, but I told him that it was too soon, maybe in a few months or so. There was no need to rush, we'd be together after we got married. His flying schedule was all over the week; he would be flying all over Canada for a year and then he'd be considered for international, but for now he was happy to travel within Canada. That way he got home more often, and had time to go and see his parents. I went with him many times, but sometimes I stayed home and took my uncle and aunt fishing, so I was always busy and it was good for both of us.

Before I knew it, it was July and Keven's birthday was on the fifteenth. He was going to be twenty-seven. I had a surprise for him. I called his old friend Chuck and asked him to see if he could give us a cabin for a weekend. I knew Chuck was after me as well, but he got over it, so he called me and said everything was in order, and Keven didn't have any flight going on his list. July 15th was on a Thursday so I asked Mrs. Geyer if I could take two days of my holiday. She looked at me a bit puzzled, but in the end, she said yes. She also reminded me that the CNE was coming soon, and I'd have to commit myself to her. I knew that, and I promised I'd do my job as always. She smiled and told me to get going and have a real good time.

I got everything ready; a bottle of champagne, a small cake, and I found a shirt that he'd always wanted.(It was Janis Joplin, he liked her songs.) So a t-shirt and one 45" of Janis's single record, I thought that was a good present for Keven. He was never a big, big spender. He always tried to save money, and I knew why, so I never complained. I called him and asked him if he could be ready at five o'clock. I told him no questions asked, and like a good man he never did, but I think deep inside him, he knew I was planning something, so he just went along.

Like always he was right on time. As I drove, he smiled and right out of the blue he said, "Are we going up north where we met the first time?"

I knww he's figure it out, so I just said, "Yup, yes we are."

"But how did you manage to get a cabin? At this time of year almost everything is booked solid."

"Well, you see, I kept Chuck's phone number, and I called him early this year, and that's how I got it. I think Chuck was hoping that you and I were not a couple, but he was happy to see us together."

"Ramona, you are an amazing woman, and I love you so much."

"Hey I love you too."

When we finally arrived it was about eight p.m., I was a bit tired from driving that far, but when we walked inside my surprise was so great, that I forgot how tired I was. Chuck had made everything so clean and had a pizza in the oven and cold drinks and lots of ice. He had done far more than I expected. There was no phone in the cabin, but I was planning to go and thank him in person, in a day or so. We had the cabin for four days because I had to go back to work, and Keven had a flight to Vancouver, so we were planning to stay until Sunday afternoon.

As we settled down, I went to get some ice, and the cake was getting soft and needed to be in a fridge. I took two glasses, got the champagne open and raised a glass. "This weekend is for you my love, and only you. So Happy Birthday and I want you to know I loved you from the first day I saw you and I'll love you forever. Happy Birthday Keven."

We spent the night listening to records and eating pizza, and we finished a bottle of champagne. By then I think both of us were in quite a good mood, and that led to our time together, a time that was one of the best. Next morning or noon, we both had hangovers, but fresh wind and fresh air cleared all that up. I made breakfast, and after that, we took a boat ride, thanks to Chuck. We had so much fun, and I wanted the day to never end. After that we got to dress up and we went to a local restaurant, which was so good. Angela, the lady that owned the restaurant, remembered me and with a smile she put her thumbs up. I laughed and said thank you.

Once we got back to the cabin, we sat on the deck for a long time; there were no words.We both were far away in our beautiful thoughts. Next day we went to the marina to thank Chuck for all he'd done, and then we went on a boat ride again. The day just went by so fast, I felt drained, all I wanted was to go to bed and rest.

We nearly slept in and I jumped up and got ready, leaving Keven sleeping for another fifteen minutes. I packed all our belongings and made some coffee, then woke up Keven. His birthday had been lots of fun, and I knew he enjoyed it.

Going home, I let Keven do the driving. We went to his place first, and then I went to my place. I was glad that his birthday was a good one.

It was Sunday afternoon, and both my aunt and uncle were home. They never went anywhere. I was happy to see them. As usual my uncle was drunk, and my aunt was making supper. I sat with them for a while then went to my room. To my surprise, there was a letter from Megan. I hadn't seen her nearly two months. These days she was working on some photos of Vietnamese life in a war torn zone. It was a very dangerous job, but she loved it.

I was lonely without Megen. When Keven wasn't home I used to go out with her, but now she was so far away, and I missed her a lot. Her letter shocked me; she said that she'd met a guy that she was falling in love with. Megan was falling in love with a man! That was shocking news. Megan would never go out with guys, much less fall in love. I thought she must be high on something. As I kept reading, her words were unbelievable coming from Megen. She said she'd be coming home in late September, and in the meantime, she'd try to send me a picture of her new love. His name was Sam, and his background was Italian. He was born in Italy but was very young when he came to Canada. I was totally shocked—my Megen had fallen in love. To me that was a big thing. knowing what she went through with her father, and now she had finally realized that not all men were as bad as she thought. It made me feel good because Megen was my best friend and the only friend that I could tell everything to.

I read her letter again and laughed at myself. Finally, my Megen knew what love was… and with that, I went to bed.

For the next few weeks, I was very much dedicated to my job. We had The Ex show coming up, and a lot of orders for new books; the place was just one big roller coaster, but it was like that every year at that time. Keven went home to check up on his father and I had lent him my car. We saw each other as much we could but both of us had thints to do, so sometimes three days would pass by. But when we got together, we were happy. He told me that he was worried about his father. Summertime was so busy for him, and he wouldn't last long if he didn't slow down, That worried Keven a lot, and one evening he asked me if we could get married sooner and go to live with his parents.

It was so surprising and unexpected that I couldn't express myself. "What about the dream you had for flying Air Canada for two years, and saving money for a new four- seater plane? Why do you want to rush? We're both young, and we have a lots of time to get married."

Keven's worries were making him change his plans. I was starting to worry myself. He never asked me to make up my mind; he just left it up to me. I was determined to help Keven as much as possible and even get married and go to live with his parents, but I wondered if marrying him was a solution or a struggle not to let go of each other.

It was almost the end of summer when I carefully asked Keven what was happening with his father.

To my surprise, he said that his dad was better because he'd gotten some help. "A young man from England needed a part-time job as a pilot and came right on time when my father needed him, so for now, everything is okay, but for how long we don't know. But I decided to stay with Air Canada until next June, and then definitely I'm going home but not without you. Please, Ramona, tell me that I'm not going to lose you because of my plan change. I can't leave my father too long to take of business; I know I can handle it with him or just with his help. I have talked to a lot of people about getting my business going, and believe me, there is so much support available there. I'm going to take that chance, but only if you come with me. Please, Ramona, I know I'm asking too much, but we still have seven or eight months, and by then you can decide. I'll not stand in your way; you're free to do whatever you wish, I'll understand."

"Keven, why do we have to get married? We can go and live together until we're both ready—rushing like this causes a problem for both of us. I'm not saying I don't want to marry you, but let's wait a year or two. I don't mind going with you and being with you at your house. I might find a job in town or just stay home and help your mom."

"Ramona, my parents are old fashioned and us living there not beeing married, it might cause a problem. I don't see why we can't get married earlier than we planned. You don't have to worry about a job or anything like that. I'll support you and take care of you, and besides that twenty-seven is old, and I'd like to start a family. So what do you say?"

"Let's just sleep on it and see what we think in about a month or so. I don't want to rush into something, just because you'd like to go home and look after your father's health and business. I want us to get married for our love and what we have now. I want this relationship to stay right forever. I trust you on everything, and I know you, believe me, so let's just give it some time."

Strangely I started to question myself. Was I prepared to get married or was I just looking to belong to someone? Crying, I left, and I went home to think about it all. I wasn't sure what to do about all this. When I talked to my aunt, she said, "Go and marry him, Keven is a nice man."

"I don't want just a nice man. I want more but I can't understand what it is."

Next day at work I cautiously approached Mrs. Geyer and told her I needed to talk to her. She saw me looking lousy and she told me to go into her office for privacy. I think she sensed that I was searching for something, or something bad had happened.

"Out with it Ramona. Tell me what's going on. Are you sick, are you breaking up with Keven, or don't tell me you're pregnant?"

I shared my dilemma and finished with, "So you see I don't know what to do. I'm so confused and unclear and don't know how to handle all this. I need your advice."

"You need my help! Okay, let me ask you this. Do you love Keven? If you're not ready to get married now, why do you think you'll be ready in a year or two?"

"Yes, I do love Keven, and I don't know why I believe that in a year or two will be better to marry. I'm so confused."

"But why, why do you think that? What's wrong now? You're both young and it's a good time to start a family. Ramona let me tell you something that I have never told to anybody before. When I was young, all I wanted was fame and to be a boss and have a good name and business, and yes I got all that. I'm happy with what I accomplished, but there is one thing missing in my life, and that is a child and happiness. I don't have anybody to say, 'Happy Mother's Day,' or 'Mom, I love you.' I never thought about having children because I was always putting that aside. My husband was always mad about that, and finally, he gave up, and at the time I wished to have children I was getting old. Now I have everything, but my life is empty and sad. Yes, I may look like a happy person to you and many others, but my heart is full of sadness. Please don't let this happen to you. If you love Keven, and you know he is a good man, I don't see why you would wait. You don't want to make something out of yourself, you told me so; all you wanted was to have an excellent job, but a good job like this one you can find anywhere. So, Ramona don't lose what you have now, just because you're confused. Get together with Keven and talk it over. I don't want to be 100 and too old to be godmother to your children."

"Thank you, Mrs. Geyer, I knew I could always count on your help. You're right, I do love Keven, and I was silly doubting my love for him. He's coming home from St. Johns tomorrow, and I'll talk to him. If everything goes the way we like it, you'll be a godmother next year at this time. You have been my mother for five years now, Mrs. Geyer. I know without you I would be lost."

Keven called me that evening, and I was surprised because he had never called me from his work before. He was due home about eleven p.m., but there was an emergency in St. Johns. The pilot that was supposed to fly out west called in sick, so Keven volunteered to take a triple shift. I knew he needed money, but he'd been traveling too much lately, and I was worried.

"Hey! Cherry Pie, sorry I can't be home tonight, but I'm helping a friend, he's very sick, and there's no one to take the flight to Vancouver. I know you worry, but I promise I'll take a good rest in Vancouver and be back in two days. You'll have more time to think about our talk, and as I said before, whatever you decide I'm with you. Now I've got to go. See you in two days...I love you."

Before I had a chance to say anything he was gone. I was so afraid for Keven when he took two or three flights a day, but I knew why he was doing it, and I thought marrying him will do him and me good. There would be no more wondering when he was coming home, so I'd marry him.

Keven came back two days later and was exhausted, so I just talked to him briefly and told him I would see him on the weekend. He sounded very tired and apprehensive, but I knew why. I told my aunt I would be spending the weekend at Keven's, and if she needed me, all she had to do was call. She just said, "That's no surprise, have fun."

Once I got to his place I gave him a big kiss and a hug like never before. "Keven, I missed you so much—no more triple shifts, no more worries, we are going to get married, and we will be living with your parents, and Mrs. Geyer wants to be a godmother to all twelve children. So if we're going to have twelve children, we'd better get started. So what you think of that?"

"Ramona, don't mess with me. I'm exhausted and having twelve children, wow, where did you get that number? Are you just trying to make me feel better, or are you serious? What about your plans that we get married in a year or two? What happened to you in the three days while I was away?"

"I'll tell you what happened. I don't want to stay home for three days, and wonder if you're safe. I have thought a lot about all this. If you work with your father, we'll be home together every day; we can work on your business. We can make it if we just give it a chance, and that's what I want for us. But if you change your mind about getting married now, there will be only six children."

"Do you mean getting married right now? Or what did you mean, when you said now? I'm not sure I understand you at this point. Our communication is not clear to me. Please, Ramona don't start like that and make it like a joke. I don't want to get married right now, but my wish was soon, so I have no idea what you're up to now."

"Look, Keven, I'm sorry, but here's a plan that I thought would be good for both of us. Your father is not too bad now since he has a helper, but that costs him money, so I thought if you and I get married on Valentine's day, and then we move to your parents' house on March first, that will give us both some time to get everything organized here. Then when we're ready we can just take our suitcases and go, and by then we can go on and start our family. So what you think of my plan?"

"Oh Ramona, you must have read my mind. I thought about us getting married on Mother's Day, but your suggestion is better than mine. I'd honestly marry you tomorrow if you wish. You are one of a kind, and I know with you I'll be happy, and by the way twelve children! Well how about four?"

"Now that we have got our marriage all in order, I have somoe news that you're going to be shocked at. Megen is coming home from Vietnam and guess what. She has a boyfriend now, and I'm just dying to meet him."

"Wait a minute! Did you say, boyfriend?"

"Yup, news to me too. His name is Sam, Italian background, raised in Toronto, and to my surprise quite a good photographer. I saw some of his work in *Time* magazine, but how those two got together I can't wait to find out. All she told me was that I was right about her. She was always confused about men, because of what her father did to her, and now she says that Sam is so understanding and one of a kind…but she did say except you. Megen didn't like you at the beginning but as time went by she truly saw that you're one of a kind."

"You know I always thought that Megen was putting on a big show about being in love with you or with any other girls. Sometimes I noticed she was looking at me, but I tried to ignore all that, hoping one day she'd find her way in this world, I somehow felt that she was not gay, and I guess I was right, so good for her. Maybe we can make a little party for just a few people, to tell them about our plan and to celebrate your birthday and our first day when I saw you. What do you think?"

"Sounds great. Megen and Sam will be home on October 5th, and I'll invite some of the people from work, and you can ask Chuck and some of your pilot friends. Your apartment is big enough to fit ten people; I think that would be great. Meanwhile, I'll make a good dinner next week and tell my uncle and aunt, and then you can call your parents as well."

"That all sounds great. In the middle of November, I'll be going to help my father one more time before winter. Every November 15th, he has some rich people from Toronto that like to spend fall days up north, and the only way you can get there is by plane. My father usually picks them up in Markham (there's a small airport there) and brings them back. These people are very rich, and my father makes good money on that day. This time, I'll be going with him, because now that I have a pilot license I can fly any plane. After that trip, my parents usually stay home like two bears, doing nothing, except my father does inventory, and my mother goes to see her sister in Sudbury for a week or so. Now you see, our life will be simple; no stress and no big worries, and then we will have lots of time to make our dream come true and have lots of children, but hey not twelve."

"Okay Keven, that all sounds great—you better rest now, and I'm going home. I'd like to organize our party, and your job is to call your friends. So see you later, I love you."

Summer was almost over, and as we were approaching fall, it was our one-year anniversary and my birthday, and our party. Megen was coming home at the end of September, and I was so excited to see her, and even more so, Sam.

I told my aunt that Keven I had big news, and we would be taking them out for dinner. They didn't go out much so I thought this would be fun for a change.

She was very excited, and I heard my uncle mumbling at the back, but even he seemed glad to go out. So I made a reservation at very nice Hungarian restaurant on Bloor St. and told them it is on September 31st, which was Friday night.

Keven had just arrived from Calgary and was a bit tired, but he made an effort to be on time. Before they served dinner, I ordered a bottle of red wine. I knew my aunt liked red wine, and my uncle would drink anything. Keven was not much of a drinker, but we both had one glass. Just as a waiter brought soup my uncle stood up to say something. That was a surprise to me because I had no idea what he was going to say.

"I raise this glass for health and long life for our newborn, and toast all the best to parents."

"Oh oh. No, no, my dear uncle. You've got all this wrong. I'm not expecting a baby, no no no, not now. We wanted you to know that we are getting married in February on Valentine's day; that's about three months from now. We decided to get married early than we said before, because Keven's father is not in good health, and it's time for Keven to help his dad. I'm okay with that, so we'll be married in February, and then I'm going with Keven to live up north where his business is and his parents.. Maybe one day you can come and see how beautiful it is up north. This is why we are celebrating to-day, not because I'm pregnant. I'm telling you this early so you'll know when I start to make some plans for the wedding. It won't be anything big, since we don't have many relatives, and his parents don't have a big family either. Now let's raise that glass, and hope that my uncle will be able to give me away, since I don't have a father, and he's the only father I ever had."

"Ramona that is the nicest thing you ever said to me since you came to live with us, and I'd be proud to give you away to Keven."

"Thank you, and let's have a good dinner, and please do enjoy. I want you both to know how much I care for you. I know I don't show it to you enough, but I love you both. I'm sure that by now you know that. Lots of times I get mad at you dear uncle, but that's because I care, and we'd all like you to have a good, healthy life."

The night out with my aunt and incle went right, and I was glad that Keven spent time talking to my uncle. I drove Keven home, and the three of us went nicely and quietly back together.

The next few weeks went by pretty fast and before you knew it, it was the end of September. Megen was coming back the next week; that meant I was in for a big surprise. Keven was working very hard, taking more flights. He wanted to go and see his father on November 2nd, so he could help him with the last trip of the season, and I thought that would be a good time for him to break the news to them about our plans. I was sure that they would be excited and happy, especially his mother.

My twenty-second birthday was on Saturday and I sure hoped Megen came home by then. Keven invited only two of his friends; Chuck, and another guy from work. As for me, I had Mrs. Geyer coming and two girls from the warehouse, and yes Megan and her new boyfriend. I was so looking forward to this.

It was Wednesday night when I got a call from Megen. Like always, she forgot that I had to get up in the morning to work, but this time I was so glad to hear from her.

"Hi, Ramona it's me, Megen. Sorry to call you so late but we just got in, and I know you wanted to know if I'm coming on Saturday. Well, I can't wait to see you."

"Megen, if I weren't so determined to see you, I would yell at you for calling me so late. Hey I'm glad you got home okay. Now say, is Sam coming? I can't wait to see him—somehow I still don't believe you have a boyfriend."

"Yeah, you aways complain. Yes Sam is coming and don't try to be funny, you know what I mean."

"Are you, saying you haven't told him about us? Our love? Your secret is safe with me."

"Shut up; you know what I mean, but I'll always love you, Ramona, no matter what. My love for you is entirely different from any other."

"I know, my friend, I was joking. I love you as well, but I've got to go now. I have to get to work in about three hours. Have a good rest and I'll see you Saturday at Keven's about sevenish."

Keven and I we were so excited about the party. It was the first one for us, and I made sure we had enough beer, wine, and sodas. I made four different kinds of sandwiches, and my aunt made us some cookies, and we had lots of chips and peanuts. I thought everything looked good. All the guests arrived but no Megen. I was starting to worry, but at about nine she showed up with Sam. My mouth just dropped. Wow! Where had she found him? Sam was a magnificent man, but I think he knew it.

Megen just laughed and whispered in my ear, " Ha ha, I got a better one."

"Shut up. Now that we're all here, let's have a drink to my best friend Megen and her new partner, and with that, I have important news to tell you."

Keven stood up. "Ramona, please let me do this. First of all, let's raise a glass to my love and wish her a happy twenty-second birthday. And to my friends, thank you for coming. And now we have an important announcement. Today it is one year since Ramona and I met, and that was the happiest day in my life so far. Now it is my pleasure to tell you all, that Ramona and I are getting married in February on Valentine's day. Then in March we are moving to my parents' house where I'll be joining my father's business, and Ramona will be my boss. Well that's what she says for now, but she also wants to have twelve children, so as for bossing me around, she won't have time. I hope that you enjoy our party tonight because the next one will be our wedding."

I was so surprised when Chuck stood up and wanted to say something. I could tell that Keven was so happy that no matter what Chuck was going to say, it wouldn't bother him.

"Ladies and gentles, please let me say how Keven and Ramona met. Last year at this time Keven was spending alone time in one of my cabins that he likes to rent. It was October 15th when he rushed into my office and was so crazy. He started to mumble something how she didn't call him yet, and he had to find her, or he'd just die. And that's where he met Ramona, and he fell in love too thick. For some reason, she never called him, and Keven was freaking out." And then he talked about Keven how tracked me down.

Mrs. Geyer put up her hand. "Okay, not so fast Chuck. Let me tell you my story." And then she regaled the party with Keven's and my meeting in her office. "So let me congratulate them both," she concluded, "and yes Keven, I'd like to be godmother to all twelve but I'll be happy with four as well."

I was touched by Chuck and Mrs. Geyer, and how they remembered our first meeting and I thanked them both.

Keven came and asked me to dance, and he whispered. "I still remember the first day I saw you."

I squeezed his hands, and with a smile, said, "Me too."

The party lasted almost until one, and it was time to stop the music and noise before the superintendent came to give us hell. Once everybody left, Keven and I were tired, so we went to bed and slept until almost eleven a.m. the next day.

On November 14th, Keven got ready to go to his parent's place for a week. This time, he took a bus. I told him I would be okay without a car, but he said it was okay, he didn't mind a coach. It would give hm lots of time to think about our future, and how his mom will be so happy about us getting married soon.

When we got to the bus station I started to cry. I was sad, I just didn't know why, and I asked him to change his mind about going

He was sad to go, but he said this was the last time we would be apart. After this trip, his parents would stay home for the winter, and his father would relax until next year, and then everything would be okay. He was just about to say something about our honeymoon, when the bus driver announced with a thunderous voice, "Last call for Sudbury. All aboard, leaving in two minutes."

Keven jumped up so quickly that I had no chance to ask him anything, but he opened the window and said, "Our honeymoon is going to be a big surprise, and you will love it. Take care, I love you, Ramona."

With tears in my eyes, I told him I loved him and I always would.

I was sad and I couldn't explain why this trip bothered me so much. I even told Megen I didn't want to go out with her and Sam. Megen knew me well. She sensed that something was wrong but never asked—she was a good friend, and if I didn't want to tell her something she never insisted.

The weather was a bit stormy—lots of freezing rain. I wondered about Keven flying in this bad weather, but he'd been flying since he was fourteen, and he always said "I love up it there. No matter what kind of weather it is, I can handle it."

It was a Thursday evening when I came from work and I was getting ready to go to Keven's apartment to make sure that everything was all right. The phone rang, and I was hoping it was Keven, but the caring voice on the other side just sounded sad. "Ramona, are you home? Please sit down and turn on the TV and watch the news. I'll be right over."

It took me a minute or two to realize it was Megen. "Megen, you're scaring me. What's wrong?"

"Ramona just turn on the TV right now. It's about Keven."

"Oh my God! What are you talking about? What about Keven? He's up north, you know that. I don't want to turn on the TV. What's wrong Megen? Just tell me."

"No, not on the phone. I'll be right over.

I was shaking and turned on the TV but I wish I never did. The announcer was showing a huge explosion in a small town fifteen kilometres from Sudbury. A small plane had hit a Hydro pole, and fell on a gas tanks right near Keven's home. There were no survivors. According to his mother, Keven, and his father had made their last trip for the year and had been hoping for a real comfortable winter.

The news was going on and on, about how Keven was a good pilot and the accident was due to bad stormy weather, which took two lives.

I must have passed out. When I woke up, Megan and my aunt were standing over me.

All I could hear was, *no survivors, no survivors*. No, that couldn't be true. Keven knew how to handle inclement weather—it must have been another Keven. He wasn't the only Keven in the world. No, it couldn't be true—not my Keven."

All I wanted was to be with Keven; nothing else mattered to me that moment. I heard the phone ring again and I jumped up and grabbed it. With high hopes, I yelled,

"Keven is that you? Please tell me, is it you?"

"No Ramona, this is Sandy, Keven's mom. I guess by now you know the news. Oh Ramona, what am I going to do? I need you right now. Please, how soon can you come?"

"Sandy, I'm so sorry. I don't know how I'm going to live without Keven. I don't even want to live anymore. I cannot believe this has happened. Yes, I'll come as soon as I can. Right now it's late, but first thing in the morning I'll drive, and by noon I should be there. Oh Sandy, I can't believe this is the truth, I just can't. Try to say calm and let your neighbors help you. Have you called your sister? Maybe she can come to be with you, until I come? Please take care, and I'll see you tomorrow."

Megen and Sam came early next morning, and slowly we drove north. Most of the time I was crying, and talking to myself and just trying to figure out how in the world I was going to face whatever was left of Keven, or anything; his mother, poor Sandy who'd lost more than I did, but we were both in for long, sad days.

I knew that I'd never forget Keven, I was very sure of that.

As we arrived in Ten Lake Village, there were so many firetrucks, police, and ambulances, but they were no longer needed for this location. We went to the main house where I found Sandy in the bedroom crying. Thank God, her sister was with her so I felt more relaxed about when I'd eventually have to go back home. We hugged and cried together for a long time, and finally I had the nerve to ask her what had happened. Keven was a good pilot and so was his father, so how did this happen? How? I needed to know to help me believe that Keven was gone.

"It wasn't Keven's or Rick's fault; it was the weather. I'm surprised you got here okay. Most of the roads are closed, because of Hydro poles that were blocking the roads and ice all over. You see the wind was going on almost ninety-five kilometres an hour, so loud and high and on top of that freezing rain that was coming down. I saw our plane in the distance, and the next thing was that I heard an explosion. The house just shook, Our gas tank got hit by a falling hydro pole and made the first explosion. But then there was another explosion; the second one came from the plane getting caught in the first explosion. Our gas tank got hit by a hydro poll and made the first explosion. Oh Ramona, it was so horrible. I watched them flying right into the fire, but I just froze, I did nothing to stop them. I think that I'm responsible for them—I should have gone out and waved to them or something. Oh my God it was so horrible, they just blew up right in front of me. There's nothing left; only bits and pieces of the aircraft, there are no traces of our loved ones. The explosion was so big that it burned everything on the site."

After I'd calmed Sandy down, I went outside; I wanted to see it all. I was looking for something of Keven's. I needed closure. As I approached the site, I noticed that one of the firemen was staring at me, but I just kept walking. A policeman came and told me that I couldn't go too close to the site because it was under investigation.

I looked at him, and he knew I was looking for something, anything that they might have found that belonged to Keven or Rick. "Sorry miss, there was nothing left, but I think that fireman over there has found a necklace under the remains of a seat. Let me get him for you."

Soon he was back with the fireman I'd spotted watching me. "Miss, this is Fireman Steve, he's been working on this site almost all night, and he would like to show you something."

The fireman stepped up. "First of all, my condolences about your loved one, I can not imagine what you're going through. I personally have never seen such a crash where everybody in town is crying. While I was cleaning, trying to find some remains of Keven and Rick, I stumbled on something shiny. It was a necklace, and I knew it belonged to Keven. You see Keven and I grew up together; I knew that one day he'd be the best pilot, but never this. We have to look into all possibilities to see if there was something wrong with the aircraft, but there was not much left to find. I only found this. I'm sure you'll recognize it.

I took the necklace in my hand and put my other hand on my neck to feel the one I was wearing. "Yes, that is what I gave Keven for Christmas," I said and started to cry. I was mad, mad at everybody. "Keven and I were going to wear these necklaces forever. What about Keven? Why can't you find him? Please look for him, maybe in the field. Have you looked everywhere?"

I was just going crazy, until the fireman took me in his arms to calm me down. "I'm so sorry Ramona; we have looked and looked everywhere but there's nothing. I have carefully searched all the fields and surrounding areas, but nothing. Believe me this very hard for me too. I'm so sorry for what happened. Please don't cry."

Crying, I asked him, "How do you know my name? I don't remember meeting you before."

"Well, the news was all over town that Keven was getting married and like I said, we grew up together. He even asked me to be his best man, and he told me all about you. Ramona, I want you to know that Keven loved you more than anything in this world. It's a shame what happened, and if there is anything I can do, please let me know."

No, that's fine, thank you for keeping the necklace for me, and thank you for trying to find something."

Struggling to keep my tears to myself I looked for Sandy. She was so heartbroken that it made me even more sad. I sat beside her, holding her hand and we both started to cry again. "Sandy, please let's go in the kitchen, and I'll make you some tea," I whispered. "I have to talk to you."

I knew that Megan and Sam could only stay another day, so I needed to find out what she was planning for a funeral, if any.

"Ramona, I don't know what to do about that, I've asked our priest to come over, and as soon as he arrives, we're going to discuss that and we'll take it from there. If you can't stay, don't worry, I understand."

"No, Sandy, I'm just thinking of my friends. As for me, I'm staying, I'm going to be with you as long as you need me. Don't worry about me. I loved Keven more than I can describe, and I'd like to say goodbye to him and Rick."

I saw Megen looking at me. She and Sam both had critical jobs, so I told her that they should go, and that I'd be staying, but for how long I don't know for sure. "Megan, thank you, just go, and I'll call you about the funeral and when I'll be home. Just please call Mrs. Geyer for me and tell her I'll get in touch with her and tell my aunt and uncle I'll call them tomorrow. Please don't worry about me. I have to do this; I have to say goodbye to Keven even if he isn't with us at the moment. Please just go, and thank you." We hugged each other, and neither one of could help crying.

Just before Megen left I heard her saying, "Please don't cry. I'll help you get through this. Take care, Ramona."

When Megen and Sam left, I went into Keven's bedroom. Funny, I'd never been in his room before. I always stayed in a guest room, and as I walked in I felt Keven; his smell. I heard his voice. I sat on his bed and wondered what in the world I was going to do now. He was the only one who understood me. He never questioned me too much, and was always easy to get along with.

I was so deep in my thoughts, I never heard Sandy knock on the door, so when I saw her standing there I thought I was going nuts. But Sandy saw my confusion and took my hand and with a soft touch she asked me if I'd like to eat something.

"No thank you. I'd just like to be alone with Keven. He's here Sandy. I can feel him."

"Ramona my dear ,you have to try to let it go. Keven is gone. He'll be in our hearts always, and that is why you feel him. We have to be strong, life is short, and we have to go on. I'm sure Keven would not like you to spend the rest of your time crying over him. One day you'll meet again, but for now we have to say goodbye to our loved ones. Also, I came to tell you that our priest is coming tomorrow morning, so that we can talk about the funeral arrangements, but if you're not up to that, I won't hold it against you."

"Don't worry about me Sandy. I'll be up first thing in the morning because I would like to hear what the priest has to say. Right now I'd like to lie down a bit, and later on I'll come down."

As I lay down, I felt my heart racing. I was so, so sad. I took one of Keven's shirts and held it so tight. I started to cry and beg God to take me to him. I was at the end of my rope. All I wanted was to die, and with crying and looking for an answer I must have fallen asleep. Next thing, I heard a knock on a door and it took me a few seconds to figure out where I was. I heard Sandy's voice, and I told her I would be right down. I couldn't believe I'd slept all night.

The priest was there, and he was ready to explain to us how you bury a person without a body. It was very so sad, I'd never experienced anything like that. The funeral was arranged for three days later, because there was a lot of work to be done, and most were painful tasks to undertake.

After the funeral, I stayed one more day. Megen and Sam came with my uncle and aunt, and after that, we all went back together. Saying goodbye to Sandy was very hard for me to do, but she understood, and we promised to write to each other. With tears in my eyes, I gave Sandy a hug, and I told her I'd always remember her and her family. She hugged me as well and whispered. "Ramona, please don't cry. Life has to go on. You are young, and you can't stay sad all your life. I'm sure Keven would like you to move on."

CHAPTER 28

After Keven's death I was sad, drained, and not worthy of anything. I was so lonely and lost, my communication with others was zero. All I wanted was to be alone. My life meant nothing to me. I went to work every day, and sometimes I worked on the weekend as well, just to make sure I was busy so I wouldn't think about Keven. Nothing was important to me anymore. Mrs. Geyer even offered me a job in Chicago in a new plant, and I was not interested. Maybe six months before I would have been, but not now. Now all I wanted was to work and go home. Megen was the only one who understood my pain and would call just to say hello, and that was all I needed.

Days, weeks, months, and even a year passed me by, and all wanted was to die. I started to smoke and often had a beer in my hand. Now I understand why my uncle drank. Drinking gives you some freedom from pain and then you start all over again. My aunt was getting apprehensive, and one day she told me that there was a big dance at a European club and most of the people who were going to be there were from back home. She thought maybe if I met some young man with the same background, perhaps then I'd come out of my sadness.

I thought about it and told her okay, I'd go.

The other girls who went were overdressed as far as I was concerned, but I just put on my pantsuit and with no high hopes or desire to meet anyone, along I went.

The club was full of young girls and men. The music playing was all Yugoslavian songs, which I did not fancy that time. They all danced in a circle, and there were just a few slow songs. A young man stood right beside me and asked me if I'd like to dance with him. Well most everybody was dancing so I thought there'd be no harm in it, but by then I'd had two rum and cokes, and I was feeling good. So then I danced with some other guys, and I gave them my phone number, but deep inside of me I was hoping not to hear from them. I was just having a little fun, and that was all I wanted. All three guys were okay in my book, but not for me. I was looking for Keven's image, and could not find it. I don't know why I gave them my phone number, but I decided I'd give myself a chance to get to know whoever called first. One of those three guys was not bad at all, he liked to joke and it was fun being with him. The other two asked too many questions, especially the blond one, I think his name was Pavle. The other two were Stefan and Rayen, but I guess they were looking to meet the right person just like everybody in there. Rayen was the one I hoped would call me.

By mid-week I got a call. At first, I wasn't sure with whom I was talking, so I had to ask. To my unpleasant surprise, it was Pavle. At first, I didn't know what to say. All I could think was this was not the one I wanted, but maybe since he was the first one to call, just maybe he is the one. We talked a bit, and he asked me if I'd like to go out with him. I wasn't so sure about him, so I told him I was working that weekend. (It was a lie.) I said I'd be free next weekend, hoping that he wouldn't call again. I was still hoping to hear from Rayen.

It was late Sunday when the phone rang. I hoped it was Megen, because she was out of town and I wanted to tell her about my night out, but it was Rayen. As soon as he asked if he could speak to Ramona, I knew it was him. There was something about Rayen that I liked; he reminded me a little bit of Keven.

"Hi Ramona, this is Rayen. How are you? I was going to call you earlier, but was thinking maybe it wouldn't be a good idea, because I was not totally honest with you that night at the club. I like you, and I was wrong in many ways. You see Ramona, I'm from Vancouver. I just came to Toronto last week for my sister's wedding, and I went to that club just to have a little fun. I wasn't planning to meet someone like you, but the distance is wrong. And this is why I'm calling you so late, just in case you think I was one of the guys that were looking for real time, but that's not me. So this is to say hi and goodbye, and I hope you forgive me for not telling the truth that night. I'm leaving Thursday night, and if you're not too mad, maybe we could meet for a coffee before I go. If you said no, I'd respect your thoughts and I'll understand."

"Thanks for calling Rayen, but I'm not looking for a long distance love or anything. You know you were my favourite that night, and honestly, I was hoping to hear from you, but not like this. So I hope you had a good time and good luck, thanks for calling."

I made sure I hung up before he had a chance to said anything. It did hurt that he hadn't told me the truth that he was from Vancouver. "There goes my chance to get back out in the world," I said to myself. So now if Pavle called I had to be ready to go out with him or lie again. I wasn't not sure. There was something about him I liked, but there was something that bothered me. I just couldn't figure that out yet, so maybe I'd go out and see what it was that was troubling me about him.

I knew I'd not have Keven again, but comparing Keven to another young man was wrong, so I'd try to look at it another way.

CHAPTER 29
Pavle....1974

IT WAS A Friday evening when Pavle called, and as I thought, he did ask me out. This time I agreed to go on Saturday night, and I wanted him to pick the place because I was sure that the places where I would like to go, he probably would find odd. I like bars with rock and roll bands or folk music, no fancy dress up, just go as you feel. I had a feeling Pavle, or any other Eastern European man would not like that kind of a date. I gave him my home address to pick me up at 7:30 pm.

Though I'd agreed to go out with Pavle, I realized my choice was unclear. I had no feeling for him, so why had I decided to go out with him? I just couldn't explain that to myself. Maybe I was looking for someone that wanted me, and what I wanted did not matter at that moment.

As I suspected, he was dressed in a very gentlemanly way, and I made sure I looked more like a young lady than a happy hippie. I didn't ask him to come in, because I wasn't so sure about him, not just yet. I had told my aunt about him and she was glad that finally, I was going out on a date, after all those years of crying and misery. She said it was about time.

And that is how I started going with Pavle, not thinking that we were going to get married. (It was one of my biggest mistakes of my life.)

Pavle took me to a small European restaurant that was playing songs from back home, and the food was like my aunt made...well maybe a little better. At first, I liked it, but then there were some young guys who had too much to drink, and a big argument started over who was better, Serbians, Croatians, or Tito. To me all that sounded so stupid so I asked Pavle if we could leave. He was surprised; I guess he loved the argument they were having. Then he asked me what I liked; a Serbian, Croatian or Yugoslavian man. I just looked at him and said, "I don't care. I thought we were all the same."

"Not in Canada," he said. "Here you are either Serbian, Croatian, or Yugoslavian."

Well, I didn't know the difference between Serbia and Croatia, so I said I was Yugoslavian.

To my surprise he said, "Good. I just don't like Croatian people, but Yugoslavians are Serbian as far as we all know."

"Pavle, I think you're wrong and so is everyone else who thinks like you. Yugoslavia is all one, but we do have different nationalities and that's all. As a matter of fact, my background is Romanian, but like all my other relatives, I was born in Yugoslavia. So in your opinion what am I? Serbian or Croatian?"

"I don't care, as long you're not Croation, and hope that you're not defending them because your last boyfriend was Croation!"

"Pavle, as far as my previous boyfriend, that is not your business, but no he wasn't Croation, he was Canadian. And now I'd like you to take me home; I've had enough of history for today."

As we drove home, I was silent. He must have noticed it and just as if we'd known each other for a long time, he said, "Are you mad at me?"

"Hello, this was our first date, and we argued about nationalities... so, not my kind of time." I was expecting Pavle to apologize, but nothing. All he said was that next time we'd go to a different club. Once we got home, I said good night and thanked him. He wanted to come in, but I told him it was too late and my folks didn't like me bringing guys home so late. So I said goodnight again and went in.

I could tell he was a bit surprised, but hey if you like me, you call, and if not, no big loss. Those were my thoughts.

Pavle and I did not start off as well as I would have liked, so I never expected him to call me again, but at the end of the week, he did. I was very cautious on what I was going to do if he asked me out again. I wanted to find out more about him; his background and just about everything. Our first date had not gone the way I liked, so I thought I'd give him a second chance. but this time we would go to a small Italian restaurant that Sam's father owned. I knew this place was charming and spotless.

He agreed to pick me up at nine on Friday night because he had to work all weekend. This time he was dressed more casually and so was I. We ordered excellent pizza with a bottle of wine, and this time Pavle looks more relaxed. There was no crazy talk about Serbian, Croatian, and Yugoslavian, we just spoke of each other, and that night I liked him. He was completely a different man. It was a bit strange to me that one could change so fast, but I ignored it since I guess the wine made me a bit relaxed, and we went home happy. Before I had a chance to say goodnight he kissed me and said, "See you next week." Not waiting for an answer he went home.

Most of the time I was home, either watching TV or just hanging around. Megen was in Columbia, and Sam was in New York. I had never seen people that loved each other like those two, and long distances never bothered them. I was so happy for Megan and missed her a lot. I wanted so much to tell her about Pavle and she would tell me if she liked him or not.

Pavle and I had some more dates, and after about two months, I ask him to be a guest at my house so that he could meet my folks. He never asked me how come I called them Aunt and Uncle, not Mother and Father. All Pavle wanted to know about me, was what I had done all day—where did I go? To me that was sometimes just a joke, but sometimes I asked him not to bother me with that kind of question. We were just a girlfriend and boyfriend, nothing too serious so far, so whatever I did all day was not his concern. I noticed Pavle did not like those answers, but I just ignored him.

I made a nice supper and told my uncle to try to be at his best. My aunt just smiled and said not to worry. So Pavle came, and as my uncle and aunt came in, I told Pavle the truth about who they were right away. Pavle was a bit surprised but never said anything.

My uncle seemed to like him right away as the two of them sat and started to drink. Privately, my aunt said Pavle looked like a good man, but I never answered her about that. We all had a good time, and when Pavle was about to go home, my uncle asked him to come back very soon. With that, I presumed he liked him.

Outside, Pavle asked me about my mother, but I told him she was ill and was not able to take care of me, before or now, and that was why I was living with my uncle and aunt. He said it was okay with him, he liked my uncle and my aunt was a sweet lady.

Pavle had no one in Canada, and that was one of the reasons he liked my uncle and aunt. It was easy for him to talk to them in our language. My uncle showed some interest in him, so Pavle thought he fit right in with us.

After that day Pavle called quite often, and if I weren't home he would talk to my uncle, I wasn't too keen on that, but I kept quiet. I told my aunt about

Pavle and Uncle talking a lot, and I thought that was weird since we were just a boyfriend and girlfriend. She said that they both liked Pavle and were hoping that something would come out of our dating. I was still not sure, so I ignored all their questions about Pavle and me.

New Year's Eve was approaching fast and Pavle decided that we would go where we met the first time. I had nothing against that, but I had been hoping to go out with Megen and Sam if they both came home early.

My wish and hope came true. Megen came back on December 18th, and Sam came the next day. So just before Christmas, we got together. I told her all about Pavle, but Megen sensed something different about Pavle. "Ramona, do you love this guy? I don't know him at all, but one thing I'm sure about is that I can't feel any excitement when you talk about him. So what's up? Why are you going out with him, and have been with him almost five months, but don't feel any love for him. Ramona, what's wrong?"

"Megen, you're right. I don't love him, but I do like him. You see he's from back home, we speak the same language, and he has a good job. He'd like to have a family soon, and my uncle and aunt like him a lot. You know my background. All I wanted was to have my family, but since I lost the love of my life, I just can't find anyone like Keven, and I can't do this to myself. The only way for me to completely forget Keven is to go with someone, and Pavle is the one that I like for now."

"I tell you what, why don't we all meet on Friday and let me see your new boyfriend, and like always I'll be honest with you. We can go to Sam's father's restaurant, and let's have a real time. So what do you say to that?"

"Okay Megen, I'll call Pavle and call you back."

"Swell. Bye honey."

"Shut up, Megen, love you too."

I was just about to call Pavle when I heard my aunt calling me. "Ramona, Pavle is here, come out."

Pavle hadn't told me that he was going to come over. I was very surprised and quite mad. I didn't remember telling him that he could just come over anytime he liked, so I came out very upset.

I saw the smirk on his face, which made me angry.

"Hi Ramona, I was in the neighborhood so I thought I'd drop by and see what you guys are doing."

Emotionally I wasn't feeling good, but I pretended I was glad to see him. "How kind of you, I was just talking to my best friend Megen about you, and I would like you to meet her and her boyfriend. So I wonder if you're are free on Friday evening? I know you'll like Megen, we've been friends since we were sixteen-year-old kids. She's a well-known photographer for the newspaper and a lovely person. So what do you say on that?" I could tell that it wasn't his favourite thing to do, to spend with other people. All he wanted was just us, and that made me mad and sometimes very unclear about Pavle. That night, as we walked home after dinner with Megen and Sam, Pavle told me he didn't like Megen or that hippie boyfriend of hers.

"Pavle they are my friends, and that is not going to change. I've known Megen for almost ten years and Sam about three, so if you don't care much for them I suggest you keep it to yourself. I don't want to get between them and you, so you and I can go out to places we like, but then I'll go out with my friends as well. I hope this doesn't change anything because as far as I'm concerned, they will stay my friends whether you like it or not."

"Ramona, they are your friends, but not the friends I'd like you to have. But you do whatever, I don't care. So let's not talk about those hippies. I have to work this weekend and I'll call you later."

"Look Pavle, you don't call my friends hippies just because of the way they dress or look. You don't see me calling your friends names, so from now on it is Megen and Sam—just don't make me choose between them and you."

I think this was our first argument, so he went home pretty upset, and he made me mad. I wouldn't let Pavle call my friends names, and would not take orders from him. If he called me and didn't apologize, then I'd have to think things over before we got deeper into our relationship.

Just before I was going to bed, Pavle called. I could tell by his voice that he was upset. "Ramona, I don't like going to bed mad, so I want you to know I'm sorry. Megen and Sam are your friends, and I don't have to like them, but I won't call them names either. I'm sorry if I made you mad, and for you to choose between us, it's not fair. You can stay friends with them for now, and in time we'll see."

"Pavle let's just drop it. You are not going to tell me who I can be friends with now or ever. Therefore have a good night and we'll talk later, in a week or so." I know he sensed my being mad and just said okay.

The New Year's Eve party was just around the corner, and I was wondering if we were going at all. Pavle didn't call me for almost a week, and somehow that didn't bother me. If Pavle thought that I had to do everything his way, he was wrong, so for now I just waited to see.

Christmas was on Sunday, and I wasn't sure if Pavle would come, because of our argument. So I asked my uncle if he'd talked to Pavle lately. Apparently they'd been talking quite a bit, and he said Pavle was coming for Christmas dinner. I just laughed and said, "Why don't you adopt him as well?"

I saw the smirk on my uncle's face when he said, "Why don't you marry him, you're getting old and Pavle is right for you."

"Whatever," I said, and I slammed the door. In my frustration, I grabbed the phone to call Megen, but just then there was a knock on my door.

"What now?" I shouted. I thought it was my uncle, but no, Megen was standing there. "You know Megan, this is so spooky you appearing at my door when I was just about to call you. Come in, I'm glad to see you. So Megen what are your thoughts on Pavle, and no bullshit, be honest."

"You want my honest opinion? Well, in plain English I don't like him at all."

"Fair enough, but Megen, you never liked Keven either at first, and later on you loved him, so maybe you'll be like that with Pavle. I know that Pavle can be a little bit demanding, and you have to take into consideration that his English is on the rough side, and that might be a problem."

"No Ramona, nothing's wrong with his English. It's his rules that you're not seeing or you're just plain blind. Pavle is a pushy guy, and he thinks he is right all the time, and calling us hippies, that is so, so… forget it. I just don't like him. If you asked me, I would tell you to leave that man and stay single until the right person comes along. Look you asked me, and I'm telling you the truth. You're my best friend, and I don't want you to make a big mistake just because you want to get married and have children. Ramona think twice about Pavle, that's all I have to tell you as a friend."

"Sorry Megen for putting you in that position, but I know you'll tell me the truth, so thanks for that, but I do care for Pavle more than you know. I know it's not the way I loved Keven; that kind of love will never happen again. I'm happy enough to be with Pavle, and if you two can't get along I can't be part of that. You're my best friend and that's how it's going to stay, so you don't have to like Pavle, but just be there for me if I need you."

"Fair enough, Ramona, I hope you know what you're doing. By the way, I have this little gift for you I found in Colombia, and when I saw it, I thought about you. Don't open it until Christmas. So what are you doing for New Year's Eve? Or I should know, you're going out with Pavle."

"Yes and no, for now. You see we had a big argument about something and unless Pavle apologizes properly there will be no more Pavle and me."

"Wow! Wow! You didn't tell me that! So what was the argument about? Wait, don't tell me. Is it about Sam and me?"

"Yes, but don't think right away that you were right. He said some things that I didn't like, so as I said if Pavle won't apologize I'm done with him."

"Well, has he called you to apologize yet?"

"No, he hasn't called yet."

"Ramona, it's not my business, and I'm not telling you what to do. I told you what I think about him, and the rest is up to you. But Ramona, think with your head not with your heart. Do what's right."

"Pavle is coming to my house for Chrismas, thanks to my drunken uncle who told him he is more than welcome to be with us on Christmas day. So if he doesn't call by then, Megen I don't know what to do. I have to have good thoughts about him and me. There's one more thing I have to do. I never told Mrs. Geyer about him. You know she's like a mother to me, and now I have to call Pavle and pretend nothing is wrong. I'd like him to meet Mrs. Geyer and see what he thinks of her since nothing went well about you and Sam. I was planning to call him after I had a good talk with you, so we'll see."

"Just don't get full of yourself, I think he likes to win all the time, and giving in to him is wrong. But do what you want, and don't tell me I didn't warn you. I've got to go now so see you between Christmas And New Year's. Sam and I are staying home for the holidays, so if you need me just call."

"Megen, hold on. I have something for you and Sam—hope you find it funny."

When Megen left, I called Pavle, and to my surprise, he picked it up on the first ring. Pretending nothing was wrong I asked him if he would like to meet me at work the next day. "I'd like you to meet someone very close to me." I was just about to give him my work address, but he said he knew where I worked. It struck me funny, because I never gave him my work address, but he said my uncle gave to him. At that moment I wasn't going to start an another argument; I just said, "Okay, see you then."

Next morning as soon as I got to work, I went straight to Mrs. Geyer's office.

"Hello my dear," she said. "What can I do for you? How are you? It's sweet to see you. You've changed, you're not working close to me broke my heart, but I do understand, so what's wrong Ramona?"

"Why do you think something is wrong Mrs. Geyer?"

"Because I've know you for almost nine years and I can tell when you're upset or sad. So set down and tell me, what's bothering you."

"I don't know where to start or how, but I'll make it short." Then I told her about how I'd been seeing Pavle and how he had insulted my friends.

"Ramona my dear I knew you had a boyfriend, but I wanted you to come to me. You see quite often I see a young man walking down the parking lot and looking through the window. The last time I saw him I told him, I'd call the police if he didn't stop. He said that his girlfriend was working here and he was just trying to surprise her for lunch or something like that. I didn't like that man, and now you're worrying me. I sure hope that's not Pavle."

"Oh Mrs. Geyer, I sure hope not. He didn't know I worked until recently, but we'll see. I asked him to come today to meet you, but I don't think he knows who you are.. He'll be here about ten. I'll go back to my job, but let me know if you see a tall blond man coming in."

"Okay Ramona, see you later."

I was miles away in my mind when I heard Sandy paging me that Pavle was there. He was dressed very nice and was smiling. I gave him a small kiss and toldl him to follow me. As as I knocked, Mrs. Geyer said. "Come in," but something in her voice was telling me the man she'd been talking about was Pavle, and it scared me..

Before I had a chance to said anything she was ready for Pavle. "Well, well, look who we have here. My, my, I Ramona I know this man. You're the young man I told to stop peeping through our windows at the back, aren't you Pavle?"

Pavle went so red, and he stormed out and said, "I'm not interested in that old bag, see you after work. I phoned in sick today so that we can talk."

As I walked back to Mrs. Geyer's office, I could tell that she was so frustrated. The first thing she said was, "Get away from that that man."

I was shocked. What was going on?

"Ramona, that's the man I was talking about before. I almost called the police one day; he came so many times. He's not a good person. Ramona, you're a young girl why are you rushing so much to get married?"

"No, no Mrs. Geyer, it's nothing like that. It's just he's nice to me; I just don't understand the things that he does. I know he's a bit jealous, but I think every man is."

"Ramona, to me, he looks like a creepy man. I'm not going to tell you what to do, but I'm giving you strong advice to break up with him. You're not a child anymore, so therefore you choose, but with your head, not your heart."

"Funny you say that; Megen said the same thing. Mrs. Geyer, thank you for your time and we'll talk later."

After work, I went home to get ready for going out with Pavle. I usually didn't like going out on work days, but this time it was important to both of us. About seven, Pavle came, and he was carrying flowers, which he'd never done before. I knew right there that Pavle was sorry for walking away from Mrs. Geyer.

"What's this for?" I asked him, pretending nothing had happened earlier.

"Ramona, I'm very sorry for everything, and you have my word it won't happen again, so if you're ready to go, let's go. I found a small cafe on Yonge Street that serves our kind of food and has a little band—nothing fancy but very cozy.

The café was very friendly; I liked it a lot. Ther was a man playing guitar and singing soft songs, something I didn't expect in a Yugoslavian café. I liked it a lot. As we ordered, Pavle start to apologize, and I could tell he meant it, so I asked him if he would like to meet with Mrs. Geyer again. I never in my life got a such a quick answer.

"NO, not now or ever. This what I wanted to talk to you about this evening. You see Ramona, I don't like your friends at all. Your friends are rude to me because of my English. They make fun of me, I can see that, I'm not blind. You can see them anytime you like but without me. Megen and Sam are not my type of people and Mrs. Geyer, she is just an old lady and should mind her own business. Yes, I came few times, I wanted to surprise you, but that old witch told me to get lost, so I don't like her at all. You have some Yugoslavian friends and that's okay with me. I'm not asking you not to see them, but I would like it if you don't see them when I'm with you."

"Pavle, that's okay with me, but one thing you have to remember is that you're not going to call my friends names. Mrs. Geyer is one of the most respectable ladies in Canada and to tell you the truth I'm very lucky to have her as my friend. And another thing, I don't have any Yugoslavian friends;

those girls that you saw at the dance are my aunt's friend's children. I just met them once and that's all. I have my friends, and I don't need to make new ones just because they're not Yugoslavian. I hope you respect my wishes and we can continue going out, but if you don't respect my friends, then we have to break up. I won't let you tell me who I can see. I like you a lot, but you have to change."

"Fine, but I'll not go out with your friends, and if that's not sufficient then I guess we're through."

"Pavle, we can't build our relationship over debating what I can do and who I can see or the other way around. We have to trust each other, okay? If you don't like my friends, that's fine, I'll see them on my terms, and I think we have to start all over again. Pavle you have to ease off, and let me be. I can tell you one thing for sure, I'm involved only with you, and for you to keep me liking you, you'll have to trust me as I trust you.

Now it's getting late, and I have to get up in the morning for work, but hey, I think this was a good talk and we'll see what the future is going to bring us. I hope to see you next Sunday for Christmas, but I'm sure we'll talk more."

Just before I stepped out of the car, Pavle spoke in a little voice. "Ramona, I'm sorry for everything, I do love you."

I turned and gave him a small kiss and went in.

Nothing much happened in the next few days. Megen called and asked about Pavle and me, but I told her that I would handle Pavle. "You, Sam, and Mrs. Geyer are my friends, not his. He just doesn't like you guys, and I'll not stand in between all this. I told him I'm always going to see you and that's that. He's coming for Christmas and we'll see. Megen, please be my friend and try to understand. I like Pavle; he has lots of good approaches towards the future, and I think I'm in that future. So please just be there if I need you."

"Ramona, you're baking your cake, and you will be eating it, you'll see. My dear, have a merry Christmas and I'll see you after the holidays. Let's get together like in the old days. We can go shopping or just pop into one one of our favourite cafés in Yorkville."

"That's an excellent idea. Say hello to your mom and Sam, and have a good one. Love you, Meg."

"Hey! Hey, what's that? You haven't called me Meg since we were kids, and 'love you'? Are you sure you're okay? Do you need me to come over?"

"I'm fine, but Megen I miss Keven so much. I just can't stop thinking about him, and I feel I buried him inside me. I think I'm with Pavle just to forget Keven and it's not working. I miss him a lot. It's just that we were planning so much before the accident, and the holidays are the worst. I'm okay, honest. Don't worry, talk to you later."

"Listen I'm only ten minutes away. Call me if you can't handle the holidays or just about anything—just call me, okay? By for now and stay good."

Next morning I went to Mrs. Geyer's office to apologize for Pavle walking out.

"Ramona my dear, you don't have to apologize for him, if he were a man he would do that himself. I have read that man, and I truly don't like him. But that doesn't mean you have to listen to me. You follow your heart and I hope everything will be okay. I love you like you're my daughter and I always will, but I'm telling you now, that if you ever marry Pavle please don't invite me to come, because I won't. He was vulgar to me. Men like that don't interested me at all. You can call me anytime, anywhere, but not him. "I have news for all of you, but I'm going to tell you first. As of January, I'm moving back to England. I'd like to spend some quiet time. I would like to be officially retired from fashion shows. You never know, maybe one day you can visit me with Megen and Sam, and we can have fun like before. This will be my last Christmas with many of you, but you, you will stay in my heart forever. Before you go, please take this and keep it until Christmas and then open it. Ramona, you will be in my heart every day. I want you to know you can reach me anytime you need me."

"Mrs. Geyer, please don't go. Please, I'll break up with Pavle if that's the reason you're leaving, please. I don't know what will happen to me if you go."

"Ramona, I'm not leaving because of Pavle. A man like him doesn't even interest me a bit. It's time for me to relax. I'm going to be seventy years old, and I do need a rest, that's all my dear. Ramona, please don't cry! We'll see each other one day."

That one day never came. She left, and my life turned upside down.

Christmas came and went and we all had a good time. Pavle was so happy to be with a family, and he whispered in my ear, "One day this will be like our home."

I just smiled and squeezed his hand, and I was thinking, *Maybe.*

CHAPTER 30

IT WAS NEW Year's Eve. This time I dressed very nicely, so that even my uncle stared at me, but my aunt said I looked beautiful.

Pavel came at about 7:30 p.m. and was happy when he saw me dressed so sweet. I guess nobody thought I could wear a beautiful dress because my favourite clothes were jeans and t-shirts, but somehow I had a feeling that this would be my special night. The club was full of people, but we had reserved our table, and we were sitting with other two couples that Pavle knew, though they were new to me. As it turned out, one man was Pavle's cousin, so I got to talk to them a lot. All of us had a really good time and then came midnight. We all stood up to kiss each other, but Pavle bent down on his knee and asked me to marry him. All the people around us started to clap their hands and they shouted, "Say yes, tell him yes!"

I took his hand and I whispered, "Yes, I'll marry you!"

Pavle lifted me up and shouted, "You're all mine now and nobody else's—all mine!" Some girls might have been happy with those words but I got chills all over and the look in Pavle's eyes made me wonder if I was making the biggest mistake of my life. (Later on it turned out I did make the biggest mistake of my life.)

He noticed that I was shaking and took me in his arms and said, "Ramona, don't worry, everything is going to be all right now that we're together. After the holidays maybe you can move in with me since we're going to be together all the time."

It was too much for me to take in on one night, so I asked Pavle to take me home. Pavle was surprised... more like he was upset. "No," he said. "We're going to my place tonight and maybe every night from now on like I said before. Just sit and try to have fun, and relax. We have a whole life ahead of us to talk. Tonight we're celebrating our engagement and soon, hopefully, our marriage. So, cheer up Ramona."

Communication between Pavle and me was not good. I was getting drained and wanted to go home, but Pavle was getting a little bit drunk, and I didn't like that. I got up and told him that I was going home. He grabbed my hand, and with fire coming out of his eyes, threw me back to my chair. I began to cry, but he finally came to his senses and took me home. I rushed to get in, and said, "See you tomorrow, and we'll talk."

As soon as I could, I shut the door and went to my room. I sat on my bed and started to cry. Looking at my engagement ring, I didn't know how I was feeling about Pavle. Maybe this was too much for me or was it possible that I didn't care about him at all? Or maybe I was just too scared to start a family. My thoughts were a mix, and the best thing was just to go to bed and see what tomorrow was going to bring. Maybe I was just not prepared for this yet.

As I was going to lie down, the phone rang. Right away I knew it was Pavle. He was still drunk and I heard loud music. I thought maybe he'd gone back to the club but no, he was at home and he'd continued drinking. All I heard was, "Ramona, Ramona, come back to me!" Pavle was out of control. It was a good thing my uncle and aunt weren't home to witness me crying and going out again in the early morning hours. So, I told him I would be right over and to stop drinking.

Pavle's apartment was only ten minutes away from me, and as I knocked on his door, he yelled, "Who's there? Get lost."

He was so drunk that he didn't remember me telling him that I was coming. I knocked again, and then he finally opened the door. The expression on his face was so funny. Right out loud he yelled, "Hey, it's my Ramona—she loves me after all. Please, young lady, come in."

Some other tenants were not so happy about Pavle's loud music; I could hear them yelling at him to shut up. I closed the door fast, and turned the radio off. He was so drunk, I didn't know what to do, so I just pushed him on the bed, and he was out. I took his clothes off, and off he went. Sitting there and watching him made me a bit sad. Maybe he was a very lonely person, and with me being from the same country he was trying so hard.

Morning came, and Pavle had not a clue what had happened last night. Staring at me he was so surprised to see me. Then he jumped up and started to kiss me and hug me. I could tell he was totally confused.

"Ramona, I'm glad to see you. I thought I took you home last night, but looking at you here with me I'm so happy that we're together. I know you were just a bit mad because I drank too much, but I was so out of my mind glad that you accepted my marriage proposal. Please don't be upset at me. I'm very sorry if I was mean to you. I just don't remember anything."

"Listen Pavle, don't worry, everything is okay, just get some rest. Then we're going to see my aunt and uncle to tell them the good news, and we'll have to figure out our living arrangement. I don't want to live with you all the time for now, but we'll talk about that later. I'm going to make some breakfast and then after you rest we'll go."

After Pavle had a rest and once we finished eating, we got ready to go. Before we went, Pavle asked me not say anything to my aunt and uncle about him being stupid. I laughed and told him that kind of stuff was only between us.

My aunt and uncle were overjoyed at the news, and I knew my uncle was ready to give us a speech, but I beat him to it saying that we would get married sometime this year if everything went well. Because it was the New Year 1974, we all had a day off, and so Pavle and I hung around watching TV and just talking. Then Pavle got up and went to the living room to find my uncle and aunt. I wasn't sure what he was up to, so I followed. I was shocked when I heard him telling them that we were planning to move in together in next month or so.

I got mad and I said, "That is not what we talked about this morning. Pavle, please can I see you in my room, now?"

"No!" he said. "I want to live with you now and forever. I can't understand why we have to wait until we get married. We can get to know each other better and you don't always have to go to my place and then yours. We will be in one apartment. I'd like to hear from your uncle and aunt what they think."

"Pavle, I don't care what they think. I'm not moving in with you now, but I'm not saying I won't move in with you later. I believe that it is up to me, and only me."

Before I had a chance to say anything else my uncle stood up, and for once he was on my side. "Pavle, I think Ramona is right this time. Let her enjoy her engagement and let her have some privacy to reflect on her future. You'll be living together for the next fifty or more years, so let her be with us little longer. She is all we've got, and we care for her. Even though Ramona and I get into arguments, I still love her; she's our little girl."

I saw Pavle's face turn so red and frustrated. I knew he was upset. He'd been so sure that my uncle would be on his side, that he was shocked. He got up and said, "Very well, if you all think like that, but I'd prefer that she moved in with me now."

"Pavle it is not what I prefer," I said. "It just gives me some time and we'll see, maybe I'll move in next week or maybe next month, but it's my choice, so please let it go for now."

Again I wondered if I was making a mistake, but all I wanted was to have my family, so I was willing to put up with Pavle no matter what he threw at me.

(I didn't think this was wrong at the time, but it was.)

Once Pavle left, I called Megen and told her the news about our engagement. Megen wasn't surprised, but she thought Pavle was rushing me into marriage. Megen knew me well, but this time she was wrong. I was the one that wanted to get married. I'd lost Keven because I wanted to wait.

Then I called Mrs. Geyer and told her the same thing. She said that I was making a terrible mistake, and that one day I'd remember her words, but she wanted me to be happy. I thanked her and wished her all the best in moving to England. I started to cry, and she did the same. I'd lost the mother that I never had. All I could hear was, "Please don't cry, Ramona." Before we said good-bye, she told me that I could come and see her anytime. "You don't have to have a reason, just come, my dear." And that was the last time we talked until I was getting married.

Winter was like winter, cold and miserable, but if you liked to ski it was an excellent time. Pavle and I saw each other almost every day. We talked about the future, and he would tell me all about his mother and father back home. He had five brothers and two sisters, so they were a big family. Pavle never asked me about my life in the orphan village or my life with my mother; he seemed not to care, and that bothered me a bit. Quite often he would ask me what I had done all day if I was not at work, or where I went and with whom. Lots of stupid questions. I just ignored them, but one day he was so demented about it he tried to find out what I did at work or after work, and he got caught. My aunty saw his car around the corner on our street, and she told me. I was going to ask Pavle what the game was that he was playing, but this time I just ignored it. I told my aunt to let me know if she saw him again, and I asked her not say anything about this to anybody. I felt he was a bit jealous, but I thought most men were like that with a new relationship, so again I ignored it.

Winter came and went and we all were looking for spring and higher temperatures. But that's not all that came about. My regular monthly period never came. First I didn't panic but then May came, and I noticed that I was changing. I'd gained two pounds, and for me who never had weighed more than 105, that was a sign that something was wrong. I kept all that to myself and planned to see Dr. Andrew, whom I'd known for almost eight years.

At work I would be sick or throw up, and one of the ladies who'd known me for a long time, took a look at me one day and asked me, "Ramona! Do you know you're with child?"

"Tina, you're crazy. How can I be with child? We're very careful, no way, I sure hope not."

I was getting used to Pavle's little remarks. He was a good man in providing food and was a good worker, but was he good to me? I never felt any of the healthy love like I'd had with Keven, but I got by.

As I walked in that night, Pavle was surprised, because I usually went home before I went to his place. "Hi, Ramona, are you okay? How come you're here so early, is anything wrong?"

Well Pavle, sit down."

"Is anything wrong?"

"Well, yes and no. It all depends on what you think. Pavle, I think I'm pregnant. I'm not sure how many monthsm but I would guess three. It's a big shock to me, so you're the first one to know. I have an appointment withDr. A ndrew tomorrow, so I'll know for sure. I'm so scared, I don't know what to do."

"Oh Ramona, this is the best news I ever had! I'm going to be a father. I'm going to have a son. Sit down, let me see you. Yes, yes, yes you are a bit bigger and look at that bright face; you're just glowing. I'll go to the doctor with you and once he tells us all the details then we can make arrangements to get married. I don't want my child to be born as a bastard."

I started to cry. "Why did you have to use the word bastard? You very well know that I never had a father. Don't be so cold Pavle, the child is a child. And you presume it's a boy—don't do that. If the baby is a boy or a girl it will be our first child. As long as it's healthy, a baby is a baby. And yes, we're going to get married and start our family, just you and me and our children."

"Ramona, I'm so sorry, but right now all I can think is that baby is mine and you're going to be my wife soon. I'm so happy for both of us."

When I got to the doctor's office, he took me in first and told Pavle to wait because he had to do examine me. My doctor was a like a father to me. All these years he'd always looked after me and my uncle and aunt. He liked me because I tried to help my uncle with his drinking.

Once the exam was complete, he shocked me. "Ramona, yes you're pregnant three months and the baby should be with us sometime in January. But before you go any further, I know you're not married yet. Yes I know you're engaged, but Ramona do you really want to spend your life with that man? You may not know it, but your aunt is apprehensive. She thinks he is a troubled young man. She says that because she lived with one just like your Pavle. Many times Pavle has gone to the house, gotten your uncle drunk, and then asked him many stupid questions that no man in love would ask. I'm concerned about you, so please, if anything goes wrong get in touch with me. Before I let him in, make sure this talk stays just between us. So, now let's get him in."

When Pavle walked in he greeted him with, "Congratulations Pavle. You're going to be a father, and I sure hope you're ready. Ramona is in her third month and it looks like the baby should arrive some time early in January..Now all you have to do is take good care of Ramona, and there should be no problem. Ramona, I'd like to see you in about three weeks. Until then, take care and give me a call if you need anything."

As we drove home I was very lost in my mind. I didn't even notice when we got home.

"Hey, are you okay? What's wrong? Are you thinking about your Dr. Andrew? To me he looks like he likes you more than a patient. And just how long have you known him?"

"Pavle, are you kidding me? What's wrong with you? We're going to have a baby, and you're wondering how long I've know my doctor? Look Pavle, let me tell you this now and only once. If you don't stop being so jealous, I don't think I can go on being with you any more. For the last time Pavle, you have to change, or I'll be gone, and both of our dreams will be for nothing. You're getting to be impossible. If I was looking for another man, then whose baby am I carrying? Don't be so stupid. I'll raise this child on my own, if I have to, so please stop all those questions. I'm with you and only you, so knock it off. This is our happiest day, so don't spoil it. We have to start planning for our marriage and a bigger apartment, not fight. I hope you understand me. Now, I have to call my aunt and tell her the good news, so let's go home."

For the next few months Pavle was like an angel. He did everything possible to make me happy, and we found a two-bedroom apartment. We also decided to get married on July first; Canada day. I was starting to show, but not that much, so getting married in July was a good idea. I called Sam's father and asked him if we could have the wedding in his restaurant. I liked his food, and the place was beautiful and clean. Pavle was not so sure he liked that idea, but I assured him that the place was right, and we wouldn't have to pay so much, and then finally he agreed. Then I called Megen and Mrs. Geyer and told them both about my plans for the wedding. Megen was happy, and she decided to be my maid of honor. Mrs. Geyer was glad to see me happy too, but her answer was no. She wanted to know if I was marrying Pavle because I was pregnant. I assured her that I loved Pavle and that he had changed.

But Mrs. Geyer knew better, and what she told me stayed in my head all my life.

"Ramona, the wolf changes his coat, but never his mind, so be careful. Keep your eyes open and take care of the baby."

That was the last time I talked to her for a very long time.

My aunt helped me with finding my dress, and she gave us a beautiful bedroom set for our new apartment and many other things. She never told me she was happy that I was getting married, and her eyes were telling me that she wasn't. I told her that I was euphoric that from now on I'd have my family, and I'd try to be a good wife and a mother. She took me in her in arms and said, "Ramona, I know you're going to be a good wife and a mother, but I'm focusing on Pavle and his strange behaviour. Ever since you started going with him, you don't have any friends and you're always sad. I remember how happy you were with Keven, and I don't see that with Pavle, so I'm asking you one more time, are you sure you want to marry Pavle? If you're marrying him because of the baby don't do that. We can help you raise that kid—you don't have to put yourself through that. Your uncle is worried as well. Even though you two always fight, he cares, and we'd both like you to know we're here if you need us, now and forever."

I gave her a hug, and we both cried, and few minutes after we were all okay. I promised I would be careful, and told her that I was happy, and I'd be glad once we got married and could wait for baby to come. (But I knew deep in my heart that I was kidding myself.)

CHAPTER 31
July 1974, Ramona and Pavle

MEGEN AND SAM came from California and the three of us went out to celebrate our good old days. Pavle, as always, refused to be with us and for me and Megen that was just fine—we had lots of fun. And then Megan shocked me with a question. "Ramona, do you love Pavle or are you pretending that he is Keven? I have a feeling that you're confusing yourself about what you're going to do. Every time you or anybody mentions Keven's name your face lights up, but when it come to Pavle, your eyes are full of tears. Not many people notice that, but I do. So, are you marrying Pavle because you're pregnant, and is it the right thing to do for you and the baby? Ramona, it's not too late, please I beg you think actively with your heart not your head this time."

"Megen, I know that you and the rest of my family and friends don't like Pavle, and I understand that. He can be so rude to people, but he 's right for me. We're going to have a baby together and all I'm asking from you is to be happy for me. Maybe Pavle is not Keven. As a matter of fact, no one can replace Keven, but I have to go on, and Pavle is the man that I want to be with now. Do I love him? Meg, you and I have been friends for over ten years, and we always tell each other everything, so to answer your question do I love Pavle, well, no, I don't love him, but I do like him. I'm twenty-six years old, and it is time to settle down. Love has nothing to do with that. I only loved one man, and he's gone, and now I'm going to be a wife and a mother, so maybe love will come in time. Perhaps this is not the right way to start a marriage, but I'm going to give it a try. Please Meg, be my friend and let it go. I'm truly okay with all this. In two days I'm going to be married, and my secrets will be carried in my heart. I loved Keven so much that no man can replace him, but Pavle is here now and so am I."

I was in my room for the last time, and I heard Megen calling that it was time to go. The wedding was on schedule at one p.m., and Sam's father had made all the arrangements for the evening at his restaurant. I don't know what happened, but my whole body froze. I felt ill, dizzy, and icy. I thought maybe it was because I was pregnant, but deep inside me, I knew I was nervous to start a new life with Pavle. I hadn't told anybody, but sometimes I thought Pavle was disturbed, because he was such a jealous person, and if he didn't change I knew my life would be one great disaster.

Then, I saw Keven. He told me that everything was going to be all right… that he'd watch over me.

A knock on a door made me jump, and I realized I was dreaming. There was no Keven—he'd been dead for over four years.

My aunt called, "Ramona are you coming? The car is here, come on. You don't want to be late for your wedding."

"No, I'll be right there." I took a look at myself in the mirror. The white dress was beautiful, but that's all that was beautiful, my eyes were so sad, and my heart was bleeding. I'd made my choice, though, so with a head up, I walked to the car pretending I was the happiest person on earth.

Megan took one look at me, and we both knew the truth.

Pavle was in church waiting for us. He looked very handsome in his gray suit, and his best man was right beside him. There were not that many people; most of them would come later, so the priest came and asked us if we were ready. We looked at each other, and we both said yes, and so after an hour or so I was Ramona Obrenovic and the ring on my finger told me that I was a married woman now. I knew Pavle was euphoric, but there was that funny smirk on his face that I never liked. He held my hand and whispered. "Ramona, you're my wife now, don't you ever forget that. We're going to have a big family, and this baby boy is the beginning of our future."

I looked at him with a smile and I never said anything, but my heart felt the threat.

After the wedding, we both took two days off from work because Pavle did not believe in honeymoons, so two days was enough for him. After that it was back to work as usual. I was planning to work until the end of November, so I had lots of time. Most of my working hours I had to spend on filing orders and all the people at work were so good to me. Leaving them after nine years would be very hard, but life goes on, and that is how my working at *Fashion and Pattern* magazine ended.

At eight months pregnant, I had a sad and lonely life. Pavle made sure I didn't have any close friends. He knew Megen was in Californa and the rest of my friends from work didn't like Pavle, so I ended up lonely. My aunt would come and see me once in a while, and Megen called me almost once a month. I never returned her calls, but Megen knew why. Pavle would check the phone bill and get so mad when he saw long distance charges, so I stopped. But I continuing writing to her.

On my twenty-seventh birthday, my aunt came and gave me a birthday card, but the card was not from her, it was from Megen. She wanted to know why I hadn't returned any of her letters! I'd thought Megen was busy, so I never paid any attention to not hearing from her, until now. I got very upset, so when Pavle came home, I asked him very nicely, "Pavle what have you done with the mail that Megen sent me?"

"What mail are you talking about?"

"Look, Pavle don't play stupid. Megen used my aunt's address to send me a birthday card because she was wondering what is going on. So tell me what's going on. I'd like to know. What have you done with my mail?"

"Okay, I just threw them in the garbage. You don't need to keep in touch with those hippies—all you need is me, and soon you will have a baby, and that's all you need. I don't like that gay woman, and I know that the two of you have some dirty secret. I won't let you be friends with her any more."

"Pavle, you cannot keep me locked up like an animal. I need to have some friends; someone to talk to when you're at work, or just some small talk. I have one more month of work, and then I won't have any friends if you act like this."

I was not prepared for his response.

He grabbed me by my hair, pulled me towards the wall, and pressed his fists under my chin. I started choking; then he let me go with a threat. "Next time you will not be so lucky."

I froze. What had just happened? Was this the man that I married, or the monster that everybody was telling me that he was. No, no, he'd just lost control, I had to believe that. I was very upset, and in a way I was scared. Pavle noticed that I was crying, so he came and said he was sorry. When it came to Megen he just couldn't help but get upset. Megan and Sam were a threat to him, but why I didn't know. After that day he never did the same thing again, but now and then he would call me names or he would not talk at all. Then the time came for me to quit my job. I was seven months pregnant and big, so I said goodbye to all the people that I'd worked with for so long. It was a sad day for me. They brought me lots of baby clothes and some gifts for me. My favourite present was a large photo of us in the early years; even Mrs. Geyer was in there. I cried because I was so sad. I knew that as of today, my lonely days were coming until the baby came.

And I was right.

Dr. Andrew told me that the baby was doing well, and that he thought it was a girl. Well, that part I did not tell Pavle because he was so sure we were going to have a boy. Often he would say that all clean woman surely have a boy baby first. I knew what he meant by clean, but I ignored the remark. I knew I was getting into something no good, but I thought it was too late to change, and I kept everything to myself.

(I was wrong, I should have left him that day.)

Staying home all alone felt so lonely. There was not much to do because the place was small and cleaning was not a big deal. Every day I would be so happy to see Pavle after work. He would ask me what I did all day and if I'd gone out. We would talk about our baby that was due in about five weeks. Christmas was coming so we got ready to go to my aunt's place, and for the New Year, we would stay home since I was getting fat. Secretly I wrote Megen a Christmas card, and in the card I told her I was just fine (which was a lie), and told her not to worry. I had to give it to my aunt to mail it, because Pavle would have killed me if he knew I was still in contact with Megen and Sam.

Christmas came, and we were at my folks' place. I had a good time and my aunt told me in secret that there was a letter from Megen in my room. I excused myself from the table to go lie down for a moment, but I was going to get Megen's letter. I was just about to open it, and there he was with a cold look in his eyes. "Are you okay?" he said. "If you like, we can go home. Come on get up. Let me help you."

As I got up, my letter fell on the floor. I froze again; I knew what was going to happen.

Pavle grabbed me, took me to the living room, and told my uncle that my aunt and I were doing things behind his back, and that if we continued: "I'll not come to your house any more. I'm Ramona's husband, and she has to do what I say." Then he grabbed me and pulled me towards the door. I looked for help.

My uncle got up and told Pavle to sit down and listen because this was the only time he'd say this. "Pavle if you ever hurt Ramona, or do any harm, you will answer to me. I have to respect you for marrying her, but I'll not let you make her your prisoner. She and that girl Megen were friends since they were kids, and you cannot break a friendship like that. Megen is like a sister to Ramona, so don't you ever make threats to her again. Ramona can come back home, and we will take care of her and the baby and you, you can go to h..."

Before my uncle finished the sentence, I stopped him. "Please, it's Christmas, let's not behave like mad people. Uncle don't worry everything is going to be okay. I'll call Megen and tell her not to write me anymore. I'll..."

My uncle stood up. "No, no you won't do that! She is your friend and she'll stay your friend. Pavle whether you like it or not, Megen can write Ramona through us and that's that—subject closed. Now let's have that dessert that your aunt made for us."

That was the worst Christmas I'd had, and going home that night with Pavle I honestly felt scared for my life and the baby's.

Once we got home, Pavle threw me on the bed and hit me so hard on my head that I got dizzy and almost lost my breath. Angrily, he said, "Ramona, you listen to me! You and your parents, I mean your drunken uncle and stupid aunty, can all go to hell. You're going to do what I say, and once the baby is born they will be going out of your life just like the rest of the world. You have me and soon will have a baby, and that should be enough. And soon we'll have another one once this one is born. All my brothers and sisters back home don't have many people around them, we all just care for our own families; that means you, our children, and me. Once the baby comes, you won't have time to think about stupid Megen and the others. So get to bed now. I'm getting so tired of all this shit."

CHAPTER 32

About 10:30 on Sunday morning January 16th, 1975, I was washing dishes from breakfast, and then I felt warm water coming. I was in a labour, so I called Pavle and told him to get ready, the baby was coming. The hospital was close by and going to the delivery room I was so excited and scared at the same time. *I'm going to be a mother, I'm going to have a child,* and for the first time in my life I knew that the baby was all I was waiting for.

Pavle left me in the delivery room; there was no way he was going in because he said it was my duty as a wife to give him children and I had to put up with the pain all by myself. That was no news to me, so I was fine and in about two hours the baby came. It was a girl, just like Dr. Andrew had told me. I started to cry; those were happy tears. *I'm the mother of a baby girl.* Dr. Andrew went out to give the news to Pavle, and meanwhile, my uncle and aunt came as well—we were still talking for now. The doctor told them it was a girl, and Pavle's expression was uneasy. He was stunned—he'd wanted a boy, and look, a girl. My uncle and aunt congratulated him, but he didn't care.

He came to my room, and without any happiness he said, "Where is my boy? A girl, how could you do this to me? Hope you're happy, now I'm going home. I have to get her room ready and will pick you up in a couple of days. For the birth certificate tell them that her name is Vesna."

"But, Pavle what kind of name is that? We live in Canada, and I think we should give her a Canadian name."

"Well, well, I wanted a boy, and you gave me a girl, so you see, we don't always get what we want, so her name is Vesna, whether you like it or not."

He never even showed a little happiness, so I was crying, and then my uncle and aunt came and congratulated me. They told me that if Pavle went on giving me a problem to pack up and come home. But no, again I said everything was going to be okay, he was jus a little disappointed, because he had wanted a boy very badly.

Once I got home with the baby, the tension between Pavle and me was unbearable. Pavle barely ever spoke to me, only if it was necessary. At night we'd go to bed, and he would actually rape me. It felt like revenge—it was foul. I would cry, and I know I was getting depressed.

After a week or so we were just an ordinary couple with a baby. Pavle learned to love little Vesna. He would go out with her, meaning I didn't have to step outside myself. But when he went to work, I always took the baby for fresh air even it was winter. Five or ten minutes made her sleep better. One day Pavle asked me if I went out at all. Pretending I didn't know what he was asking me, I just said no, it was freezing outside. Then he got so upset, he grabbed my hair and punched me in the head. The reason he hit the head, was so that no one could see marks on it.

"You, you are a lying bitch! I know you were out almost every day, so don't you lie to me. From now on you better stop lying, and everything will be okay, otherwise you might regret it. I saw you looking at that guy across the street. He's good looking, hey? Blond like me, so perhaps the baby is his? What do you say to that?"

"Pavle, let me go, and I'm telling you this—this is the last time you are hitting me and treating me like that. I will go back to my family and you'll never see the baby or me again."

After that big argument, Pavle was an angel. He would take us out, maybe to a mall or just a short walk to the park. So, I thought he had changed. But at night in the bedroom, he was a heartless madman, and I figured a man like him could not change everything. And like before, I felt obligated to him because he was my husband. My loneliness no one knew and I never complained, so, months went by so with my disappointment in life. Many times though, I would talk to my little angel and she would laugh and make my day.

One day Pavle called to tell me that he had to work overtime and would be home very late, so I decided to go to the park since it now was summer and the day was perfect for Vesna to be outside. As I was pushing the stroller, I felt that someone was following me. As quickly as possible I went back to our apartment, wondering who.

Since Pavle never made any comment about me going out when he came home, I told him that we went to the park, but something weird had happened, I told him. "I believe that someone was following me."

He grabbed me, and this time he didn'tt hit me but gave me a funny look. "You stupid bitch. That was me. I wanted to see where you go and with whom you talk all the time. So you see, you never know where I am, so be extra careful when you go out. Make sure that your boyfriend knows that I'm watching you both."

First, I figured, *Oh God! Here we go again.* To me it felt like every six months this man went nuts, I didn't care anymore, I just didn't care if he killed me. I had no desire to live anyway. So I turned around and looked at his face, and right out in the open I asked him if was crazy. "If I have a boyfriend why are you still with me? You are nothing but a madman!" and I slammed the door and went to the bedroom.

Pavle was shocked and never said anything. Just like nothing had happened, he came, and went to sleep.

So, that's how my life went on; sad, miserable, and heartbroken. Many many times I thought to run away, but where? He would find me, so I just continued living like a prisoner, because no one knew Pavle like I did.

I was even lying to my aunt that Pavle was a good man. I didn't want her to worry, so I kept it all to myself. And then my worst nightmare came. I got pregnant again. I thought about what to do, but maybe this time it would be a boy, and Pavle would change. But no such luck, I had another girl. She was born on August 7th, 1977, and this time Pavle was at work when the baby came. Dr. Andrew called him and told him that he was the father of another healthy little girl. Pavle didn't come to the hospital for five days. He didn't want to see the baby or me. For the birth certificate, I gave her a name that I liked and my new baby girl's name was Sandra. While I was in the hospital, our best man and his wife looked after Vesna, which I was happy to hear.

Finally, Pavle had no choice. He had to come and take us home, but he was cold as an ice cube. He never even looked at Sandra and never asked her name, so I just ignored him and went on with my life. Now I had two girls, and they occupied my time. Pavle and I never spoke for almost a month or so, but that never bothered me. He would come from work, eat, and then he would take Vesna out, and only return for her sleeping time. I think he was so disappointed that he had a girl again he was blaming me for it. One day he told me that Sandra didn't look like him and maybe she was not his. Sandra looked like him more than Vesna did, but Pavle refused to see that. Anyway, time went by and so did our lives. No one noticed my pain and my sorrow. I couldn't remember anymore when I had been truly happy. Yes, when the girls were born but even in that time, I had no one to share it with. My aunt and uncle finally gave up on me leaving Pavle, so I was truly on my own. Pavle knew that and took advantage of it to abuse me, and sometimes he would hit me.

The girls were growing pretty fast, and they both looked like Pavle more than me, so finally after a long time he started to play with Sandra, and would take both of them out to the park. I think deep inside of him, that he loved them, but his male pride made him think it would better if the girls were boys. Eventually, he was so fond of them that he would go and buy them things so expensive that it would make me mad, but like always I tried to ignore it, though it was hard on many occasions. Pavle would buy them everything, but as for me, I could go around like a bag lady, he wouldn't care.

Magna Tools and Mechanics was an excellent company where Pavle worked, and in 1979 the company was moving from Toronto to Ajax, which was not that far. That move was on September 15th, so before Pavle had to travel to work that far he decided that we'd move to West Scarborough. I didn't care. What I suggested was that there was a building in the area where Pavle was looking to move, where they were looking for a full-time superintendent/manager who was willing to live in the building. The offer was a three-bedroom apartment and a full salary for one person. I talked to Pavle and suggested that this way we could save some money, and maybe in a few years, we could have a down payment for a house. And this way I could stay home with the kids. Or if he didn't like it, then we would go on living on one salary.

To my big, and I mean big surprise Pavle agreed with me. He that if I could get that job, then before we moved, we could go on a vacation. I was thrilled because we were married four years by now and we'd never had a holiday. But my happiness did not last long. Pavle wanted us to to Yugoslavia so I could meet his family. I knew he loved his mother; in secret he was sending her money, but I just closed my eyes like I always did. I hoped that one day I'd have enough courage to leave him, but not yet.

So next day we drove to the office. Pavle was working night shift, so he came with me (no surprise to me), to see the building and the owner. The owner was a very nice man; his name was Mr. Samul Browckyski. The job was that one person, that would be me, would stay home and do all collections for rent on each month, and would look after maintenance, to keep the lobby clean at all times, and to assist the superintendent if needed. In addition to the salary and free three-bedroom apartment, there would be vacations after three months. The apartment was on the second floor, and the office was on the main floor, where I would work if hired. It sounded excellent. The school was nearby, right behind a park. I liked it very much, and I think the owner was pleased with my working history, which was in one place for nine years. The job would be available on January first, but since it was only September, we would have to stay in the old apartment for another four months. I was willing to that, so it was all up to Pavle.

Mr. Browckyski told us he had one more couple to interview, and he'd call us in a day or so. Before we left, I asked Mr. Browckyski if he hired me, if it would be possible that we could have a vacation in July for three weeks, because Pavle' mother would like to see us, and we hadn't had a holiday in four years.

"Mrs. Obranovic, I don't see any problem, but you have to prove to me that you can handle the work. Having two small children it won't be so easy, but like I said, I don't see any other problem. According to your last name are you both from Yugoslavia? I have one small building downtown, and its superintendents are from Serbia, I presume it is the same thing. Those people are very friendly, and we like them, so we will get in touch with you, and thank you for coming."

The opportunities were there; it was all up to Pavle. As we drove home, for the first time since we'd married, he asked me what I thought. Quietly I told him it would be much easier on the budget, and I thought I won't have any trouble handling the job.

He looked at me with an approving smile and said, "Okay, Ramona, let's do it. That way we can save a lot of money, but I want you to remember I'll be watching you, so you better know what you're doing. That means do your job and nothing else."

"Pavle, if you're going to be suspicious of me in any way then let's forget it. I can stay home, and you can lock the door and buy some more tape. You can tape the doors again to check if I went out or not. I never told you, but I knew you have been putting tapes on the bottom of the door so that if I open it, you'll know I went out. You have done some stupid things, and this time I'm dead serious…you better stop. You being so jealous is getting out of hand, so you better make up your mind. If you'd like to keep us in person, just grow up and let's try to make our life little better."

"Okay, okay, stop. I do admit I have done a lot of stupid things to you, but I'm a changed man now, and I know you're a good mother, and I don't want to lose you. I'd like you to call Mr. Browckyski and ask him if he has decided on which couple he'll take. Tell him that we're very interested and we can start right in the new year.

In the next four months Pavle never said anything on my birthday, or for Christmas. He had lots of toys for the girls, but totally ignored me, and I was sorrowful. I had no one to care for me. As I was packing, I found old pictures of Megen and me. Looking at her picture made me start to cry. Why had I not listened to her and the others, what had I done to myself? But it was all too late now. I had children, and I needed them to have both parents. I'd grown up with no one, and I did not want that for my girls. I knew I was going to take a lot from Pavle; I knew he wouldn't change, but as soon my girls got to be in their early teens, I'd leave him forever. That's the promise I made to myself. I put Megen's picture back in the box.

The next day we were ready to move to our new place—it was the year 1980.

CHAPTER 33

NEW JOB, NEW apartment, new surrounding area, I loved all. I thought maybe with this move Pavle and I would be better. What I mean is, I was hoping Pavle would be happy. The girls were so happy for having separate rooms. Vesna was almost five, and Sanda would be three in August. We didn't have enough furniture for three bedrooms, but it slowly added up. I loved my new job. I got to know the owner of the building and most of the tenants. The girls were always with me, but we did go upstairs for break time, and I had to make supper. So I was working from nine to four, and then I went upstairs. We had regular superintendents, a couple from Romania and they had three children, and we got along good. The building was kept immaculate because that is the way I like it and the owner did notice a lot of changes. Many times he gave me a compliment, and I knew I was doing a good job. Pavle was all right... well most of the times, and I knew why. All he cared about was for us to go to Yugoslavia for me to meet his family. We never had too many friends, or we never had any, except the godparents to our children, and they were from Pavle's province in Serbia, I was from the north. Anyway, they would come now and then, and that was all. I had lost all my friends so my life was lonely and sad. I called my aunt and told her that we had moved. I gave her my office phone and explained when to call me. She understood and was somber that I was so unhappy. My uncle was drinking more now, there was no one to bug him about it, and he had been ill, mostly due to the drinking, but there was nothing I could do. I had my own problems.

In early May I had to go downtown for a passport, so I took a chance and went to a women's shelter to find out what my chances were if I had to leave Pavle. The place was not too far from the passport office. As I walked in Vesna was curious as to why we were there, because there were so many kids and women there. I told her that one of my friends lived there and I wanted to talk to her. She somehow did not believe me, but then a lovely lady came and asked me if I need help. Before I answered her, she said, "Let me take the girls to play with our children in the other room." The girls were a bit shy to go, but I told them I wouldn't be long, and then as they left I went to a room for a talk.

The first thing she said was, "Look Mrs….or is it Miss?"

"I'm married."

"Okay, what's your name.?

"My name is Ramona Obranovic…".And suddenly I found myself pouring out my heart to this nice woman, about my growing up and the abuse in my marriage, and how I was afraid of my girls growing up without two parents. So, you see why I'm looking into this," I said. "The truth is I don't know if I can do it. I know I need help, and I would be grateful for any advice you could give me."

"First of all Ramona, you see this is the city of Toronto. You live in Scarborough, so there is no way we can keep you here, we do have a long waiting list for families like yours, and we only take emergencies right away. But what I can do for you is give you the address of the Scarborough women's shelter. I know the woman that works there. Let me write down the phone number and then you can call her, and she'll help you. But my honest and truly best advice to you, Ramona would be don't wait too long. I have seen lots of men like your husband, and we always say that a wolf changes his coat, but not his mind, which is always ready to kill, So my dear be careful and take care."

I thanked her, and looking at my watch I knew I'd better get home soon. Vesna was asking me many questions, but I just told her that my friend needed my help.

Later that evening after supper Pavle asked me about passports and I said they would be ready the next week. Just then Vesna laughed and said, "Daddy we went to a big building. There were lots of kids there, and Mommy was talking to a lady, and we played in the other room."

I scrambled for an excuse because I knew that he wanted to grab me and kill me, but Vesna was there, so he just stayed calm. But after the girls had gone to bed I knew what was coming. Pavle grabbed me by my hair, pulled me into the washroom, and with his fist hit me right in my stomach. I almost passed out, but he grabbed me again and demanded for me to tell him about the man I was with today.

I got up carefully and tried to explain to Pavle that there was no man involved. "I went there to see a girl that used to live in our old building. She works there, and since I was in town I wanted to say hello, nothing else. Vesna has a wild imagination and she likes to say things just to please you, but you better be careful Pavle—I have also learned where I can get help. So go ahead, beat me or do whatever you like, but my time will come. Vesna is almost six, and Sanda is a little over three, they are too young to understand what goes on, but it won't be long, mark my words."

"Ramona, I told you when we got engaged that you're going to be only mine and that is how it's going to be always. If you like, you can get the hell out, but the girls will stay with me, or I'll fight you for them, for the rest of my life, and maybe I'll strangle you or something. Now mark my words, you fat whore."

That night was the first night that I slept on a couch, I was honestly scared, but next morning for the children's sake I pretended everything was good. Pavle ate his breakfast and told me that he was not mad at me. He whispered in my ear, "Tonight I'll be your handsome prince; I won't now or ever live without you, don't forget that." Because the girls were there, he kissed me.

Something went through my body like an icy shiver. I looked into his poisoned eyes and said, "I can't wait."

Once Pavle left I told Vesna that I'd like to talk to her. I knew she was only five and a half, but I had to say to her that lying is bad, she was hurting mommy. Sandra was playing with the superintendent's kids, so I had a chance to talk to Vesna alone.

She looked at me and said, "Mommy are you mad at me?"

I think she knew that she'd been telling lies to her father, so I went right out and asked her, "Vesna my dear, can you say one thing to me? Do you know the difference between truth and lies? Do you understand?"

She looked at me and smiled. "Sure, Mommy. I know the difference. Daddy says if I tell him things he'll buy me new toys, and I mean all the time. I know you see your friends, but Daddy likes to hear different, so I lie to him. I'm very sorry Mommy, but you never buy me things, and daddy does, so can I go now?"

"No, you can not go now. Sit here and listen to me. Vesna my dear, I'd like you to stop lying, that is terrible. Nobody likes liars, and nobody will play with you if they find out you are a liar. You must always tell the truth; lying won't get you anywhere. Maybe you are too young to understand all this, but I'd like you to promise me, No more lies. I love you and I always will, but please be nice and from now on listen to your mom, no more lies."

Poor child, she was so confused and scared. I gave her a hug and told her I loved her.

"Okay, may I go and play now? And I won't lie anymore."

That night after supper we sat and watched TV, and then Vesna got up and went to her father, and right out she said, "Daddy no more lies about Mommy. I love her more than your toys."

I almost fell off the chair. I saw Pavle's face turn so red I thought he would shoot me right there, he was so sure I had put Vesna up to this. "Honey what are are you talking about?"

"Well, Daddy, you ask me every day did Mommy do this and that, so I always say, yes, and next day you brings me a new toy, but I don't want to lie anymore. I'm sorry Daddy."

Poor kid, she was so scared but brave at the same time.

Once we were alone, Pavle just stood up, and with no signs of anger or anything, he just spoke very quietly. "Ramona, I'm sorry. I'm going to bed. It was a hard day at work today."

After that day everything seemed to be a little bit different. I noticed how Pavle ignored Vesna on many occasions, and the poor kid was so sad. One day she was crying and told me that she thought that Daddy didn't love her anymore. She thought maybe it would be better if she started to lie again. I almost had a heart attack. Talking to her I told her that Daddy loved her even more now, he was just so sad that he'd made her lie to him. "Don't worry about anything he'll buy you more toys, and I'm sure he loves you a lot."

A week after, I went to pick up the passports, but this time I left the girls with the superintendent. I came home very fast, and the girls were okay. Pavle asked me if I went to pick up the passports and wanted to know if I went with the girls or just me. For a moment I was going to lie, but no, I just said, "I went by myself. Why are you asking me this?"

"No reason, just wondering." That's what he said, but I knew different. Pavle's face was full of anger, and as soon I put the girls to bed he just blew up. "Ramona, if you have someone, please tell me. You can not respond to me like that. Running around with another man, I can not take it."

For a moment I wasn't sure if he was sad or mad or if he wished I'd just disappear. I took his hand in my and told him, "Pavle, you are the only man I have, and you will be the only one as long as we live. I want you to know that. I have never been with any other man except you ever since we got together. So don't do this to yourself, you've got to trust me, or you will destroy the family, which I know you love."

For the first time since I knew Pavle, I saw tears in his eyes. He took my hand and made me go to our bedroom, and that night Pavle was the man that I always wanted.

Three months passed by, and I hadn't heard from Mr. Browckyski about my new contract or if I could go on vacation for three weeks. I was a bit worried, but then his son came one day with a big apology from his father. "I'm Mr. Browckyski's older son Mosha. Mr. Browckyski is very ill, but he wanted you to know you that you can have your three weeks vacation and he is willing to give you a raise. But he'd like you to promise him that you will be back and will stay in the building at least two more years."

"Mosha, may I call you by your first name?"

"Yes, yes Ramona by all means."

"I'm sorry to hear about your father's illness and sure hope he'll be better very soon. I'll call him tomorrow, and personally thank him. I have no attention to move for at least three or more years, so no worries there."

"Ramona, please don't call him, he is very ill, and I'm not so sure if he's ready to be disturbed, but I'll take your message to him. And one more thing.. When are you planning to go on vacation? I need to know so I can have a temp covering you while you're away."

"As of now we're leaving on July 3rd and will be back on July 28th. Right back to work on time for August rent."

"That sounds good. Thank you Ramona. You are the best building Manager we ever had, so I'll see you before you go on your vacation, and your pay is more as of April 15th. I'm sure you,l will be satisfied with your new contract and pay."

As Mosha was living Pavle walked in and he looked upset. "Who the hell was that in the office with you behind a closed door?"

"Calm down Pavle; that is Mr. Browckyski's son." Then I told him about our conversation.

"So, your new boss is cute, is that what you think? But you'd better watch it, that pretty boy is not cute for me."

"Pavle stop that, we talked about your jealousy before, you have to stop it. It's not my fault if some good looking man walks in and talks to me, that doesn't mean I'm going to jump in bed with him. Maybe if you were working here and a good looking woman walked in, just maybe you'd jump in bed with her. What about that!"

I think I got him where he wasn't ready to answer. Instead, he walked out slamming the door. I just laughed to mysel, *What an idiot.*

Later when we were leaving for the airport Mosha came upstairs to wish us a good vacation. His father was getting little better, and they all hoped for the best. I thought it was sweet of him, but Pavle was furious. "Why did he come to say goodbye, is he going to miss you or what? You're so stupid Ramona, I can't deal with this now, at least back home you will learn how to obey your husband and always look down. Let's go; I can't wait to get the hell away from here and your lovers."

I just said thank you to Moshe and gave a Pavle dirty look, just like he gave me one. More and more I had been answering him in a bad way. I was struggling to stay quiet these days and deep inside me I kept saying, *My day will come, you're going to be sorry for everything.*

Come to think of it, I was getting just as bad. I had all wrong though in my head. I just did not care anymore. Going back to Yugoslavia to his hometown was good for me because I'd search until I found out who in his family was like him.

Pavle had been away from his hometown for nearly twelve years. And when we arrived I had a big shock; there was no one waiting for us at the airport. With two small children and suitcases, it was very hard to travel, and I was wondering if they even knew that we were coming or was he worthy of them, to come and bring him back home? Pavle must have read my mind and was saying how hard was for his folks to get all the way to Belgrade to greet us, but I smelled dirt. That is no way you treat your brother, son, or new family member; not sending at least one person to help, but I kept my mouth shut. I knew somehow that I'd learn something.

As we arrived at his house, his mother was the first one to welcome us. Pavle totally ignored me for a while, but his father, old Bora, came right to me and gave me a big hug, and kissed both girls. Bora was a gentleman. I could tell by his eyes that he was happy to see us, but there were no happy greetings for his son, not like his mother. There right there, I noticed a story behind Pavle, his mom, and the rest of the family. None of his brothers or sisters came to see us, but Pavle had an excuse for everything.

The house was slightly small with only a kitchen and one large bedroom, which had one bed. I looked at Pavle and wondered where we were all going to fit.

"Ramona, don't worry about living space. I have arranged for two small beds which are right under the big bed, and my mother will sleep in the kitchen on a sofa, and my father sleeps in the summer house, so no worries at all, we will manage. Once we get rested and settle down, we will be going to meet my brothers and sisters. They all live not too far from here, so a country buggy with the best horses will take us everywhere, and I think that my older brother has a car. If possible, I'll ask him to let us have it for few days."

The girls were happy, to them rooms and beds didn't make any difference as long as we were all together. I personally noticed that house was spotless. I had a funny feeling it wouldn't stay clean as long as we were there, but this was a county home so for me it was okay.

It took us a couple of days to rest. Meantime lots of neighbours came to say hello to us, mostly to meet the children and me. Not many people came to say hello to Pavle, and I wondered why. Why didn't they like him? Was the whole world against him, or what was it that I didn't see? My goal was to find out once and for all and to add that I did not have to wait too long to see what was really going on or what had been going on a long time ago. Pavle's father noticed that I was alone with Sandra, so he came and sat beside me. I saw that he wanted to say something but was somehow afraid. I took his hand in mine and right out I asked him if there was anything I should know about Pavle, and why was everybody in this village not so happy to see him except his mother? Before he answered my questions, he asked me if Pavle and his mother went with Vesna to town or just to the neighbours.

"Father, Boro, why are you afraid of Pavle or what's going on?"

It took him a minute or so to answer me. "If they went to town, then we have lots of time to talk, let the little one play with the chickens and cats, and I can answer a lot of your unanswered questions. Ramona my dear, I'm not afraid of Pavle, but I'm afraid of what his mother is going to put in his head, which is always wrong. It all started a long time ago when Pavle was in his late teens or early twenties, I can't remember any more. His mother did not like our older son's new bride, and she put lots of evil thoughts in Pavle's head and told him to watch every move she made. After that, she groomed him to learn how to lie about things that never happened. It did not take Pavle to do what his mother wanted him to do, because he was a strange child from the beginning. Most of his problem is or has been that he is a very jealous, intense, and disturbed man. He told lots of untrue stories to his brothers and one sister. One time he tried to end his life by drinking some kind of poison that was unfamiliar to any doctors in our area, but his evil mind was with him all the time. Lots of folks in our village don't like him, thanks to his mother. Pavle is a good man when he wants to be, but can be just as dangerous as well. One of his sisters was divorced because she believed that her husband was cheating on her because Pavle told her he saw him with another woman, which was a lie. Many, many things he has done…many wrongdoings. I only hope that Pavle has changed, but we all know that the wolf does modify the fur but not his mind. I see you are a very kind person, you have two lovely girls, but are you happy with Pavle Ramona?"

"Father Boro, I'm going to be very honest with you. Pavle is a good man as far as providing for a house and the girls, but as for me, I'm just a rug that he walks on. I do care for him, and I felt sorry for him many, many times. But there were times I just had enough, and I wanted to leave him. Pavle has hit me many times, and abuses me by telling me all the nasty things, and sometimes if he feels like it, he just throws me in bed and rapes me. I have lost all my friends because of him, and my aunt and Uncle don't want anything to do with him, but I keep hoping he'll change, and for the past six years he hasn't changed. I know I should leave him, and I will, but not yet, and I sure hope it won't be too much later. One day he came and asked me if I'd like to kill myself. He said it would be easy for me, and he'll tell the girls I was a sick person. Is this a man I should stay with? I honestly think Pavle is crazy, and he needs help, but he won't admit that, so I just go on until my time comes."

"Ramona, I can give you one piece of advice. Whatever you're going to do, don't come back to live with Pavle here. There is no protection for a woman, no matter how bad the husband is. I know in America it's a little better, and please don't wait too long. You see me. I'm a man, but your mother-in-law is and has always been abusing me, in different ways, but as you see I stay in the summer house. I just stay with her because of custom. You don't have to do that. I'm your father-in-law, and I should be happy that you love my son, but not this one. All my other daughters-in-law are happy, and all of them don't like your mother-in-law. So you see Pavle is the black sheep in the family and it is all because of Tanja, your mother-in-law."

"Father, I can hear a car coming, maybe Pavle found a car so that we can travel easier. He'd like us to go and visit all of his brother and sisters, and I'm so not looking forward to that."

"Don't worry about his brothers or sisters, they'd all love to meet you and the girls, but don't be surprised if some of them won't be home or pretending they're gone somewhere. One more thing, Ramona. Please let our talk stay between us. Otherwise, both of us will pay the price."

"Father Boro, you have my word and thank you for everything that you told me. I'm sure that it took a lot of guts to tell me the truth and for that, I'll be forever thankful."

When he came in, Pavle had a big smile on his face, but his mother looked so miserable and scared.

"Hey Ramona, look I found a rental car, so now we can go everywhere with the girls and if my mom likes she can come as well."

All I could think was, *Great, that's all I need her behind my back all the time,* but I just smiled and pretended I was happy.

The next five days were so tiring for girls and me. We went to see all his brothers and two sisters, but like Father Boro said, some probably wouldn't be there, and he was right. Pavle's older brother and his wife welcomed us very politely and with a great lunch. They had five boys and one girl, and poor thing, she had to do everything, but I guess that is how they treat a woman in that part of the universe. As we were ready to leave his brother said goodbye to me. Then I saw him whisper something to Pavle. I saw tears in Pavle's eyes, but I just kept my mouth shut. I don't know what he said, but for the rest of the trip Pavle was sorrowful and soundless. Once we got back to the village he told his mother to leave him alone, and he looked at me and gave me a dirty look. I had no idea why, but I just turned and walk away. Father Boro was sitting under a tree, so I sat beside him and told him what happened. He wasn't surprised at all, he just shook his head and walked back to his summer house.

The next day we went to see Pavle's second brother; they were only a half-hour car trip away. This time the old woman came with us, and she made me sick. She gave me a sly smile, and I just returned the same. I wanted her to know that she couldn't control me, and I think she was getting the message. His second brother was home with all four children; two boys, and two girls, but his wife went to see her mother because she was ill. I was getting the message. Pavle was not welcome in his village at all. His brother apologized for his wife's situation, but I told him not to worry. As he was saying goodbye to us, he too whispered something to Pavle, and the same thing happened. Pavle was so sad I actually felt sorry for him. He thought that time had passed and people would have forgotten what he did, but I guess not in that part of the world. Both Pavle and his mother were miles away, but I knew better. No one wanted to see them, or they were afraid that he might cost some problems again. Communication between Pavle and his mother worsened.

After of two days of dramas, Pavle decided next day we'd go to town where the circus was in. The girls were so happy to do something different, and so was I.

After a good day in the city, we were all so tired but happy. Pavle was in a better mood, but I knew that would change as we planned to go and see his third brother, Toma, the one is with the most children; total seven. I didn't know what was with this person having all those children? Next morning, as we were ready to leave Pavle asked his mother if she'd like to come with us since the trip would be only half an hour or so. She was so happy, but not so much me.

Once we arrived at Toma's house, there was a bunch of kid outside standing with a woman all smiling and happy. I couldn't believe she took care of the four boys and three girls. She gave me a big hug and just a handshake to Pavle but as for her mother-in- law, she never even looked at her. A bell rang in my head. This one didn't like our mother-in-law, hurray for her and me.

The kids stayed outside to play with the others while we went inside. The place was so messy and kind of dirty, but with all those kids I wasn't surprised. She offered us coffee and fresh bread and some fresh plums. The food was delicious, but I didn't know what I had drunk. It wasn't coffee. She must have noticed my surprise and told me she made coffee by herself from some wild grasses. Okay, I thought, as long as it wasn't poison it was fine with me. Her name was Rada; I liked her. She got up and asked me if I'd like to come with her, she'd like to show me the rest of the house and all the pigs, cows, horses and many other animals. But I got the feeling that's not what she wanted. Once we were a bit far from Pavle and his mother, Rada opened up to me.

"Ramona, my husband is home, he is hiding in the barn. You see Pavle has always called him names and me too. He called his brother a drunken, stupid man, and he called me a Gypsy. You know my skin is a bit darker than yours, so he told everybody in the village that Toma married big fat Gypsies. They don't like each other at all, and Toma thought it would be best if he doesn't show up at all. So, please accept his apology, and you are always welcome to my home, no matter what."

"Oh my dear Rada, don't worry I'm not mad at you or Toma, this same thing happened when we went to see his other brothers. A younger brother wasn't even at home, I mean no one, his sister was the only one that welcomed him, but I know now that Pavle has done a lot of wrong things in his youth. But I wonder how come no one thought to forgive him. After all, that all happened long time ago."

Ramona that's so true, but Pavle has not changed all, not for all these years. Many times some of us would get a postcard with a funny question like the one Bora got that said, 'Is that Bypsy still with you?' or one of the others would get a card like 'I'm always watching you.' Mind you this had stopped, just about when you and Pavle got married, so we were all relieved and thought he must have smartened up, so you tell me Ramona, and tell the truth, is Pavle a good man or is he the man we all knew from before?"

"Rada, there are two answers to that. Yes, and no, more likely no. He is excellent when it comes to providing for a family and children and he is good to fix just about anything, but when it comes to me that's a different story. He treats,s me like dirt. He calls me names, and there were some nasty slaps on my face and head, but I always forgive him because he is so kind to the children. But you know Rada, one of these days I'm going to get my revenge. I'm ready to leave him, but for now, I'll just wait patiently. If I put all this together, my actual answer should be, 'No, Pavle is not a good husband.'

Okay, I can hear them coming. Listen please let this stay between us, and I promise you I'll keep in touch, and thank you for your honesty. Tell your husband goodbye for me."

We got home very fast, and the old lady made a funny remark. "Children go and wash up; you came from a dirty place, wash up before you come in."

I thought that was so not nice. I gave her a dirty look, grabbed my girls and told them not to worry. As we were going to change, the girls asked me a funny question and got me worried at the same time. "So, do you think we can send them some of our toys?"

I looked at them and told them that as soon as we got home I'd try to send them everything I could. "And with your help, we can send them some of your clothes as well, but we have to talk to your father before we do all that."

"But Mommy, I don't think they like Daddy."

"Vesna why would you say something like that?"

"I don't know Mommy, but I saw most of them didn't even said hi to Daddy, only you, and why is that?"

"Okay, you guys, why don't we talk about that when we get home, and I can't wait until we do that."

Eventually, our trip to Pavle's village was over and was time to go home. His sisters came to say goodbye and some of his neighbors, but the sad one was the old man, Boro. He gave me a big hug and whispered in my ear, "Ramona, please look after yourself and the girls, and I sure hope you have found what you were looking. Take care."

As for the old lady, I just looked at her and me whispered in her ear, "This is the last time you'll ever see me."

(Not knowing it was the last time, she died the year after).

CHAPTER 34

THE FLIGHT HOME from Yugoslavia was the quietest one I ever had. I don't know why the girls were so quiet, but Pavle was sorrowful and devastated by how his brothers and father had treated him. I felt a little bit sorry for him, but finding out what he did to each and everyone, I don't see how he was expecting anything better. I never said anything about my knowing, and he never offered to tell me. But, I knew soon or later he'd open up, for now, I was glad to be flying home.

Once we got home, I called the superintendent, to let her know that we had arrived and she was happy to see me. "Ramona, as soon as you have time please call your aunt. She told me that she must speak with you, it's critical."

That got me scared. First I thought my uncle was very ill, because of his drinking, or she was very sick herself. It got me worried, so as soon as we unpacked, I told Pavle that my aunt was calling and I had to see what the problem was.

On the first ring, she answered the phone. "Ramona is that you?"

"Yes Aunty, what's the problem?"

"Ramona there is no problem, but I have big, I mean big, news. Your mother is coming to Canada August 23rd from Australia. I got a letter from her, while you were in Yugoslavia. Your Aunty Jana give her my address, and that is how she know where we are. So my question is what are we going to do, or what are you planning to do with your mother? I don't know what to do now. Please come over this weekend and talk about it. Tell Pavle this is important, and hope he'll drive you over, and I'd like to see the girls. Okay, I'll call you later."

As we were all sitting at the table and having supper, I decided to tell Pavle about my mother coming after my not having seen her for fifteen years.

"Wow! How nice is that?" Pavle spoke with a smirk on his face. "So your mother finally decided to find you after eighteen years or so, and if I remember right, that's what she did to you while you were in the orphan village. To me it looks like she only likes to see you every fifteen or eighteen years. Why is that? Ramona? Would you like her to come to our house? I don't think it is a good idea at all. You don't even know your mother, it would be like a stranger coming, not a mother."

What Pavle didn't know was that I had a plan. My mother coming into my life would be just making my project come true. I looked at him and I gave him that smirky face right back. "Yes, you are right about her coming to see me after all these years, but we don't know why she's coming now so, let's just wait and see. One thing I'm sure of is that she'll have only one person that won't be happy to see her, it won't be as bad as what you went through with your family."

As I said that Pavle's face went red, and I thought he'd blow up like a balloon.

"You don't know anything about my family, and don't you ever repeat that. My family is my problem not yours, and your mother will be your problem, not ours. She can come and stay with us only for the time being, and then she can go whereever she likes after that. I'm only doing this because of you; I'd like to prove to you that your mother is not a mother. After all these years she's coming to see you—not fair and not very smart. My hope is that she'll only stay for a little while.

"Pavle, I don't care what you think, and I'm not going to pressure her to stay with us, but I'll give her a chance to get to know her grandchildren. Time will tell us the rest. So girls, what do you say to that? Are you excited to meet your other grandmother? She's coming in two weeks."

"Mom, I hope she won't be so mean like Daddy's mom was."

"My dear Vesna, I'm sure that she's not like that, but for now, we'll just wait and see."

I called my aunt and told her we would come Sunday afternoon, but wouldn't stay too long because Pavle was going back to work and it was a morning shift. The girls were happy to see my aunt, she always made sure that she had something for them, but neither one liked my uncle. He was always drunk, but he would not hurt the girls, in any way. He always cried for some reason that I hadn't been able to figure out.

My aunt was excited to see her sister. The last time they'd seen each other was in 1956, but my uncle didn't care much at all. He knew that no one in the family liked him. The girls were asking lots of questions about their grandmother. My aunt told them that she hadn't seen her in a long time, but when they were kids their grandmother was always bossing her because she was older. But she assured them that everything was going to be okay. After a short visit, we came home exhausted from the trip and now from the news that my mother was coming. I had thought a lot about why she was coming now after all these years. Perhaps she was getting ready to be a mother or a grandmother, or God knows why. Once she got here, I'd try to pressure her to stay for good. That way my plan to leave Pavle would be faster, but that all depended on my mother's plan, I'd just have to wait and see.

The next two weeks were like needles and pins for me. I just could not believe that my mother would be there. Whatever her motivation was, I didn't care. Pavle was in his same old mood. He told me that he hoped I would not turn out to be like my mother. I wondered what prompted him to say that, but it was probably something my uncle said because he knew that my mom didn't like him. So, I'm sure he told Pavle lot of bullshit, and Pavle was happy to hear the worst of my mother. As far as I could see, his family was the worst I ever saw, but I didn't care. I was happy to see my mother and I sure hoped that she'd be glad to see me and would maybe even stay.

I had told Mr. Browskyski about my mother coming from Australia, and he was surprised that I had a mother because we never talked about her. He said if he could help me with something just to let him know. I thanked him and my plans were getting better. All in all, I was hoping!

August 23rd came very fast. Being excited, I had a big puzzle in my head, wondering why my mom was coming to see me after all these years. After all, she had given me away. As the airplane from Australia landed, I thought my heart was going to explode; I wondered if I was going to recognize her? But with all the power, in me, I stayed calm.

And then there she was. I recognized her right away. She hadn't changed much except she was getting a bit chubby, but I thought she looked good for her age. As she was approaching us, I started to cry, and my mother was crying as well. We hugged each other like no one else could. Holding her in my arms, I whispered to her, "Mom, I'm so happy to see you. Let's go and meet my family. Mom, this is my husband Pavle and your granddaughters. Vesna is almost six, and Sandra, she is four."

She took my girls into her arms, squeezing them, kissing them and crying at the same time. It was a moment I won't forget for a long time.

Then she pulled two beautiful dolls from her bag and the girls went nuts, they were so happy. They both gave her a big kiss with a big, "Thank you, Grandma, we love you."

Then, she approached Pavle. Unexpectedly she gave him a big hug and welcomed him to the family.

Being drained from all this, going home, I was in deep thought. The girls and my mother had fun, but I could tell Pavle was confused. I don't think he expected her to be so sweet to him, so he was quiet. At home, we made the third bedroom ready for my mother. The girls were to stay together until we saw what was going to happen. Once we got home, my mom wanted to go and have a rest, because coming from Australia is very tiring and the trip was very long. It was about 7:30 p.m., so I gave the girls a bath, and they watched TV a bit, and then off they went to bed with a doll in each arm. My mother was asleep before she had time to said anything.

At first, Pavle didn't say much, but then he spoke in a low voice. "Your mother looks like brilliant person, showing up with those big dolls, and giving me a hug and kiss. I can tell she is up to something, but I m not stupid. She can stay with us for a while, but if she decides to live in Canada for good, then we will have to discuss her living arrangments."

"No problem," is all I said. Knowing Pavle, if I said something different he'd insult me, so I just agreed for now. I, myself was more curious to see what her plans were, but for now, I'd just hold on to my ideas.

The next few months were very happy.. I thought my mother finally loved me and she was there to help me anyway I needed. We took her everywhere to see Canada, I mean only in Ontario, and she loved it, but I had a feeling she wasn't going to stay. One day she asked me what my plans were, as far as for Pavle and me. I was shocked; I had no idea that she was noticing that anything was wrong. Pavle was most of the times as sweet as he could be, and for her to ask me that was a surprise, so I just pretended I didn't know what she was talking about.

"Ramona my dear, I m old but not stupid. I can see how Pavle treats you and how he talks to you. If he was my husband he'd be gone a long time ago. Even your boss Mr. Browckyski told me that the only reason he is giving you this job for as long as you like is because of you. They don' like him at all, and many people in the building think he is a disturbed man. You can't even have free time to yourself, and you don't even have any friends. All you do is look after children, and you cry when no one is watching, and why? Because of him. I have watched all this, and I'm willing to help you. That means, come to Austalia with me. Forget this lonely and sad life you have. Even your aunt and uncle don't like him. They both think Pavle is a jealous man and always ready to put you down. I can see he loves his children, but you are just a rug that he walks on, and I can't take it anymore. So either you come with me, or I'm going back as soon as I can find a suitable reservation for a flight to Australia."

"Yes, Mother, you are right, and so are the rest of the people I know, but how can I come with you? It's not so easy. You can't just pack up and go. Do you honestly think Pavle will let his children go with us and leave him here? Pavle would rather kill me before he'd let us part him from his girls and that is a fact I know. Pavle may not love me, but he would kill anyone that tried to touch his children. I do have a plan to leave him but in later years. I wanted my kids to grow up with both parents not just one, so my answer to you about going to Australia is no. I'm sorry Mother, but I'm willing to take anything Pavle throws at me, and I know my revenge will come. I'm so sorry if I disappoint you Mother but it has to be my way."

"Ramona, perhaps you are scared that I would abandon you when we get there. I know what I did to you, leaving you in another woman's arms was wrong, but I had no choice.

Ramona, please sit down, and let me tell you everything—everything that I should have said a long time ago, but I was so ashamed, and I had a nervous breakdown, and many other problems." And then she told me about her husband's tragic death and about the police chief who had raped her.

"You and I had a similar tragedy," I said. "And I think it is best that we both forget about the past and go on with the future. I won't get mad at you if you go back to Australia, I can see you're not happy here, but I'll not go with you. I'm truly sorry."

The fact is I was was hoping that she'd say she wouldn't go without me, but that never happened. So, I had a feeling that my mother would abandon me again. The girls just loved her. She would take them to school and always make sure she was there to pick them up. If she left this would be a big shock for them.

It was very close to Christmas when we were getting to go shopping, but my mother stayed home, saying she had things to do. I had a funny feeling about that. Before we went out, she gave the girls hugs and kisses and kisses, and told me, "See you later," just like that. The girls laughed when she was kissing them, but to me it was obvious she was saying goodbye to them. I was the only one who felt that, but I'm pretty sure my mother sensed that we weren't going to see each other anymore.

It was about 8:30 p.m. when we came home, and before we went up, the superintendent came down, with tears running town her face and mumbling in a caring voice, "Oh Ramona, she left us. She's gone. I don't know if she told you that she was leaving, but I had a feeling that you didn't know. She asked me to inform you that she was very sorry, but it was time for her to go. Staying here would only make things more complicated. She hated Pavle; how he treats you and she couldn't watch it anymore. I'm so sorry Ramona. I loved her. She was a sweet old lady."

All I was able to say at that moment was, "Thank you, Peggy."

Once we got upstairs the girls ran to her room and there was a loud scream and crying and a panicked, "Oh no, no, where is she?" Then a big slam at the door. "Mommy, Mommy, Grandma is gone, where did she go? Please mommy call her, we want her back."

I just stood there and hugged my girls; I was speechless. I'd been disappointed and destroyed again by my mother. She'd left me again. Pavle was happy but I was just numb. I knew that I had to explain to the girls why my mother left me. It wasn't easy but it went well. After all, both were hoping that she'd come back one day.

As the days went by, and Christmas was in aa about a week, I got a phone call from my mother. She was crying and said that she was very sorry for leaving like that, but it was for the best. I could not help it, I just asked her right out openly, "Mom, best for whom? You or me? I had plans for us, and you couldn't wait for just a little longer. I think it would be best if you try not to hurt me anymore. Just take care of yourself and don't worry about me." As I hung up the phone, I started to cry. How could a mother do this to a child! I personally would not leave my kids like she did. I could never forgive her, not this time, and that was the last time I heard from her. My phone calls and lettelrs were never answered or returned, so I guessed this time she was gone for sure, and finally, I gave it up.

It was 1980 when I saw my mother for the last time. As a new year was just around the corner, I was hoping for a better life with Pavle and me. Ever since my mother left, Pavle was in a good mood, but once in a while he would swing his mood to abuse, like telling me that I was not any better than my mother. I knew he was just looking for a reason to make me upset, but like always I just swallowed and kept my mouth shut. That made him more violent, he would push me against the wall, and he would hit me in the stomach, begging me to admit that I had a boyfriend. Many times I honestly wished that I had a boyfriend, then he would have a reason to be so violent, but how could I admit to something that wasn't true? Every time we had an argument with a punch or two I was ready to pack up and leave him, but my girls were the one that stopped me. I truly did not have enough courage to pick up just like that; I was always scared. There was no one to help me, and I focussed on hiding things from people.

The only one that noticed my sadness and my sorrow was my boss, Mr. Browckyski. He would approach me many many times and ask me if I need help, but I always assured him that everything was okay. I hated lying to him, but I was so ashamed for him to know me well. He said he'd been a doctor a long time ago. His practice was treating people with stress and emotional problems. H said he could tell that I fit in that category, and if I didn't get any help soon, I might end up in a mental hospital just because I was scared to tell someone what was going on in my life. He told me that if I liked, he could call his son. He was the one who had taken over his practice, and he could give me advice, and not tell anyone, though he suspected the advice would be, "Get your girls and run."

"I know that you want to help me Mr. Browckyski, but I have to do this my way. You don't know me, and I don't want to be a burden to you, but my sadness and miserable life will end soon, and then, perhaps then I'll find peace. Until then I'm ready to take any punches, abuse and crazy times. I know my time will come.

"Oh my dear Ramona. You can not wait for revenge. Hate is wrong. Please take my advice and look for another solution. I'm willing to help you. Revenge never worked for anyone, you will always remember your pain and sorrow, but with revenge, you won't be able to heal your wounds, never. Trust me on that. I have lived with revenge for a long time and it took me years, and years to realize that I was hurting myself and losing the best time of my life because I was full of rage and revenge. Please let that go, and you'll see the difference, just try o understand that better days are coming. Ramona, I won't pressure you to do anything. That you have to do by yourself, I can only help you to gain a different view of life."

"Right now is not the time for my revenge, but it os in my future. I'm sorry, but you can be sure that I'll be careful, I know what I'm doing. All I want is that my girls grow up with an entire family and one day I'll tell them everything. Mr. Browsckyski, I know that revenge is an unyielding word, but that is how I feel, and no one can stop me. I know you're trying to help me, but I have made up my mind, and one day I'll be free, free of pain and arguments. Mr. Browsckyski what was your revenge? Why were you so upset about life?"

"My dear Ramona, I was in a labor camp in wartime in Germany. They took us from Poland, threw us all in trains and we ended up in Germany. My brothers and I survived, but our parents were nowhere to be found. We're pretty sure they were some of the millions that died in Germany's gas chambers. I was very young, but I do remember everything and I told myself that when I grew up and if I survived that, I'd come back one day and kill every German man I saw. That was wrong; I know that now but then I was full of rage, and I wanted to make them pay for all the pain we had. I lived with that anger for a long time, and one day I realized that my life was slowly disappearing and I hadn't let myself enjoy the beauty of the second chance I had. So I threw out all my revenge thoughts and started a new life. I never forgot what happened to us, but I forgave them all. It was wartime and soldiers just did what they were told to do. Your life Ramona has a different range, but it is easy to change. Leave that man, look up in the sky and ask God for help. You will feel much better if you let your rage go. This is coming from a much older man that you, and much more pain that you ever had. Trust me, you're going to be okay, just let it go."

After that good talk with Mr.Browscyski, I tried to change. I tried very hard to speak to Pavle; I tried to be the wife that he wanted. Every time he accused me of something I begged him to forgive me, and that was all he wanted to hear. I'm sure that he knew it wasn't true but it somehow made him happy. I never could understand that man. He was glad to hear me lying instead of knowing the truth, so I played along. Pavle's game went on and on, and to everybody we looked like a happy family, but no one knew what went on inside of our minds, just Pavle and me. We lived a difficult life, and it went on like that for a long time. It was now four years since we'd lived in the apartment and one day with a big smile on his face Pavle gave me keys and said, "We're moving to a house. I want you to be happy the rest of your life with the girls and me. The place is peaceful, and I know we'll be happy."

All I could say was "Wow." What kind of man goes and buys house without telling his wife? He was always in control, and that showed me that even something important like buying a house he did without me. I did not even smile. I just looked at him point blank and laughed.

"Are you serious Pavle, a house? Where is it?"

"The house is in North York, not too far from here, and tomorrow we're all going to see it, and they need your signature. The house is in both names, so neither one of us can sell it without the other knowing. Although you'll be happy about that since you never had a house in your life, so I wanted you to see how nice it is when you have your own place. I sure hope you are going to like it and the girls too. For them there is a school within walking distance and a big shopping mall not too far. Everything about the place and the area is so beautiful; you'll see."

"Okay Pavle, but buying a house is not like a new toy for a kid, you should have talked to me as well, not just go and buy it. I'm happy that we're going to have a house but it would have been nice if I knew anything about it as well."

"Don't be like that Ramona. All I wanted was to surprise you, that's all, You see with or without your permission I wanted a house. I'm so, sick and tired of this apartment living, all I wanted was for us to have a better life."

"Pavle, for us to have a better life is up to you. You're the one that needs to change, not the apartment. A house won't make us happy if you are always so jealous and moody and you look for issues to use your fist, and I'm always this and that. A house is a house, but you are the one that has to make a significant change. Let your negative emotions go away, be a man and most important be a husband, not only a father to the girls. Show me some love and care as a spouse should do. You have to stop hitting me and calling me names. All this is up to you; the comfortable house is not like the way you are now, but it could be happy if you change. So Pavle why don't you just give it a try, and time will take care of the rest? Anyway, I'm happy for all of us; you'll have to give me all the details, so I can let Mr. Browckyski know that we're going to move."

"Well according to these documents, the house is ours November first, so, that gives Mr. Browckyski plenty of time to replace us, since this is only July."

News about us moving went fast enough in the building. Since I'd made many friends, they were sad to see me go, but there were lots who were happy that Pavle wouldn't be around any more. A few tenants called him a watchdog, some would say mad dog, but he was my husband so I always defended him.

Mr. Browckyski was the saddest of them all. With me being manager of his large building for five years, it was hard for him to let go. He and I had gotten to know each other well. He was like a father to me, the one I never had. Mr. Browckyski was worried that Pavle was making a big trap for me, because here in the building I had friends, but living with him alone and with no one to look after me, it sounded to him as if Pavle was going to be in control forever. I had thought about that too, but I was determined to make it work this time. Since Pavle was so jealous, this would be the perfect time for him to change, since I wouldn't be talking or going anywhere, and I was willing to go through all this just to make our family happy, with no pain, and no hiding behind doors.

The girls were happy as well, and together we went to see our new house. The house was beautiful and big, well for me it was big. I'd never lived in a house like that, so it was huge for me. There was a large backyard and lots of trees. School for was just a one block away. Everything looked perfect and lovely. A lawyer came with the documents, and once we both signed, the house was ours. I did have a few tears in my eyes but they were happy ones. I finally had a house, and a family. The only thing I had to do now was try to meet Pavle halfway to improve our relationship. I was going to do my best, all for my girls. The hardest part of leaving the apartment was saying goodbye to all the friendly people I'd met. I started to cry when I hugged Mr. Browskyski, but I heard him saying, "Ramona, Please don't cry. You can call me anytime if you need a friend, I'm going to be only a phone call away. Take care, my dear."

CHAPTER 35

THE GIRLS HAD already started a school, and I was so happy that they were be going to the same one. Vesna was in grade four and Sandra was in grade two. So, now that I was home alone all day, I talk to Pavle saying it would be a good idea if I looked for a job in this area. To my surprise, he agreed. It took me only five days to find a job. There was a company that sold hospital operating instruments, so they called me for an interview, and my only concern was if I could work from nine a.m. to three p.m.—that way I could take the girls to school, pick them up, and have enough time to make supper. Work involved picking up orders and shipping them to customers all over Canada. I knew I was able to do that, so I was confident that there was no reason not to get that job, unless they had a problem with the hours I wanted. The company was within walking distance of the house, so that was why I was hoping I got the job.

The interview was set up for November 18, at 1:00 p.m., and I was very much sure that I'd get it because I had lots of experience in picking orders and organizing the workflow of a warehouse thanks to Mrs. Geyer. The company was called Health Supplies Inc. and it was from Sweden. As I walked in, right away, I noticed how clean the place was. The young receptionist told me to sit in a meeting room where she took me. I was a bit nervous, but then a young man walked in with the most beautiful black hair and the darkest blue eyes and a big smile. He made me feel welcome, and that helps my nerves. His name was Hendrik Frechen. I got little bit embarrassed for staring at him. He reminded me of Keven, and I asked myself, if it was possible that there were two of them. He spoke in a very soft voice with a German accent, and he was very straightforward. After we talked about the job and all the benefits, he asked me if I could start as soon as possible. My working hours were okay as far as he knew, and if I liked maybe I could work on weekends if they needed me. Before I got up to leave, he asked me if I don't mind he would like to know where I came from, since English was my second language.

"Mr. Frechen, why is it so important to you to know what my background is?"

I think he got a little bit surprised and his face got red, so I jumped right back to his answer with a smile. "Mr. Frechen, I came from Yugoslavia, and I have been in Canada for the past fourteen years. If that's a problem, I'd like to know why."

"Oh! No, no Mrs. Obranovic, I asked you that, because of your name. I have not heard that name anywhere, and I have been in a lot of different countries. I think your name "Ramona" is so different from all other names, that was all. I sure hope I haven't crossed the line asking you that, and if I did, I'm sorry. I just like your name that's all."

I just smiled and asked him if that was all.

"No, one more thing. I'd like to take you to the warehouse and show you where you'll, be working and I'd like you to met the rest of the warehouse staff. You're going to be the only female there, and if that's going to be a problem, please let me know."

"I don't think that's going to be an issue for me, actuallyy I like working with a man better than a woman but don't tell them that."

"Okay then, let's go. There are nine people working in there and they all have different responsibilities, but they all help each other as well. We have a few old timers. They think that they own the place, and we let em because good working staff is hard to find, so don't let them boss you too much. You can always come to me, my office is in the warehouse, and I'm always on the floors. You see Mrs. Obranovic…"

"Please just call me Ramona, it sounds better to me and since you like my name then just call me Ramona."

"Okay, I'll introduce you to the guys as Ramona, and you're right, it is better like that, too formal would be kind of Ah."

The introduction went well, and I could tell I was going to like it there. The old timers were very helpful and one of then even winked at me. I just gave him a friendly smile and told them I would be happy to work with them and any help they could give I would take kindly."

As we walk back to the front, Mr. Frechen told me that he could tell the guys in the warehouse liked me, and one more thing he wanted me to know was that everybody in the warehouse called mhim Henk, and he would like it very much if I did as well.

"You know, Henk I like your name as a Hendrik, but if they all call you Henk, then I will too. If there is nothing else, I would like to say thank you and see you Monday at nine a.m."

"Ramona there is one thing I'd like to ask you, and if you think it is too personal you don't have to answer me..You see, when I walked in the meeting room and introduced myself, you looked at me like you saw a ghost and your eyes were glued to me all the time. I did get little bit uncomfortable, not knowing what the story was here. Do I look like someone you lost, or do we know each other from somewhere? As I said you don't have to answer me if you don't feel up to it."

"Henk, yes you look like my first boyfriend, actually my fiancé. I loved him very much, but he died in an accident a long time ago. You look like so much like Keven, I thought I saw a ghost. I'm very sorry, and it won't happen again."

"Okay, Ramona, I don't mind, so I shall see you Monday morning. And Ramona, I'm very pleased to meet you."

Going home I was so happy, for me it was as if I'd come out of a prison that I was in for nine years, and now the warden was letting me out, but I knew there would be a price to pay for all this. I was focusing on how Pavle was going to handle the news that I had a job, but with a new job I was sure I would be okay in the coming days. Now we had a new house, and I had a job. I was smiling knowing that my plan to leave Pavle was getting better. I just had to be careful around Pavle, because he was so emotionally disturbed he could snap anytime. He was home when I got in, all smiles and happy, and when I saw his face, I just froze. Pavle was so red and full of anger; I thought he was going to explode and I was sure he'd hit me. The first thing that came to my mind, was that something had happened to the girls, or even him.

"What's wrong? Pavle?"

"Where have you been all morning?" He grabbed me and threw me against a wall and was about to hit me, but this time I grabbed his hand.

If you hit me again or try I'll go to the police; I've had all I can take from you, for no reason you want to hit me, but no more." I was going to the kitchen, but he stopped me.

"Where have the hell have you been all morning? You took the kids to school and then what, where did you go? I told you many many times; you are not allowed to run around like a mad stupid lying bitch. One of this days God help me, I'll fix you for good."

"Pavle, are you going nuts? Don't you remember I had an interview for my job? You must have forgotten, so you better calm down, sit and listen. I got the job." And I explained about the hours. "Therefore the girls won't be home alone at all. Hope you are happy now."

He was speechless for a second, then just pushed me and went to the basement.

The next two weeks Pavle was working the night shift, so I had plenty of time to get to work, and I was looking forward to that. Getting out of the house was my ticket to freedom, which I was the only one to know, because it was my plan. Because my manager looked like Keven that made me even happier, I just could not wait to get there. Once I got to my work, I forgot Pavle's words, threats, and his moods; I was a new person, I felt free.

The girls were doing good in school, and I loved my job for the next few years. I got to know all the men that worked there, and for some reason, I got to know Henk more than I wanted. He would come and sit in the lunch room with us, which was strange to me, considering his position in the company but something about Hank was so confusing to me. One day just before lunch he asked me if I would like to go and have lunch with him outside the company. I looked at him, and with surprise, I said yes, why not. I don't know why I said that, but I was glad I did.

The restaurant was just across the street from the company, so I knew right then that he was trying to tell me something that had to be outside of work. At the beginning he acted a little bit strange and then right out of the blue, he asked me if I was happy. I wasn't sure what he meant by that so I just said, "Yes, I'm euphoric," but it was clear that wasn't what he wanted to hear.

"Ramona, you have been working with the company now for almost three years, and I have never heard you talking about your husband. You do talk about your girls, and I can tell you love them, but I can't figure out you and your spouse. I saw him a couple of times looking around. At first I didn't know he was you husband until he asked me to speak with you. To me, he looked a man that likes to give the orders, and he did not look very friendly at all. He wanted to know how many men worked with you, and what do you do. I was open with him, and I did ask him to come in and see, but he just said no and went. I found that very strange, so I never told you that, and I know he never mentioned that he met me, either. I came to the conclusion that you're not happy and I was wondering are you going to spend the rest of your life with someone you can't get along with? Maybe I'm crossing a line asking you all this, but I do like you a lot Ramona and it breaks my heart to see you so sad all the time. Is there anything I can do for you?"

"Henk, I'm thrilled that you care about me, but I'm a married woman. No matter if I'm happy or sad it is my marriage, and I think you have crossed a line about that. I like you very much as a friend, I feel we can talk about everything, but Henk right now, as far as my marriage goes, let it be. You are right, Pavle never told me that he met you, but he has done that every place I've worked, so that's not news to me. I'd like to stay being your friend, and that's all for now, and don't forget you are my boss on top of that. Henk, it is a shame that you and I didn't meat before I knew Pavle. Anyway, we better go back to work, otherwise there will be rumors about you and me and I don't want that.

"Ramona, just one more question. Do you know I own this place and some more? If you do, how come you never said anything about it? You never ask me why I'm working in a warehouse instead of having fun like most rich people do."

"There is nothing to talk about it. You are wealthy and working with your employees is your business. I'm not the one who's going to ask you why. We all have some secrets and you working with your staff is your secret, just like I would not talk about my marriage."

"Okay, fair enough, let's go back to work and thank you for being so honest with me."

After our lunch together Henk and I would every now and then look at each other with a question, but at the end, we just let it go. We became good friends, and slowly he opened up to me about his life as a wealthy man. I knew more about Henk than I was prepared to know, and now I knew why he was working with us. Hank was looking for an answer in an unusual way. He was seeking to find out if any woman could love him if he was just an ordinary man, not rich. He was married, but the marriage had been over for a long time. His wife would not give him a divorce because she'd lose everything, and because Henk was Catholic, he had no choice but wait and hope that one day he'd be free. So far that day had never come, and he told me it had been like that for the past five years. I think he was at the end of his rope, Henk wanted a family, but not with the wife he had now. She was always only interested in his money that's all, but now Henk desired to find some real love. He told me that he was planning to sell all the companies they had, but not while his father was still alive, and according to him, that wouldn't be long. After that, his plans were to go somewhere and change his identity and start his life all over. So, so, sad I thought. Hank and I both had something that neither one of us wanted and couldn't do anything about it. Well, not so true. I could leave Pavle, and I knew my time would come, and I'd be free

Then one day everybody at work was so sad when I walked in, and I wondered what in the world happened? Norman, the old guy, came and told me that Henk's father was very very ill, and Henk had gone home. No one knew anything else. I got sad, because if his father died Henk will put his plans into action and I'd lose my new friend. I hoped that he would change his mind. I didn't want to admit it to myself, but I cared for Henk more than I thought, so I was sorrowful. We were all working hard to make Henk proud of us, and no one was talking about what could happen. Once I got home, I told Pavle what was going on at work, and his reaction was like someone had stuck a knife in my back. I just looked at him and walked away before I said something to trigger his buttons. It was March break for the girls, so we all went to Walt Disney World. The girls were so happy—me too, but my mind was on Henk, and I think Pavle noticed that I was quieter and tense.

The girls were having so much fun, and Pavle was in a good mood most of the time. I just followed them pretending that I was having a really good time, but my mind was far away, I was thinking about Henk. So, one night when the girls went to bed Pavle asks me to sit down; he has good news for all of us. The first thing that came into my head was, *Oh no, we're moving again.* And I was right.

Pavle was a bit uneasy, it was like he wasn't sure how to start, and then he just blew up.

"Ramona, I don't like our neighborhood anymore. Those Yugoslavian friends of yours get on my nerves, and I can see that you like them and one of those man is always staring at you. God knows what's going on between you and him. So, I decided we're going to move to a brand new house in Markham. The house will be ready by September, so the girls can start fresh in a new school. I have picked out a house for us, and once we get there, I'll show you our new house. I'm sure the girls will be so excited, and I hope you will be as well. You don't have to quit your job. You can buy a small car, and that would do it. So, what do you say to that?"

"You have done it again? You went and got us a new house without even a word to me? Why, why are you doing this Pavle? I know I don't have a choice. Markham is a new sub-division, and you haven't even asked the girls if they'd like to have a brand-new house. You always think that you have the answer for everything. I just don't understand you. Do whatever you like."

I had seen Pavle mad but not like this. He grabbed me and held my neck so hard that I was starting to choke, and then he let it go, but his threatening words made me shiver. I knew that for some reason this house would be the last one for us. Vesna was thirteen and Sandra was eleven, so that meant an easy three years for me with this monster. As he let me go he threatened me. "We will finish this talk at home."

When the girls walked in Vesna noticed, we were so quiet, and she wondered what happened. Pavle just looked at them and said to both of them, "Girls, I have good news to tell you. We're going to move to a brand new house in September; you'll have a new school and new friends, so, what do you say to that?"

For a second I thought they would be upset, but no, they both jumped around and kept asking where we were moving. I was so surprised by their reaction that I never opened my mouth. I'm sure the girls noticed me not responding happily but neither one cared. The girls were so glad to have a brand new house because I'm almost sure neither one liked the place we lived in now. I had a good idea why the girls didn't like this house. According to Pavle someone had broken in, came inside through a back window, and went in Vesna's room, but when the police came to investigate, I caught Pavle in a lie. I knew he'd staged all that. The police asked Pavle what was missing, but before he could answer them, I spoke. "I think the only thing is missing are two bottles of wine that I purchased two weeks ago."

Pavle looked at me and told the police that he could not see anything else missing. So, when they left I asked Pavle why he'd done this. "There was no wine, I just made that up; I knew you were lying. What were you hoping to accomplish with that? To the scare kids?" Which he did.

I loved the house, and I loved the neighborhood, and to move again was his punishment for me. I know it would be wrong telling the kids that their father made it all up, just to scare them, and I didn't want to upset them. So, now in five months we were going to move again, but I decided this would be the last move as a family. I eas the only one who was going to miss this old neighborhood; all the houses are different and very nicely kept, but in the new place all the houses looked like the same and cold. I convinced myself it would just be for a short time.

CHAPTER 36

THE NEW HOUSE was partially complete by the time we went to see it, but it was to be completed by August 15th. It looked so big… I know, more work for me, and I bet you that was the purpose of buying a big house just to keep me busy all the time. As always I meant to do it all. After the school year was done for that year, the girls were looking forward to moving day. Every day, they would pack some of their belongings, and some were given to the Salvation Army because Pavle promised them lots of new stuff. We sold our old house very fast, and the money we got was plenty for the new one. So we had some more money left for my car and for the girls' new bedrooms, which I didn't think was necessary, but that is how Pavle got to them; giving them new things even if they didn't need them. I had nothing to say in that, but I was sure that one day, they would realize that their father was wrong.

At the beginning of August, I got a car. Nothing special, but good enough to get me to work. Now my work was about a twenty-minute drive, and since the girls were old enough to look after each other, I decided to work longer hours, from eight a.m. to four p.m. That way I made more money and I was happy, sad to say it, but I was happy to be with all the guys in the warehouse. They were the only one that gave me some respect, and I did miss Henk. He was still back in Sweden, there was not much change in his father's health but Henk told Nacy who worked in Human Resources that he was coming for a short visit in November. I don't know why but I was so happy to hear that news. I wanted to hear everything about his parents and his wife.

Moving was a bit hard, because this time we had lots of furnishings and loads of other stuff for the house, but all in all, everything went okay in a short time. The girls started a new school, and both met girls their age and made friends. Since Vesna was thirteen and a half, I'm sure that boys were among her topics at the new school. Sandra was happy as well; she had two girls that lived on our street, so everything was going well. I started my job earlier now, so I was out at 7:30 a.m. and when I got home at 5:30 the girls would be home.

But that all changed quickly.

One day I needed a hammer for something, and I went to the basement to find one. I looked everywhere, and finally, I found one under the table, but what struck me odd and funny was that Pavle had taped everything, just like he'd taped the door on our first apartment. I looked and looked, and so to piss him off and get even I moved everything just to see what he was going to say. A few weeks passed by and Pavle said nothing about me messing up his tools, so I went to see what he'd done, and like before he'd just taped everything again. I was sick of trying to play his game, so I just forgot about it. I was getting drained every day. On weekends Pavle would take the girls out to the mall or go wherever they asked, and no one even bothered to stay home to help me. One time I got fed up and told Vesna and Sandra that they had to clean their rooms, and not to wait for me to do all that, but Pavle said that was my job to do, so the girls never helped me at all. Pavle enjoyed seeing me so tired every day. He never offered me any help; he would throw stuff in the basement and ask me to clean it up. Sometimes he'd get frustrated because I never fought back. And he said if I was busy doing all the work at home I wouldn't have time to look for a new boyfriend in this new place. I knew that was the only one reason we'd gotten this house, to take me far away from the friends I had left.

I was always sad and lonely, with no one to talk to or to be happy with. No one cared about my happiness or even to ask me to sit down and relax. On many occasions, I felt like a slave to them, nothing else. Pavle never bought me anything for my birthday, Mother's Day or Christmas, he would give the girls as little as possible to spend on me, but he told them I was old, and I didn't need nice things. I don't know why but the girls were on his side all the time. Perhaps I was too strict with them, but Pavle would let them do whatever they wanted. One night when I went to bed earlier Pavle came and said if I wasn't happy why didn't I kill myself and make it easy for everybody. I was stunned, but not surprised because he'd asked me the same question before.

I actually wished I was dead in those days.

In the middle of October the girls got a letter from the school that there was a field trip Ottawa; all students, grades five to eight were invited with parents' permission, and the cost would be $350.00 a student for the seven days. There would be supervision by parents and teachers. Space was limited so it was first come first served. I thought $350.00 was a lot of money, but to let one go and not the other would make this house so miserable—not that our house wasn't unhappy anyway. I thought Pavle would be working night shift so I would have a peace and quiet for a week, therefore I said okay. "But you have to wait for your father in the morning to see if he agrees with me."

He was on night shift and I'm sure they sat all night waiting for him, and soon as he walked in, I heard them begging and begging, and like always he gave in. He signed the note, but in the morning I told them if one was accepted and the other wasn't neither could go. Vesna did not like that but took the check for 700 dollars for both. I'm pretty sure they ran to school, like never before.

That day at work I was wondering if I'd made a mistake signing the note for the girls to go. Me being alone with Pavle sent shivers up my body. Perhaps it was time to find out if Pavle loved to be home with me or if he had any plans because he signed those notes so fast. It made me wonder if he was up to something. I forgot about that and went back to concentrating on my orders. And then to my surprise, I hear someone saying "Hi." I turned around and there was Henk. I almost jumped to give him a hug, but I pulled back very fast.

Henk didn't—he hugged me and whispered to me. "I came back fast, and I have good news to tell you. Can we go out to lunch? I'd like to tell you everything."

I knew Pavle was on night shift, so he would not be sneaking around to spy on me, so I said okay.

Once we got to the restaurant and ordered, Henk could not wait to tell me the big news.

"Ramona, thanks to your advise I did give my wife a second chance, and you won't believe the changes in her. She told me that living without me would be bad for her, and she was very, very sorry for all the bad things she has done. I believe her, and I'm going to try very hard to forgive her. My father would like to have grandchildren before he dies, so Silvana, that's my wife's name, and I are going to try to have a baby. She is here in Toronto for a little while, then she'll be going back, and I'll stay until the new year and we'll see what will happen by then. Anyway, how are you? How's your new house, and are you and Pavle in better shape than before, or should I ask?"

"Oh Henk, I'm amazed at the difference in your face, you look happy, and I'm so glad, but as for me, I'm almost sure in a year or two my marriage will be over. Pavle is always bullying me and calling me names, and I'm like a zombie.

I just don't know where I find the energy to put up with him. Don't tell me to leave him now and ask me what I'm waiting for, because Hank you don't know my background at all and you don't know why I'm putting up with Pavle. That's between him and me. I don't want to put you in any awkward position. I'm happy for you, so let it all stay like that. I'm so glad to have a friend like you."

"Ramona, tell me just one more thing and then I won't ask again. Have you done something in your life that you think I would be disappointed if you tell me about your background story?"

No, Henk, you would not, just the opposite of that, but that's my story, don't ask me again because I would need a week to tell you everything. Henk, you owe me nothing, so don't worry too much, and let's go back to work."

Once I got home that day the girls were waiting for me, with big smiles on their faces. I knew right away that they would be going on their trip. I never had so many hugs and kisses from them and it almost made me cry. The next project was to get them ready for the journey, which was in an about a week, but then I got a shiver. Pavle would be on day shift, so much for my rest, but there was nothing I could do now. I wondered if I'd made a big mistake letting them go and leaving me alone with Pavle. I felt sick thinking of Pavle and me home alone, but it was too late now. Perhaps I was was exaggerating; maybe Pavle was looking for quiet time with me, or was he?

It was Thanksgiving day when the girls left, I cried, because it was the first time I wasn't with them. It made me bit sad, but then looking at Pavle made me a bit scared. As we drove home, he told me he had changed his shift. He'd be working the midnight shift, which he never did before. His shifts were always seven a.m to three p.m, or four p.m.to twelve a.m., so that was telling me to be more than careful. He said it would be good for me to have peace and quiet at night. I knew he was lying about something. He was up to no good, I could tell by his smiling face.

It was a long weekend, so we went to see the godparents of our children, since I hadn't seen them for a long time. Spending time outside our house was a treat for me since Pavle never took me anywhere without the children, so I enjoyed my day out. They were surprised to see us without the girls, but I told them they were on a school trip to Ottawa and it was time for Pavle and me to enjoy seven days. We had fun, and once we got home I told Pavle that I was exhausted, and I went straight to bed. I must have been really tired...I went right out, which was very weird to me, but next morning I woke up and there

there was Pavle with fresh coffee and with a big smile. He asked me if I had a good sleep. Half awake, half asleep I just smiled and took the fresh coffee. Then after about a half hour, I felt very sick. I dropped the coffee because the bedroom was turning and turning. I felt sick and dizzy and my throat was so sore. Pavle was standing by the door, I tried to reach him to tell him I wasn't feeling good. I wanted to talk but no words would come out. That was the last thing I remembered.

I was so relaxed this time, but I heard someone calling my name. "Ramona, Ramona wake up, wake up girl, let me see your eyes." I tried to open them, but I had no strength in me. Something was wrong, but what?

What's going on, where am I? Where is Pavle? Then I must have gone into a deep sleep. I don't know how long I was asleep.

When I woke up, I realized I was in the hospital, but could not understand why. I saw Pavle sitting in the corner of my room. I tried to say something but my throat was so bad; it was so sore, and then I remembered it was like that just after I'd had the coffee. I had enough energy to sit up and made a little noise on the bed so Pavle could see that I was up.

Pavle came closer to me and asked me how I was feeling. I looked at him; I wanted to know what happened. Deep inside of his eyes, I saw he was laughing, but just then the nurse came in.

Well, well, looks like you're up; it's about time. You gave us all a big scare there. I'm going to get the doctor, and he'll have some questions to ask you. If you can't talk just nod your head. You don't have to force yourself to talk, you had a big big problem in your throat, but it's all okay for now. Right now I'm going to give you some pills for the pain and please try to drink some water; it is crucial."

"Good morning Ramona, my name is Dr. Richard Samuel, and I have some concerns about what happened to you. I'm well aware that you can not talk for now, but just yes or no will do. Do you know why you are in the hospital?"

I managed to whisper, "No."

"Okay, then let me explain to you. I think you were poisoned by some chemical that is unexplained to us. I have seen this kind of a poisoning from rat or mouse poison or just plain old windshield wiper fluid from the car. So, my question is, do you have any of these things at home?, Just yes or no for now."

"Yes."

"One minute, please. Mr. Obranovic, can you step out for a moment? I have to exam Ramona."

When Pavle left, the doctor whispered, "Okay, Ramona, I have your husband outside, I need to ask you this. Is there any chance that your husband tried to poison you? Are you two having trouble at home? I need to know, so I can come to a conclusion to figure this out, if this was planned to kill you, or if it's some mystery illness. I'll be honest with you. We can't prove anything, but my personal feeling is this is not an accident or some unknown thing; I think someone has poisoned you. I know you can't talk but if you take your time I'll be patient to hear your answer."

I was startled and didn't know what to tell him. Did Pavle try to poison me? The answer wass for sure yes, but I couldn't say that to him. Pavle always insulted me; he had hit me many times, he asked me repeatedly why I didn't kill myself, he called me all sort of names, so my answer would be yes. But if I told the truth, what was going to happened? They miight arrest Pavle, and he probably would go to jail; I couldn't let that happen. I couldn't hurt my girls; they were innocent, and they didn't know how their father treated me every day. I couldn't do this. Maybe one day I'd tell them the truth, but not now—now I had to pretend we were a happy couple and what happened to me was a mystery. I had an opportunity to get even with Pavle for all the things he had done to me, but who was I going to hurt in the process? I knew the answer.

So, in a soft voice I told the doctor that there was no way Pavle did this, Pavle and I were married for fourteen years so far, and we had problems like any other couple, but nothing that would make him do this. Telling the doctor this big lie was one of the hardest things I had to do for my girls.

"Okay, Ramona. I'll write in my report that you were made ill by something unknown, and I sure hope you were telling me the truth. I'd like you to stay until Friday, just in case your throat gets worse. I'll come to see you before you go home. For now, try to drink as much water as you can and eat some Jello."

"Thank you Doctor, and yes I'm telling you the truth."

Once the doctor left Pavle came in, and he was so pale, it got me worried. Maybe he did this to me, and now he was scared not knowing what I told the doctor. He spoke in a very soft voice. "What did the doctor tell you? Are you going to be okay? Can I stay for a while to keep you company?"

According to the doctor they can't figure out why my throat was like that, and came to the conclusion that I must have been poisoned by some kind of chemical. It's very hard to figure out, so I'll be staying until Friday. You can stay if you like, but I'm so drained, and I like to take a rest. Just go home, and we'll see you tomorrow. One more thing. Are you going to call the girls and tell them what's going on?"

"Ramona, if you don't mind, I don't think that calling the girls would be a good idea. You'll be home by Friday, so why bother to get the girls worried about nothing."

"About nothing! I almost died Pavle, and you know that. How can you say nothing? Please just go home, and I'll see you tomorrow."

Next thing I knew I had to do was call Henk at work. He had to know, and I wasn't going back to work for him. I needed a new start, which meant a new job, and I was going to ask Pavle for a divorce. Henk was out with his wife, so I left a message with Norman and I gave him the hospital number. I told Norman not to worry, I was going to be okay, and later on I'd call him. Norman was a kind old man, and he was concerned, but I assured him everything was going to be okay.

Next morning I got up, and I felt much better. The doctor came to check on me and told me that everything was going good, but he gave me a sad look that told me he didn't believe that I'd told him the truth. In my heart, I said I was sorry to him, but I made sure that he wouldn't ask me again. Then about eleven a.m., a nurse came and told me I had a visitor. I wondered why she would call Pavle a visitor, but to my surprise it was Henk. My face brightened up so fast, I almost jump out of bed. But Hank came very close and gave me a small kiss on my cheek. I must have blushed because I felt my face was burning.

I was happy to see him, but I never heard him talking, I just stared at him. At first again I was sure that he was Keven, but then Henk touched me to wake me up from dreaming. "Ramona, are you okay? What's wrong? You were looking at me the same way you did when we met the first time. These flowers are from the rest of the people at the company and me. We all wish you a speedy recovery."

"Oh Henk, I'm so sorry, my mind was playing tricks on me, I thought you were Keven again, so sorry."

"Okay, Ramona tell me what happened to you. When you left Friday you were not sick looking to me, so what happened, and the truth, please."

I found myself telling him that Pavle had given me coffee and that the next thing I knew I was in the hospital.

"So that bastard poisoned you, did he? What are the doctors saying?"

"Henk, you don't know that for sure and neither do the doctors. To them it is something they can't understand. It is poison but what kind of poison is hard to discern. The doctor said it must have been rat poison or windshield fluid; the two things are hard to tell apart once they're in the body. He said I must have been using this for more than a one day, and finally, my body couldn't take it anymore, but as for pointing fingers, no one is sure. One nurse told me things like this happened more often then they like to see. One more day of that poison in my body I would be dead, but for now, everything is cleaned out and I'm much better. I'm going home Friday afternoon because Pavle is working the day shift."

I started to cry, and could not help getting upset. Henk was right, but I wanted him to be my friend now, not a judge.

"Ramona, we have been friends for four years now, and we've told each other lot of secrets, but this time I know you are not telling me the truth. I can't see why but aren't you scared that Pavle will do this again? And don't say it wasn't him. I know him by now, and he is the most disturbed man that I ever met. Can't you see what he has done to you? Look at you, you don't have any friends, your children will never know to this day. Why can't you just walk away? I'll help you if you like. You saved me when I was most vulnerable to any woman who wanted to take advantage of me, and now it is your turn. Please, Ramona, let me help you.

And, please don't cry."

"Thank you, Henk, but this time I'm going to be all right. You see, once I'm well enough, I'll get a new job, and after that, I'll ask Pavle for a divorce. This time he has gone too far. I could have been dead, and he just laughed, so no more . Please, don't ask me to come back and work for you, I can't, and let it stay that way. I'm strong, and I know I'll survive this, just like I survive everything."

"So you do admit he did that to you. I can just go to the police and get him out of your life forever. But yes I won't do it because it's not what you want, but right now Ramona, I'm going back home, and in a year or two I'll be back, and if you're still married to that creep, I personally will face Pavle and will report him. It is my promise to you."

Thank you, Henk, but this time I'm going to do what I should have done a long time ago."

Hank sat with me another hour or so, and then he left, and that was the last time I heard from him, not because he forgot me, but because I wanted to forget him.

CHAPTER 37
No more Stress, Fears, Anxiety,

ONCE WE GOT home Friday evening, I told Pavle that I would not sleep with him in the same room anymore and we had to talk about our future together from now on. He never said anything; I could tell he was a bit scared, because Pavle had no idea what the doctor said to me, and I wasn't going to tell him. I wanted him to suffer a bit, so he agreed with me. We had four bedrooms, so I took the empty one and made it my room. Not having an extra bed was a little problem, but I took lots of old blankets and made it okay for me. Once I got to settle down I told him that I would tell the girls that I had a back problem and that was why I was sleeping on the floor. I just hope that they would not notice anything that was going on. Eventually I'd tell them, but not now. "I don't care what you'r going to do," I said, "but Pavle I want you to know I won't ever forgive you for what you did to me. You know, and I know I was sick because you did something. The doctors will keep an eye on me, so you better not try this again, or I'll tell them it was you."

"What are you saying? The doctors had no idea what was wrong with you."

No, I did not mention that doctors are investigating more, for now, and I have to go back for a complete checkup in two weeks. Right now I'm exhausted, and I'd like to go to bed." I was drifting away and wanted to go to sleep right away. "One more thing, Pavle, don't ever and I mean ever bother to make coffee for me again. Make it just for yourself and enjoy it,: and with that, I slammed the door right in his face.

As he walked away, I heard him saying, "Bitch, this is not over yet."

I knew I had to get out, very soon, but the first thing was to get a new job and some security and then I would take action. Meanwhile, I had to bevery careful around Pavle.

On Sunday morning the girls were coming home. We were going to pick them up together, but I told Pavle he could go by himself, because I wasn't feeling so good.

I had something else in mind. I knew he didn't believe me but I just wanted to be home alone, to see if I could find poison; that mouse or rat kind that the doctor talked about.

"Yeah okay, but what should I tell the kids if they ask me where Mom is?"

"Maybe tell them the truth. How about that? But I know you won't, so just tell the girls I'm not feeling well."

After he had left, I went downstairs to make something to eat. I was almost in tears when I saw a cup of coffee on a table with a note:

"This is for you, my dear, Try it; it is not poison."

I took the cup and threw it on the floor. Not realizing what I was doing, the crash woke me up. I couldn't believe that Pavle was that kind of a monster—who in the world had I been living with? At that moment I did not know what to do or think. Was I safe from now on? Then I remembered to go downstairs to see if I could find something like the mouse or rat poison. I didn't know why we would have that stuff; we didn't have any mice or rats in the house, the house was brand new. But then it dawned on me. Pavle had been planning this for a long time, just like the doctor said—that poison had been in my body for some time.

I looked and looked everywhere but nothing. He must have put it in his car, I don't know. Just as I was going up, I heard a car pull in. The girls were happy to be home, and to my surprise, they did not even how come I never came with their father to pick them up. But then I knew that in our house no one cared much about me, not even my children. At some point, they were happy. Pavle made sure of that, buying them everything the girls asked for, so their mother was just a person at home who cooked and cleaned. As they walked upstairs they both noticed that the extra room we had was made into a bedroom, only the mattress was on the floor. I managed to explain to them that I had hurt my back and I needed to sleep on a hard mattress, so that is why that room was for me. "And because my back is hurting me I'll be staying home about a week or so, and in the meantime I'll be looking for a new job, closer to home."

Once the girls went to school and Pavle went to work, I went and got a local newspaper and read the wanted ads. There was one that caught my eye. It was a warehouse not too far from our street, almost within walking distance. Work was advertised for a person with warehouse experience, mostly in picking orders and shipping and receiving. It was a godsend to me. I called them, and made the appointment for Wednesday at one. The company's name was Muller&Wiser; they were originally from Holland.

After my phone call with the new business, I was almost afraid to say it, but I was somehow and don't know why I was happy. When girls came from school I was cooking and humming, which made both of them look at me with eyes wide open. "Mom, are you okay? You are singing or humming orwhatever, but you look different. What happened to you?"

"Well for starters I made you your favourite pita with cheese, and I got me a new job. I can walk to it. Well, I didn't get it yet, but I'm 100% sure the job's mine. I have an interview on Wednesday, and for that, I'm in a good mood."

Then Vesna out of the blue asked me, "Mom, you had a good job. What happened? I know you liked Mr. Henk, he was your friend. So what happened when we went away. I feel something strange, like there's something you're not telling us."

"Nothing happened, I just don't like driving every day, traffic is always bad, and when I think of that big snow, I don't know, I just don't like to go that far anymore. No other reason than that."

"Okay Mom, but I'm almost sure that's not the whole story. But good luck on your interview, hope you'll be happy."

Vesna was noticing that her father and I weren't talking much, and for now, she was getting a bit confused, but I hoped it wouldn't be for long. She was fifteen now and I couldn't hide the truth from her for too much longer. As for Sandra, she never asked much, she always just looked so sad, and maybe, just maybe she felt that there is trouble in the household, but we were hiding it from them. I wanted to cry for lying, but for now, that was my only solution.

Just as I finished talking to Vesna, Pavle got home as well. I told him I was going for an interview on Wednesday, and hoped to get that job because it was so close to home. He never said anything, and that just killed my mood.. He was never happy about anything when it came to my happiness, but I just hoped that job would give me the chance to start making some money and then, *Goodbye, you asshole*, which was how I felt about Pavle. The thing that hurt the most was how my girls never noticed anything strange about their parents not talking or laughing or even kissing. To them as long they had everything they needed, happiness was there.

I did have happy days with my girls. I remember teaching them how to fish, which was lots of fun, how to swim, how to ride a bike, but those days were more happy for them than they were for me. Tjey were happy lies, but I never showed them. No one knew how I was spending hours of crying, hours of sadness, longing for someone to love me. I was loved once, and when he died I think I did too, and so did my first unborn child.

Keven never knew I was expecting. I was going to tell him that weekend, and that weekend never came, we all died that day. From all the sadness and stress over what happened to Keven, our baby was not ready for us. I had a miscarriage before the baby developed at all, so that secret went with Keven. My doctor wanted me to slow down but it was all too late.

I was very excited about my meeting at Muller & Wiser. I had no idea what they made, but I didn't care, a warehouse job is a warehouse job, what could be different from delivering a book, pattern designs or medical products, so I knew I can handle it. As I walked in a young lady came and walked me to the HR office where I met a warehouse supervisor and an HR woman. They both looked German to me, but so what, all I was interested in was a job. The H.R lady got up and introduced herself as the general manager of the company. Her name was Noemi Kohenil, and the man that was a supervisor was Bram Stringer. Mrs. Kohenil was holding a notebook, and made notes on my answers to her questions. She explained to me that the job responsibility was picking up orders and some receiving. They were not such a big company but big enough to have about thirty-five people working at the moment. In the warehouse there was a supervisor and three more men. I would be the only woman in there and if that was a problem I could tell them now. The company head office was in Holland. Right now my responsibility would be as a warehouse shipper. I'd pick up some orders as well, and there was a chance to move up. She asks me about my previous jobs, so I handed her my resume. She read it and said I was just a person they were looking for. I loved the sound of that answer. The supervise hadn't talked much, but at the end, he asked me if I could drive a forklift? He liked my answers, and told me that if I liked, he could take me to show me the warehouse.

Once we went, I met the three guys and some other people that were there. To me the warehouse needed a big clean up, and I knew I coul do it with no problem. I told Mr. Stringer that I'd like to work there if he gave me the chance. After that, we went back to HR to see Mrs. Kohenil, and Mr. Stringer told her that he would be happy to have me. He asked me when I could start and it didn't take me to long to answer. "I can start Monday."

He liked that answer, so then he put his hand out to shake and told me to call him Bram. "We're all on first name basis here, no need to address me as a Mr. and I'm sure that Noemi feels the same" After that, he said, "See you on Monday at 8:30 a.m. and he left."

Once Bram left Noemi laughed and said, "Please sit down. Let me tell you about the company, your salary, and benefits. But first, let me say this. You are the first person that Bram hired without any doubt in his mind, so if he thinks you are good enough for the warehouse it's fine with me. Ramona, can I ask you a personal question? Looking at your last name, I just wondered for no reason at all, where did you come from?"

"I came from Eastern Europ, I don't know if that matters to you, or for my job, but I came from Yugoslavia in 1963."

"No, no, nothing to do as far as work Ramona, I was wondering, because I came from the Czech Republic, and I'm happy to have you aboard. We probably have lots in common since our countries are so close to each other. (At that moment neither of us knew what good friends we were going to be.)

She checked my resume and references and seemed impressed. "Fair enough. I'll do all that later on, but now let me take you around the office and introduce you to our customer service staff and the rest."

After I met all the staff, or most of them, one person caught my eye. She had just started working there on computers and she told me to hang on, that everything would be okay. From that moment I liked her. Her name was Maka, and from the beginning until the end Maka and I were friends. In some ways, she reminded me of Megen, just in some respects. I don't know why but she was always there to help me even though I worked in the warehouse and she worked in computers, she was very helpful in everything that I needed to know.

That day when I got home, I was as happy as I could be. No one was home, so I put my favourite Beatles record on and when I was singing and dancing I never noticed Pavle. He almost scared me, I thought he was at work, but I was wrong. He started to clap his hands and with his smiling face full of rage he said, "Wow, you must have an excellent day so far, I haven't seen you happy like this for a very long time. Have you had a good time with your German boyfriend? Did you kiss him goodbye, or are you so happy that you forgot that I was going to work later on because I had to change my shift? Oh so sorry, I forgot, you didn't know. How stupid of me." And with that, he kicked my radio and smashed the only record that I'd been able to save.

At that moment I was so mad, and at the same time so, so sorrowful. This man was a very sick person. I came home with good news of my new job and all he thought was that I'd gone out to score with someone. How sick is that? With tears in my eyes, I told him I was happy because I had found a job and I was starting on Monday, but Pavle did not care for that. He would rather I'd say I was out with a man.

With tears, I started cleaning up the mess Pavle made. Breaking my radio and my records was so stupid and unnecessary, but that is Pavle. Anyway, he left for work and I was relieved that I was home alone, the monster was gone. I began talking to myself like I was losing it. Since Pavle went to work, I felt like going out for dinner, not at a big restaurant but somewhere that would take my mind off this house. Once the girls came home, I told them about my new job, "And to celebrate we're going out for dinner."

Vesna asked me if we were going to wait for their father, but I told them he switched shifts for some reason, so wasn't home. She give me a look with a question on her face. I knew I probably looked stressed, because I'd been crying and she must have noticed that, and she asked me if I was okay.

Vesna had been noticing that things were not so shiny at our house, she was slowly seeing things like how her father talked to me or how he acted differently when he was with them. Them being teenagers now, her father was very strict with her and Sandra. They were not allowed to talk to boys, and only could have a few girls for friends. There were times that a boy would call and ask for Vesna, and then Pavle would get upset and then it all began to be my fault. He told Vesna she was not allowed to give boys her phone number, or he'd disconnect the line. I knew trouble was coming; the girls were at that age and keeping them locked up was wrong. Many times Pavle would follow them to school, or if they went to a mall, he would be there. He was doing to them everything that he had done to me, and I knew that I had to make a break soon and I mean very quickly.

The girls and I had a great time out, just the three of us, like I always pictured how it should be; free and not worrying if someone was looking at you. But for now, this was just the beginning. I told girls to try as much as possible not to give their phone number to boys because their father would be very upset if anybody called. "I'm not saying you can't talk to them, but keep your talking in school," I cautioned them.

The weekend came and went, and our house was like no one lived there, it was always so quiet. Nobody talked, and Pavle and I we weren't talking at all. I was almost sure for now that the girls were paying more attention to what was going on between their father and me. I could see in Vesna's eyes that she was a bit sad that now she could see that her father and I weren't getting along at all, and the talk was only about them or something for the house. Vesna did ask me to tell her the truth about why I was sleeping on the floor. If my back is hurting me how come I had a new job—she wanted the truth. The girls were so innocent in all this and it would not be fair to tell them all at once. Therefore I told them that their father, and I were having some bad times, but we were trying to work it all out. (And that was another lie I told.)

Virtually out of the blue Vesna asked me if we were going to get a divorce.

"No, no Vesna, not now anyway. As for later, I'm not so sure. I don't want you to worry about things like that. If we're going to get a divorce, I'll have a talk with you girls before we decide on something like that. For now, go and enjoy yourself."

Very calmly I walked to my room and tears were just pouring down. I hated to lie, but for now, I had no other choice, and with tears and a broken heart I must have fallen asleep.

The alarm clock woke me up. I jumped up so fast, went downstairs, made some coffee and toast, wrote the girls a note, and off I went. I think I was flying; I wanted to get as far as I could and fast as I could from the house and that man I lived with. I went straight to the warehouse, and Bram was waiting for me. He showed me how the orders looked and how to pick an order. To me that was nothing, and in the first half an hour or so Bram was pleased. Later on in the afternoon he showed me the receiving, and again it was nothing new to me. The only difference was this was a new company, but the procedures were all the same, so I liked it. Just before time to go home, Neomi asked me to come to her office.

Neomi was an excellent person; I could tell that the first day I saw her, so I thought she was probably calling me to the office because she needed some more information for my medical or whatever.(But I was wrong.)

"Ramona, please sit down, I'dlike to talk to you, and please be honest with me. If the questions are too personal you don't have to answer me."

"Neomi, don't tell me I made a mess on my first day? Honest, I was very careful on all the orders, but I guess nobody is perfect."

"Oh no, Ramona. As a matter of fact, Bram said you are the best he ever had, and he's pleased with your work, and he can tell that you do have a lot of experience in a warehouse, so I'm very happy about that. The reason I called you is I'd like to talk to you about yourself. I have called all three places you have worked, and I'm amazed at how they all missed you, but I got some warnings about your husband. None of those people liked him. On your last job just two weeks ago, you were a great worker and a healthy woman, but somehow you ended up in a hospital last Monday. Everybody was shocked, and they think that your husband is probably the reason for that. Now Ramona, you don't have to tell me anything if you feel that situation with your husband is under control, but if not, please let's talk. I'll keep this strictly confidential, so feel free to tell me everything. You see, I probably understand you more than you think, because I left my husband—he was a terrible man. Do don't be scared, I'm on your side."

"Thank you Neomi, I'm not afraid. I was scared a long time ago but not anymore. You see I married a jealous, disturbed man, which I didn't know then. Yes, I could have left him just like you did, but no, I'm different from you. I have lived with this disturbed man for sixteen years now, but it will end very soon. I'm very sure of that. As for my husband, you will meet him at the Christmas party that Bram told me we're having. You will see a person who is very uneasy and tense, but he'll also try to impress you. Noemi, my life has been very complicated since I was a baby and there is so much I could tell you but not for now. I want you to know that working for you is the best thing that has come along, and I won't let you down. Just be patient with me. You won't have any problem with my husband; he is my problem but not for long."

"Okay Ramona, but keep this in mind. If you ever need to talk to someone I'm right here, So then we'll see you tomorrow. OH! Yes, one more thing. A man from your last job, said that you are welcome back anytime, and he personally misses you. I think his name is Henk. Was Henk your boss?"

"Yes, he was my boss, and he's the owner of the company—he and I care about each other. We were good friends, that's all."

From that day and for next the next twenty-three years Noemi and I were friends, and we stayed friends. Work was going excellent, and I loved it, but there was a one man that didn't like me because I was an immigrant, even though I had been in Canada for a long time. He would call me names like a "stupid immigrant" or say, "go back to your country." It went on and on, but one day I just had enough, and so I went and told Noemi that I didn't like working with Tom because he called me names. Noemi called Tom in and asked him why he was picking on me. Without thinking, or else he was just stupid, he told Noemi he didn't like immigrants. He made a terrible mistake saying that, because Noemi was an immigrant just like me, so next thing we saw Tom leaving, but not without having the last word. "You are a b

The company was doing magnificently, and one day Noemi said that she was getting me some help just for a while until we caught up with the orders. I had nothing against that, but a man that she hired was strange to me in the beginning. His name was Khan, and he was a young man but I had a feeling he had some issue with working with me. If I asked him to do this or that he would give me a dirty look. One day Khan came and told me to get lost, he said, "Why don't don't you go home and cook, clean, and take care of the children and wait for your husband. Your place is at home, not a place like this to work with lots of men." I know right there I had met another Pavle. He made me so mad, I went to my supervisor and reported him for bullying me, so he stopped for a couple of days, but one morning he came and told me to go and get him a coffee. Well, I did go but not to get Khan a coffee. I went and told Noemi what was going on. She was surprised because our supervisor had never reported this. Noemi got Khan in the office along with my supervisor, and she wanted to know what was going on. Khan claimed that he had just been joking telling me this and that, but he forgot that he'd also told me to go and get him a coffee. Noemi asked him if that was true.

"Yes," was his answer. "Ramona wasn't busy, so I thought maybe she had time to go and get me a coffee."

Well, Khan, we don't treat anybody in my company like that. If you have any issue because Ramona is a woman, then please pick up your personal belongings and leave."

After that unpleasant day, work was going well. There were no more bullies or anybody like Khan or Tom.

CHAPTER 38

Working at Muller & Wiser was going well. After six months I got a good raise and a bonus at the end of the month like everybody. The company had a really good policy; if you came in under budget, there was a bonus, which added to your monthly pay and helped a lot. Noemi had met Pavle by now and she, just like my other friends, did not like him. When they met at the Christmas party she noticed that Pavle was only interested in what I was doing. His eyes were like the devil's, but that was no surprise to me. Now that Pavle was not getting my money anymore, he sensed that the end was coming between us, and before I know it he cleaned out our bank accounts so that I wouldn't get any of it. I knew that would happen, though, that's why I opened an account in my name only, and every penny I'd earned since working for M&W, I deposited in my bank. Pavle never said anything, and I did not care.

Ever since I came home from the hospital, Pavle had a feeling that I was through with him, and he was right. On January 1990 Vesna turned sixteen, and that weekend I planned to talk to the girls before I approached Pavle.

Pavle was working that weekend, so I told the girls that we were going out for dinner, and they could choose wherever they liked to go. Their favourite restaurant was Mr. Greek, so we were ready to go, but then Vesna asked me what the occasion was—her birthday wasn't till the next weekend. I just looked at her, and I started to cry. Sandra was getting ready, and she noticed I was sad too. Like Vesna she wanted to know the reason we were going out. At that moment I told them to sit down because I'd like to tell them something.

Immediately Vesna looked at me and said, "Mom, Are you getting a divorce? Is that why you're taking us out—to tell us that news?"

Then Sandra starts to cry; she was very upset. "If you'd like to go and celebrate that news, you can go without me, or take Vesna with you; I'm not going."

"Okay girls, let's sit down. I have some questions for you. Do you honestly think that your father and I are happy together these days, or for years? Do you see us smiling and talking to each other in a happy way? Haven't you ever noticed that your father and I are not sleeping in the same room anymore? Did you ever see your dad get something nice for me, like for Mother's Day, my birthdays, Christmas or any other occasions? Ask yourself this, and be honest about it. Your father only loves you both, and I'm all for that, but I'm so tired of just being a woman who cleans, cooks and looks after the children. I need someone to care for me as well, and your father is not the one. The situation between your dad and me has not happened overnight. We were not happy, or should I say I haven't been happy for a very long time. I'd like to tell you more, but you are just kids. One day I'll tell you more about your father and me, but for now, I'm asking you to be my friends. I'm going to need your support, for now, and for the rest of our time together. You can always choose to stay with me or go and live with your father. You girls are teenagers now, and you do have a choice. Either way, I only know that I love you both, no matter what you decide to do. We will be staying in this house until you finish this school year, and in August I would like to move. I haven't told this to your father yet; I wanted to talk to you first. Please try to understand; this move will be good for all of us."

I knew I was hurting them both. The news was a shock to them, and all because of me. Pretending that we were a happy family and that everything was all great between Pavle and me went on for too long. The girls never know how badly their father treated me, and if I told them the truth now it would probably destroy them, so I let them think it was all my fault. Anything was better than staying and living with that disturbed man.

I sat between them, and I started to cry. Then we all begun to cry, and then Vesna got up, and with a small smile on her face, she said, "Mom, when I grow up, and get a job I'll buy you anything you like, please don't be sad anymore. We didn't know all that. Daddy was or is always good to us, and we never paid any attention to how or why you have been so sad. I do know that you cry at night. I have heard you many times, but I thought maybe you had a headache or something. Oh Mom. I'm so, so sorry, I'll stay with you as long as you need me."

Vesna's words made me feel a little bit easier, but looking at Sandra I knew she was in a lot of pain, and she never even looked at me. Sandra was always or how to put it, she was always so quiet, you never know what she was thinking. In some ways, she was like her father, but I wasn't going to say that. I took her in my arms and tried to calm her down. With a very shaking voice, she said, "Mom, I'm sorry as well. I'll go and live with you now, but I'd also like to see my dad every day or whenever I can. I hope you won't be mad at me if I do that."

"Sandra, and Vesna, you can always go and see your father, I would not ever tell you no. What happened to your dad and me is not your fault. It is your father and I who can't get along any more. As we get older, we all change. Some couples stay together forever, and some don't, and your father and I tried but it didn't work out, and I think this is best for all of us. You both can feel free to go and see your father and stay with him anytime you feel like it. And Vesna, as for your birthday party for next Saturday, there is no change there; we have to act normal just like we always do. And your graduation party is still on. Sometime in early May, I'll take you to a place where I know they have very cute dresses for young girls, so no worries there. But if you'd like to talk about it to your teachers for some advice you can, or you can speak to your friends. Both of you please don't worry too much; I'm going to be here to listen to you if you have any questions at all."

After all this talk we all got hungry, and I asked them if I should call for pizza, or if we should go out. So we ordered pizza, and watch some TV. It was getting late, so we all went to bed. :ater on I'm sure I heard Sandra crying, and I cried as well.My tears were for different reasons.But as my girls cried I felt sorry for them, not knowing the whole story about their father but I didn't want to get into "he said, she said."

I think I was awake most of the night. I heard Pavle coming upstairs, and then the house was soundless like a ghost lived there, not a family. Eventually, I fell asleep, but not for long. I got up very early that morning, made some coffee and was preparing to tell Pavle of my decision about the family and us. I made a good breakfast, knowing the girls liked pancakes and egg with lots of beacons. As I was getting everything on the table, Pavle walked in and with his smiling face he asked me how come, I got up so early.

"Well if you have to know then I'll tell you, but just one moment, please. Vesna and Sandra, can you both come down? Breakfast is ready, and I need to talk to you."

It was so hushed, and I was very calm. I knew exactly what I was going to say.

"Okay, now that we're all here I can start. Girls you and I had this talk last night, and now it's time for me to tell your father. Please put your feelings aside for now and let me talk."

I looked at Pavle's face, and I can say he knew what was coming, so he never said anything at all. He just sat there and was waiting for me to start.

"Pavle, please realize that we can not go living like this anymore. You've hated, and abused me for so long now, and I don't feel that our communication is there anymore, I'm asking you for a divorce. I have explained to the girls that we have changed, and it is time to move on. I'm pretty sure that you agree with me, and let's make this as easy as possible. I'd like us to sell the house by the end of July. That will give us plenty of time to organize our lives the way you and I would like."

I'm not sure how long was I talking before Pavle got up end left with a terrible response.

"You, you are the biggest bitch that I know, and yes I'd love to give you a divorce, but you have to know one thing. I'm not giving you anything, no money or any support except for the girls," and he slammed the door and left.

"Mom, what a filthy mouth Father has. Why did he say that? Oh Mom I'm so sorry, and I'm moving in with you, not him."

"Girls, I knew he would say something like that, but I have told you that your father is not all that you thought he was. That was only a small portion of his abuse towards me. Please, girls, let's finish our meal, and then we can go to the mall, or we can just sit at home and try to go on with our lives. I'm not sure how your father is going to react toward you with this news, but you are both smart, and you can calm him down."

Pavle came home very late that night—where he was God knows. It was very nice and quiet all day without him. Next day the girls went to school, and I went to work a bit earlier than usual. I didn't want to see him or talk to him, and I think he felt that way as well.

We tried to stay away from each other as much as possible, but it was hard to do then since we both lived under the same roof. While I worked longer hours, Pavle was taking the girls out to the mall, and he was spending money on them for just about nothing, trying to get me mad. But it didn't work. I was sure he wanted me to go crazy over his spending, but no, I just ignored everything. The girls told me that Dad was looking for an apartment with two bedrooms, and that he would like one of them to live with him, but they both agreed that for now, they just would visit him all the time, and later on would see.

I was under stress, and more, and more emotionally drained. I couldn't believe that after seventeen years I was finally going to get a divorce. Deep down in my guts I knew I should have done this a long time ago. Now our family was torn apart, and we would never be the same. Maybe it was all my fault, but living with Pavle was getting worse and worse.

At work, I was at peace; no one questioned me at all. The people at work were excellent, but there is always someone you end up not liking, and I met few like that. Then there were ladies like me with a big secret in their personal lives. Once you are an abused person you can tell the next one but knowing these ladies I never said anything. I just wondered why they stayed in their marriages. Was it like me, because of their children?

Anyway other than that I was happy at work, so I decided to be honest with our H.R., I mean with Noemi. I asked her if we could have lunch together because I'd like to talk to her. At first, she was thinking that I was leaving, but before she said anything, I told her it was about Pavle and me. As we were going out for lunch I saw some looks on my fellow workers' faces; I'm sure they were wondering what was going on. Most of them thought that I was leaving, but with a mischievous smile, I let them guess.

"Ramona," Noemi laughed. You made some people wonder what's going on. I like that, you are my trouble maker, and I just love it."

(And for the rest of my eighteen years working with Noemi she called me a trouble maker, and she even continued to call me that after she quit, when we stayed friends.) I wondered if calling me a trouble maker was an insult or a compliment, but either way, I didn't care, we were friends, and I had a secret name for her too. I use to call her Big One, so we had our little jokes.

"Anyway, Ramona, since you had your fun, what's so important to talk about that we had to go out?"

"Well, I have good news. I'm getting a divorce. And I told her what had been going on and how Pavle was hiding money. "I know he's lying, but Noemi all I want is to get it over with. I can't stand him anymore and to be honest with you I'm also scared of him. I'll need your support, and please keep this just between us, although I'll tell Maka about this as well because she and I also have become friends."

"Ramona, this is good news, but are you going to be okay with just your paycheck? How are you going to handle the rest of your expenses? I can give you an advance, but is that going to be enough?"

"Thank you, Noemi, I'm going to be just fine. You see the house is in both names, so whatever we for it we each get half, and right now we don't have a mortgage, so I'm sure more then 150,000 will be mine. I don't care about the money he keeps, I don't care. All I want is to get out of this marriage. I have suffered for seventeen years, and it is time to start a new life. I'm very scared, because, Pavle was in charge of my life for a long time, and now I have to do it all by myself. How did you manage to do your breakup? Was it hard?"

"Yes Ramona, it was very hard to do, but like you, all I wanted was to be free from him. You're going to be just fine, you'll have your girls with you and time will heal all the wounds eventually, but it will take time."

"Noemi, what does it take to be happy? A long time ago I was happy, and that happiness died with the man I truly loved, but that is another story that I'll tell you one day. I think we better be going back, or the gossip will be too unbearable. Thank you, Noemi, for listening to me and for being my friend. I won't forget that."

....

For starters, Pavle moved out on May 15, 1990. For some people that was a regular day, but for me it was a new beginning, a new life. I wasn't so sure if I was happy, sad, or both. One thing I knew was that there would be no man in my life anymore. I'd had one that I loved more than life itself, and then I had one that I hated more than anyone else. Now in the next few weeks, I was peaceful and happy to be left alone. My nightmares, my revenge thoughts, they were all gone. The girls were still sad, but we all needed time to adjust. Vesna and I both tried to explain to Sandra, that it was for the best for all us, but I knew that Sandra was heartbroken. Many times I heard her crying, but if I tried to talk to her she wouldn't speak to me. I wanted to tell her about her father; how he never even touched her for almost six months; how he claimed that Sandra was not his; how he never took her in his arms; but no how could I tell her that? She wouldn't believe me because I didn't believe it myself; that one man could be so cruel to his child. I knew that down on the road I'd have a hard time. The girls were in their teens, and one parent looking after them wasn't easy. In other words, the girls took advantage of that. I was working most of the time, and looking after them was not my priority, (which was my big mistake). I thought they were old enough to know right from wrong, but down the road the girls were just innocent children and confused. The freedom they got only having one parent came at a cost.

The house sold with no problem, and we found a two-bedroom apartment with a den. So, the girls had their own bedrooms, and one part of the living room was my room. Life went on and on, until one day Vesna called me at work and said that Sandra was giving her hard time. She had destroyed some of Vesna's clothes and thrown them in the garbage, and was going out of her mind. I was not so surprised. I came home and I made a deal with them. Those sad eyes of Sandra's were breaking my heart, but I had to do it.

The girls were arguing back and forth about who did what, so I came right out with words that shocked them both. "Okay girls, this is what's going to happen. I can not come home every time you two are fighting; I can not be a judge, so I have decided one of you has to move and live with your father. You can determine that between you; I'll not be against any result. We can't live like this anymore. I have lived under stress for seventeen years, and I don't want to reap that in my life. You are not a babies any more. You are still young girls, but you have to give me a break as well. I'd like to live a simple and quiet life, and you two fighting is not going to work out. I'm sorry about this approach, but I don't know what else to do."

Their decision wasn't unexpected to me. Sandra spoke first, and without any sorrow in her eyes she said thunderously and clear with a cold voice, "You both make me sick. I'm more than happy to move in with daddy. He is going to give me everything, and I don't need you." Looking at me, and pointing the finger at Vesna she said, "You, you can rot in hell."

I was in shock. Was that my baby, talking to me like that? Oh my God, she sounded just like her father. I had no idea that she hated us so much. With tears in my eyes, I tried to give her a hug, but she pushed me and went to her room.

The sounds of Sandra's voice was every mother's nightmare. I cried so much that night, that the next day I phoned in sick, but I did call Noami and tell her what happened.

After all the chaos we had, Sandra moved to her father's house, and she never called for a long time. I knew she needed space to work thins out, but I never expected for her to be so cold towards me. I called her many times, but she wouldn't answer, so I thought just to let it go for a while, but a while was very long. Sandra never got over our marital decision. She always blamed me for everything, and her living with her father didn't help me at all. Even when she grew up, she would come and stay with us once in awhile, but it was a frigid visit. It was like talking to a stranger, not my child. I just don't understand what I did wrong with her, but I've learned to live with it, then and now.

As for Vesna, she enjoyed her freedom from everybody. I was working all the time, sometimes even a six days a week. Vesna never complained, but deep in my heart I knew she missed her father, so most Saturdays she would go to see him and always came home happy because her father give her money and she was grateful for that. She didn't do badly in her last year of high school, and we talked about her going to university, but she wasn't sure of what she wanted to do. I never pushed her to do this or that. I wanted her to have her freedom. I didn't want her to have the life I'd had, and she understood that. We were very close, and when she finished her high school and got her diploma, I was very proud of her. She also decided to go to university. By now she was eighteen and she had her own mind. Many times she would wait until I came home and she'd take my car and go out with her friends. I wanted her to have fun, but down the road, I think I gave her too much freedom. Still, at age eighteen there wasn't much I could do—at least she was home with me.

Meanwhile, Sandra started coming to see us more often than before, and I was happy about that. She stayed longer this time because it was summer. She was sixteen now and was very mature for her age, but she was like that all the time. She and Vesna would go out together sometimes, but not often, but at least there were no fights like before, I guess because they were older. And then the summer was gone, and it was back to school. Sandra went back to live with her father and Vesna went to try university.

After my uncle's death, I spent many days going fishing with my aunt and talking about how I would like her to come and live with me one day. She loved going fishing with me, and now that Pavle was not in my life she would come and see me quite often, and we would talk about our good old times.

After a year at university, Vesna decided that continuing it was not for her, so she never went back. Instead, she found a job in a mall in a clothing store, and at night she would work in a bar. I wasn't happy about that at beginning, but she was twenty now, so there was not much I could have done. Vesna was working every day and night, so we didn't see each other often, she would be sleeping when I got up to go to work, and in the evening when I got home she would be working. The arrangement was weird, but it worked out okay. On the weekend we would laugh, saying to each other, "Hi stranger," but we had our lives in order. Then one day after her twenty-first birthday, she met a guy, and they moved in together. It was sad for me to see her go, but every mother has to let go one day. Meanwhile, my aunt retired, and she moved with me. I wanted to live by myself for a while, but I couldn't tell her that, so Vesna moved out, and my aunt moved in, so there I went again.

As for Sandra she stayed in university and got her degree, and with that, she got a good job in government. I was so proud of her, and we still saw each other whenever there was a special occasion. Like Vesna, she met a nice young man, and she moved with him. It didn't take them long before they got married. After a year they had a baby; my first grandchild. I was very proud of Sandra. Even though we were not so close I was proud of her all the time.

Eventually Vesna did the same as Sandra. After few bad relationships she met the man of her dreams. They moved in together first and then later got married, and I was a grandmother again.

Everything seemed to be going well, but then my aunt got ill. One day I got home from work and she was lying down on the kitchen floor. She scared the hell out of me. I thought she was dead. She told me she wasn't able to move, because her arm was hurting her bad. From that day on I noticed she was saying things that didn't make any sense, I knew there was going to be a problem. I was still working, so I'd ask a lady in the building to look after her from time to time until I get home from work, but she was getting worse. The doctors told me she had Parkinson's disease and dementia, so she was not able to be home alone anymore. On top of that, she was having trouble walking due to the Parkinson's. She was in bad shape. I felt so sorry that she only had me, and now she was getting so ill that there came a time she didn't even want to live anymore. It was a strange thing that all this struck her so fast. One day she was okay, and then it all went down. I had no choice but to put her in a nursing home. It broke my heart. I'd always loved her. She had the biggest heart in the world, but never any luck. Her first husband was like Pavle, and her second one was an alcoholic. She never had any children, but I know she would have been the best mother. She was in the nursing home for a long time, and meanwhile, I retired from work. Since both girls had their homes and children, my apartment in the city was too big for me, so I sold it and moved to a small town called Burlock.

My aunt lived for few more years and then she passed away. I think that was the second saddest day of my life. My first saddest day had been when Keven died, and now I was entirely alone. I went out to my balcony and looked at the peaceful lake, and Toronto was in my view as well. All that was incredible, so I asked myself, "What now, Ramona?" Then I started to cry. I don't know exactly why but the tears just wouldn't stop, so I said to myself, "Please don't cry Ramona—start your life all over, your time is yours now."

And so, I decided to go home where I'd had my first home as a child, in the orphan village. After fifty-four years I wanted to see if anything was still there.

Because I was alone for the first time in my life, I was going to do things my way and only my way, hoping not to hear the words, "Please don't cry."

EPILOGUE
One year later

MY GRANDDAUGHTER IS starting grade one, and my grandson is in junior kindergarten. I don't know how time passed me by so fast, but I am sad and happy for no practical reason. My grandson makes me laugh every day, but not seeing my granddaughter often makes me sad. Sandra is the same, I don't see her enough, but that's all due to her father always being at her house. Vesna is doing okay, always trying to be kind to her dad and me. I always say Vesna is sitting on two chairs. She never wanted her father to forget her, so they were close as well. I broke down our family, and I know I'm paying for it. Perhaps Sandra one day will understand why I did, why I left her father.

Now all they have is "he said she said," but I carry the scars of an abusive and dark and lonely person. I have promised myself to go on, but it is hard. Trying will take lots of power and willingness.

Since I don't have any primary responsibility, I think I'll try to find my best friend Megen that I have missed so much, and Mrs. Geyer, if she's still alive.

The orphan Village where I grow up, wasn't there anymore, but there was a great bronze plaque saying, "An orphan village for girls was here from 1941 to 1963."

Noemi and Maka are still my friends and once a month we get together. I also keep in touch with some other coworkers that I liked via e-mail or Facebook.

Now my goal is to try to put the past behind me and go on with the life I've got left. I'm hoping that one day my girls will get together and live in harmony because not having brothers or sisters or anyone to talk to who actually cares is a very lonely life and sad. I know. I've been there.

... END...

This book is dedicated to my children and to all who are in abusive relationships.

Abusive relationships aren't comprised of only one thing. There are many, many, many different kinds of damage that can occur, but they all belong to one word: Abuse.

Look at my history. You'll find in my book that I was sexually abused as a child, but then almost the worst violence came later on when I got married. Yes, many times abuse starts at your home. Most of the time it's a husband abusing a wife, but it could be the other way around. In any case, it's pure hell for those being abused. How do I know that? Well I've been there.

As a child, I was told if I told anyone I'd be in big trouble...as a wife I was scared to be alone. I didn't know how to get help, and in the early sixties and seventies, there was not much talk about abuse; it was all brushed under the carpet.

I did try at one point to leave my husband but did not go through with it, because I was scared to be alone. My point is, don't be like me—go out and get help. Help is out there now, don't let your abuser win because in the long run, no one wins.

Just get help and live.

Printed in Canada